A Feminist Voyage through
International Relations

Oxford Studies in Gender and International Relations

Series editors: J. Ann Tickner, University of Southern California, and Laura Sjoberg, University of Florida

A Feminist Voyage through International Relations

J. Ann Tickner

OXFORD
UNIVERSITY PRESS

OXFORD
UNIVERSITY PRESS

Oxford University Press is a department of the University of Oxford.
It furthers the University's objective of excellence in research, scholarship,
and education by publishing worldwide.

Oxford   New York
Auckland   Cape Town   Dar es Salaam   Hong Kong   Karachi
Kuala Lumpur   Madrid   Melbourne   Mexico City   Nairobi
New Delhi   Shanghai   Taipei   Toronto

With offices in
Argentina   Austria   Brazil   Chile   Czech Republic   France   Greece
Guatemala   Hungary   Italy   Japan   Poland   Portugal   Singapore
South Korea   Switzerland   Thailand   Turkey   Ukraine   Vietnam

Oxford is a registered trademark of Oxford University Press
in the UK and certain other countries.

Published in the United States of America by
Oxford University Press
198 Madison Avenue, New York, NY 10016

Library of Congress Cataloging-in-Publication Data
Tickner, J. Ann.
A feminist voyage through international relations / J. Ann Tickner.
pages cm
Includes bibliographical references and index.
ISBN 978–0–19–995126–0 (pbk. : alk. paper)—ISBN 978–0–19–995124–6 (hardcover : alk. paper)
1. International relations.   2. Security, International.   3. Feminist theory—Political aspects.
4. Feminism—International cooperation.   I. Title.
JZ1242.T58 2014
327.101—dc23
2013028661

9 8 7 6 5 4 3 2 1
Printed in the United States of America
on acid-free paper

To the memory of Hayward Alker:
Lifelong partner and friend

CONTENTS

ACKNOWLEDGMENTS

Acknowledging all the people who have guided, supported, and offered their advice and friendship to me on this remarkable twenty-five-year journey would be impossible. By recognizing some of them, I wish to pay tribute to all the feminist scholars who have contributed to the growth and success of this vibrant field, as well as those who have directly advised and helped me with my own work. Many have supported me in ways that go well beyond my own writings and, through their support and friendship, have helped to make feminist IR such a comfortable intellectual home for me.

For me this journey began before I was doing feminist work when, as a graduate student, I wanted to write a dissertation about a topic and use an approach that did not lie within the norms of political science/IR as conventionally defined. I am grateful to Robert Keohane, who fully supported my choosing a non-conventional thesis. Even though we have often had our critical engagements in print, some of which motivated several chapters in this volume, he has always been a constructive critic (and supporter) of my work and a true friend. I owe my interest in political theory, which became an important part of my dissertation, as well as my introduction to feminist theory, to the late Susan Okin who, as well as being my teacher at Brandeis, later became a close friend and mentor. I miss our conversations that took place in many different locations, even on the beaches of Block Island, a special place that has provided a quiet and beautiful refuge for writing many of the chapters of this book.

When I began to embark on my feminist research in the late 1980s, Peggy McIntosh, Associate Director of the Wellesley Centers for Research on Women, used her prodigious skills to help me write a proposal to the Ford Foundation that funded a conference at Wellesley College in 1990, out of which came one of the early feminist texts, *Gendered States*, edited by Spike Peterson. Attendees at that conference included Carol Cohn, Cynthia Enloe, Anne Sisson Runyan, Spike Peterson, Craig Murphy and Robert Keohane. All have remained lifelong friends and supporters from whose work and advice I have benefited in all my writings.

My appreciation goes also to former colleagues at the College of the Holy Cross who gave me my first job, even though I was not doing what was considered conventional IR research. Even though feminist IR was fairly new to the field at that time, they had enough faith in my non-traditional path to grant me tenure some years later. My subsequent years at the University of Southern California (USC) were also marked by the generosity and support of many wonderful colleagues and friends in the School of International Relations and beyond. It was through the support of USC, the School, and its Center for International Studies that we were able to hold two subsequent conferences, one in 2001 (also supported by the Ford Foundation) and one in 2010 celebrating twenty years of feminist scholarship. Attendees at both these conferences have had a formative influence on my own ideas and scholarship.

One of my early moments of feminist conscious-raising was the anxiety that accompanied attending professional meetings in the 1980s when there were few women attendees and even fewer on panels. Thanks to the wonderful group of women who have played such an important role in launching and nurturing the Feminist Theory and Gender Studies Section (FTGS) of the International Studies Association (ISA), this is no longer the case; ISA is now a place where many of us, myself included, draw inspiration and ideas for our research. Going to ISA is now an empowering and positive experience for women IR scholars, full of fun and friendship, as well as more serious academic matters. I cannot possibly acknowledge all the FTGS members who have had such an important influence on my work—Cynthia Enloe, Spike Peterson, Carol Cohn, Lily Ling, Marysia Zalewski, Christine Sylvester, Lisa Prügl, Anne Runyan, Jindy Pettman, Brooke Ackerly, and Jacqui True, to name a few. In 2002, when I was director of USC's Center for International Studies, Brooke and Jacqui came as post-doctoral fellows. It was then that we began weekly conversations about feminist methodologies that, besides leading to their joint publications on the subject, were very formative for my thinking, particularly for Chapter 7 of this book.

My academic travels, over the years, have taken me to various places in Europe, Australia, and New Zealand. All my work has benefited enormously from learning from scholars in these various locations outside the United States. Many of the chapters in Part One build on the concept of comprehensive security, reflecting the influence of Scandinavian peace research on my writings. The special recognition of my work by the Department of Peace and Conflict at Uppsala University in Sweden, as well as the support of its director Peter Wallensteen, is much appreciated. Teaching and writing about peace research has challenged me to think about how to foster better communication across disciplinary boundaries, reflected in many of my writings, particularly in Part Two, and especially Chapter 8. My first trip to Australia in 1996, hosted by the Department of International Relations at the Australian National University (ANU), gave me time to think further and write about the methodological issues in this section. It was also where I first met and had long conversations with Jindy Pettman, who kindly welcomed me to her house on the beautiful Australian coast. Jindy has remained a friend and inspiration. On a subsequent visit to the ANU in 2009, when I was hosted by Hilary Charlesworth, Director of the Regulatory Institutions Network, I was introduced to the work of many wonderful feminist international lawyers and wrote the article that became part of Chapter 12. I have learned much from Hilary and others at the ANU, all of whom have become good friends also. Among them are Bina D'Costa, Katrina Lee-Koo, and Cindy O'Hagen. Greg Frye, Paul Kiel, and Margaret Jolly, also at ANU, supplied me with many references and insightful ideas for Chapter 11, which was completed during my stay at the University of Auckland in 2010, graciously hosted by Jacqui True.

None of my writings could have accomplished without the input, research, and teaching assistance of my graduate students, many of whom are now launched on their own careers. It is so rewarding to watch their successes and to see many of them playing visible roles in the ISA and FTGS. Teaching has always been the most rewarding aspect of my career. It is through our students that our work continues, and it is from them that we get many of our best ideas. This list of my wonderful students is too long to mention all of them, but special thanks to Angela McCracken, Christina Gray, Eric Blanchard, Abigail Ruane, Catia Confortini, and Laura Sjoberg, who have all provided me not only with research and teaching assistance, but with friendship and support—in hard times as well as joyful ones. It is humbling when one's student evaluations say that what they particularly liked about the course was the TA, but this happened to me on many occasions! It was due to Catia's administrative skills that the 2001 conference went so smoothly. A special thanks to Laura Sjoberg, who has always done more than is humanly possible for one person and who has pushed me to think in new directions, Laura has been my co-author on several projects, always doing more than her share of the work. We continue to work together through our co-editing of the Oxford series in which this volume appears. Laura has done a wonderful job in soliciting some fine manuscripts.

During my years in Los Angeles my "West Side" group of feminist friends, Jane Bayes, Judith Stiehm, and Jane Jaquette, who lunched and talked together, deserve a special mention. Jane very ably co-organized two of the USC conferences and she has always been an insightful reader of my work. A special word of appreciation to Sandra Harding. Although she is not an IR scholar, at least in the disciplinary sense, Sandra's work is among the most frequently cited in this book. I have learned, and continue to learn, even more from her through our conversations and have valued our many years of friendship that have made this possible.

Much of the editing and putting this book together was done at my new institutional home, the School of International Service (SIS) at American

University, where Dean James Goldgeier has been generous in giving me research and institutional support. I thank my RA Karen Flores Garcia, who helped me update some of the material. A number of the now senior IR feminist scholars, including Spike Peterson, Anne Runyan, Elisabeth Prügl, and Christine Chin, received their PhDs at American; all of them have been important sources of ideas in this book. SIS has provided a welcome new intellectual home for me. I have appreciated the friendship of Christine and of James Mittelman, whose own intellectual voyaging was an encouragement for this project, about which we have had many lunchtime conversations.

The publication of this book would never have gone so smoothly and quickly without the efficient team at Oxford University Press, especially Angela Chapnko, who first encouraged me to take up this project. Angela has done a great job of guiding the manuscript through all its stages, reading and paying careful attention to every detail. I could not have asked for a better editor. I know she does the same for all the books in the series and has played a large part in its success.

My move back to the East Coast has put me closer to my all my immediate family: three daughters, their husbands, and seven grandchildren. My family has always been such strong supporters of my work, as well as helping me through some difficult times. Some of them, including some grandchildren, have even traveled across the country to various ISA meetings. My granddaughter Emma Walsh-Alker provided much-needed research assistance during the book's final stages.

As I went through assembling these chapters, on every page, I see the influence of my late husband Hayward Alker, to whom this book is dedicated. Hayward encouraged me from the start when, as a mother of three small children, I never imagined I could go back to school and get a PhD. Everything I have published reflects Hayward's help and support; he spent countless hours reading and making suggestions about everything I wrote and was always pushing me, not only to think outside the box and travel to new frontiers that I would never have thought of myself, but also to appreciate and take seriously the IR discipline and the best it has to offer. My current research about voyages of discovery and seeking out new voices bears the marks of Hayward's influence. I only wish he was here to take these voyages with me.

INTRODUCTION

No academic discipline would be complete without its origins stories. Since the beginning of feminist international relations is so recent—dating back about twenty-five years—it has been documented frequently. Putting together some of my writings over these years has given me an opportunity to look back at my part in this collective effort and reflect on how far we have come, thanks to the dedication and creative work of so many committed feminist scholars. It is a pleasure to have the opportunity to revisit some of my earlier work and reflect on how my thinking has evolved over the past twenty-five years. Before presenting this work, I will offer a few reflections about my own personal journey and how remarkable it has been to find so many others in different parts of the world and in different disciplines embarking on similar journeys. Creating feminist knowledge has always been a collective effort, and the first twenty-five years of feminist international relations (IR) has been no exception.

It is always easier to look back and detect a coherent pattern in the development of one's intellectual interests than to see it while living it. Nevertheless, I do see a number of connecting themes that eventually led me to my feminist journey through international relations. I was born in London in 1937 shortly before the beginning of World War II. Though I was too young to understand its causes and consequences, my wartime childhood gave me some firsthand experience of the effects of war on ordinary people's lives, a concern that has been central to feminists when they study war and conflict. Nightly bombing raids that forced us into shelters seemed "normal" to me. However, for adults, war was not a normal reality; they coped with bans on driving, putting up blackout curtains every night, lighting fires each morning to keep us warm with small amounts of rationed coal, making sure our gas masks operated correctly, and staying awake at night waiting for the sirens that warned of impending bombing raids.

Postwar Britain was slow to recover. It must have come as a relief to my parents when, in 1951, my father was invited to join the staff of the United Nations Secretariat. These were times when the United States was optimistic about the United Nations' future success; Americans welcomed UN families enthusiastically. Assuming that my family would go back to Britain, I continued my education at a British boarding school and later at the University of London, becoming a transatlantic commuter, mostly by sea, in days when air travel was still a luxury.

This transatlantic lifestyle unsettled my sense of national identity; chastised by my severe English boarding school teachers for losing my British accent but always appearing quite British to Americans, I could never decide where I belonged, a question that frequently arises, albeit in a different context, for those of us who have chosen a feminist path through international relations. Although relatively few young people went to university in England at that time and in spite of my choice of an all-women's college, most of my fellow graduates expected to go into secondary school teaching. This was the best option for women in Britain with a university degree at that time and one that was often regarded as a temporary stage on the way to full-time motherhood. Having studied history as an undergraduate I decided to pursue a master's degree in international relations at Yale. The realities of war and the promise of peace, enshrined in the UN Charter, were foundational for my interest in international relations, especially my evolving interest in peace studies. Yet even after I received a master's degree, it was hard to imagine a career in what was then not a very hospitable environment for women academics in IR—a very male-dominated field. I left academia, somewhat gratefully, and devoted the next ten years to full-time motherhood—"not working," as it was always described to me. Although the irony of this label escaped me at the time, I always try to remind my students that indeed their mothers do "work," even if it is not remunerated work.

Ten years later, I went back to graduate school to pursue a Ph.D. in political science at Brandeis University. I had spent the previous year in Geneva, Switzerland, where I participated in a course at The Graduate Institute taught by Norwegian peace researcher Johan Galtung. His particular interest at that time was small-scale self-reliant development as a strategy for newly emerging economies. My decision to pursue this theme for my Ph.D. thesis was not particularly feminist—indeed, I had not yet been exposed to feminist thinking at that time—but the topic was still unconventional for IR. *Self-Reliance versus Power Politics: American and Indian Experiences in Building Nation-States* (1987), the title under which my dissertation was published, compared strategies of building national-power favored by both the United States during its early development and post-independence India, with small-scale agrarian strategies, favored in the early writings of Thomas Jefferson and by Mohandas Gandhi as his vision for India's development. In retrospect, one could project a gendered analysis onto these two very different strategies—one dedicated to building national power, the other toward the development of basic needs; in both cases, the national power strategy won out.

Entering the job market to teach international relations with a somewhat unconventional dissertation, I was fortunate to be offered a position at the College of the Holy Cross, in Worcester, Massachusetts, a small liberal arts college where the quality of one's research was more valued than whether one was working in an "acceptable" IR paradigm. When I started teaching in the 1980s, nuclear strategy and the Cold War rivalry between the United States and the Soviet Union were central issues in introductory courses in international relations. Well before I was exposed to any feminist literature, I became aware of how many of my women students were quite uncomfortable with, or unmotivated by, my introductory IR course, often seeming quite alienated from the material. Besides the problem that there was nothing to assign by women authors, much of the subject matter—a great deal of it on war and nuclear strategy—seemed to leave them feeling fundamentally disempowered and disinterested. I myself had been trained in conventional IR in graduate school, and I had never thought to question the absence of women either as creators of, or as subject matter in, the discipline of international relations. It was not until a few years into teaching and going to professional conferences where women seldom appeared on panels that I began to develop a feminist consciousness or even ask the basic question, where are the women?[1]

Trying to figure out why extremely capable students felt so alienated from the material, with its emphasis on national security and conflict, motivated me to start thinking about IR as gendered masculine. A defining moment for me was reading Evelyn Fox Keller's *Reflections on Gender and Science* (1985) and attending her class on gender and science at MIT in 1986. Keller, a physicist by training, claimed in her book that the natural sciences are gendered, and gendered masculine, in both the questions they ask and the ways they go about answering them. This is a claim that I thought might equally be applied to IR. My first article (Chapter 1 in this book) began to develop this idea, applying it to Hans Morgenthau's principles of political realism.

My first encounter with feminism and international relations was when I was invited to attend a conference on Women and International Relations at the London School of Economics (LSE) in 1988. It is safe to say that before that the presence of women and gender issues had been completely ignored by the IR discipline.[2] As Fred Halliday noted in his introduction to the *Millennium* special issue that published the conference papers, there had been some recognition of women and gender in the social sciences, mainly in history and sociology. However, as he claimed, women remained hidden from international

---

1. The person with whom this question is associated in IR is Cynthia Enloe. I remember Enloe visiting my classes, picking up the students' textbooks, and searching, usually in vain, for the words "women" or "gender" in the index.
2. This is not to say that feminists were not writing about global issues before this date. Significant work was being done on women and war and women in the military. See, for example, Elshtain (1985), Enloe (1983), and Stiehm (1983).

relations (Halliday 1988). The following year Halliday introduced the first course on women and international relations into the MA program at LSE. I was fortunate to be able to participate. There was little material that we would call IR in the disciplinary sense that we could assign to the students. Guest speakers were mostly development specialists from international agencies who were responding to calls from the international women's movement of the 1970s to consider women's needs (for the first time) in development planning.

Bringing feminist perspectives into the discipline of international relations began through conferences and collaboration—a feminist way of doing things. Shortly after the conference at the London School of Economics in 1988, Jane Jaquette and Spike Peterson, professors at Occidental College and the University of Arizona, respectively, organized a second one at the University of Southern California (USC) in 1989 entitled "Women, the State and War: What Difference Does Gender Make?" Close to seventy participants attended from a variety of social science disciplines, including feminist scholars and a number of senior international relations scholars who had had little previous exposure to feminist analysis. In the following year a third conference, which I organized, together with Peggy McIntosh of the Wellesley Center for Research on Women, was held at Wellesley College and funded by the Ford Foundation. Collective efforts, such as these, and the sharing of ideas have been important aspects of building this new discipline, which has since evolved into a thriving academic community. Since academic feminism was born out of the women's movement of the 1960s and 1970s, an important aspect of these collective efforts has been an attempt to broaden conversations to include policy-makers and activists. To this end, ten years after the initial Wellesley conference, the Ford Foundation funded two additional conferences entitled "Gender in International Relations: From Seeing Women and Recognizing Gender to Transforming Policy Research," held at Wellesley College and USC in 2001. Participants included policy-makers, activists, and academics; many IR feminist scholars are explicit in their normative commitments to effecting social change and identify themselves as scholar-activists, an identity that appears somewhat unconventional in a discipline committed to "objective scientific" research but one that is extremely important in feminist research. By 2001, I had moved to take up a position in the School of International Relations at USC, an institution that supported non-conventional approaches to IR. This position gave me an opportunity to train graduate students who, together with many other young scholars from all over the world, are continuing to push boundaries and produce innovative work beyond what those of us could have imagined at the beginning.

When these efforts at introducing feminist perspectives were first launched, at the end of the 1980s, it seemed like a promising time for new thinking in the international relations discipline. The Cold War was ending and, not coincidentally, I believe, IR was both broadening its subject matter and opening up to critical approaches in terms of methodological perspectives, described at the time as "a post-positivist era" (Lapid 1989). There was the optimistic sense that feminism was one of a number of new and exciting critical approaches that would enrich and expand a field that had been so caught up with explaining the national security behavior of the great powers and with using neo-positivist methodologies to do so (Waltz 1979).

With the exception of some subfields of sociology, most of the social sciences were late in adopting a gender perspective—particularly in matters related to global affairs. Nevertheless, when this did happen, it was remarkable the extent to which scholars in different parts of the world, and in different disciplines, began to think along similar lines at about the same time. In 1993 Jan Jindy Pettman published an article in Australia's leading international affairs journal entitled "Gendering International Relations" (Pettman 1993).[3] Two years earlier, Hilary Charlesworth and her coauthors' article in the *American Journal of International Law* had already drawn attention to the gendered foundations of International Law (Charlesworth et al. 1991). That same year, Marianne Ferber and Julie Nelson edited *Beyond Economic Man*, which made similar claims about the masculine foundations of the discipline of economics (Ferber and Nelson 1993).

What were we doing in those early days? Some of us were trying to find women. Cynthia Enloe suggested that international relations was so thoroughly gendered that no one had noticed that women were missing (Enloe 1990). Besides finding women in places not normally considered within the boundaries of IR, feminists were also attempting to redefine some of the core concepts of the field—concepts such as security, anarchy, and sovereignty. In the words of Spike Peterson, these initial feminist endeavors were engaged in three knowledge projects—first, exposing the extent and effect of masculinist bias; second, attempting to rectify the systematic exclusion of women by adding women to existing frameworks; and third, and by far the most radical and least understood, reconstructing theory by recognizing gender as an analytical and structural category (Peterson 2004). It continues to be the case that the third goal, recognizing international relations as gendered (both in the disciplinary and "real-world" sense) is the most radical move and remains the least understood by the wider discipline.

This book presents some of my interventions into a field that, in the last twenty-five years, has produced a rich array of scholarship that has developed from these initial goals. Happily it has now extended beyond its Anglo-American/Australian foundations to include scholars in all parts of the world; like feminism more generally, it is paying increasing attention to

3. Pettman's subsequent 1996 book *Worlding Women* was an important early statement, introducing feminist perspectives into IR.

the issue of the intersectionality of race, class, and gender. While feminist research has been successful in making women visible, it has gone much deeper. Getting beyond women *and* IR, and even beyond gender *and* IR, it has successfully demonstrated—though maybe not as much as we would like to the discipline as a whole—that IR theory is thoroughly gendered, both in the questions it chooses to ask, as well as how it goes about answering them.

One of the most creative moves feminism has made is to challenge disciplinary boundaries and to bring in new issues and voices. Rich empirical case studies—using methodologies not normally employed by IR scholars—have shed light on those on the margins (both women and men) whose lives are deeply impacted by global politics and economics. Feminists have successfully demonstrated how the lives of sex workers, domestic servants, home-based workers, and those who work at unremunerated caring and reproductive labor are intertwined with global politics and the global economy. They have also suggested that the security of states is sometimes dependent on rendering insecure the lives of certain, often marginalized, people and that the global capitalist economy could not function without unremunerated labor, the majority of which is performed by women. IR feminists have also pointed to the inadequacies of social scientific methodologies for answering many of the questions they want to ask. There is now an emerging literature on feminist methodologies—much needed for our research students who have often gone outside the discipline to seek the kind of methodological training necessary to do empirical feminist research. Two books, one edited by Brooke Ackerly, Maria Stern, and Jacqui True (2006) and the other authored by Ackerly and True (2010) provide important guides for the many different methods and methodologies that IR feminists are using to do their empirical work.[4]

This rich array of interdisciplinary scholarship is evident in an increasing flow of books, book series, and journal articles. Much of this has been supported by workshops at the International Studies Association (ISA) and by its Feminist Theory and Gender Studies Section (FTGS). As I mentioned earlier, in the 1980s large professional organizations such as the ISA were inhospitable territory for women scholars and feminist research. Happily, this is no longer the case, and a rich array of feminist scholarship is presented at annual meetings of the ISA and other professional organizations.[5] Thanks to Jindy Pettman and many other capable and innovative editors who have followed in her footsteps, feminist IR now has its own journal, *The International Feminist Journal of Politics* (IFJP), which was launched at the Australian National University

4. Ackerly and True first worked together as postdoctoral fellows at the Center for International Studies at USC in 2000–2001 when I directed the Center. They have continued to collaborate and bring young scholars together around methodological issues concerned with doing feminist research.

5. At the 2012 annual meeting of the ISA, FTGS sponsored or cosponsored fifty-five panels.

(ANU) in 1999. In her introduction to the tenth anniversary issue of the *IFJP*, Pettman pointed to the 1990s, when the journal was launched, as optimistic times for feminist IR (Pettman 2009, 3) A transnationalist feminist movement was being built and was having some impact on the international stage; this created an interest in feminist publications across the fields of development studies, international political economy, international law, and cultural studies. In the same issue, Meghana Nayak (2009, 22) praised the *IFJP* for providing a sense of community for feminist scholars, one that they often lack in lonely spaces within academic departments. Since its launch in Australia, *IFJP*'s editorial home has moved to the United Kingdom and Canada. In 2013 it moved under the coeditorship of three scholars in the United States, South Africa, and the United Kingdom, making it a truly international journal that attracts articles from a wide array of disciplines and many parts of the world.

When I tried to explain to Peggy McIntosh, the co-organizer of the 1990 Wellesley conference (not herself an IR scholar) what IR was about, her reaction was that IR seemed to be neither international nor about relations. I think that, in the last twenty-five years, feminists have demonstrated that IR can be truly international and that it can be about relations. IR feminists have engaged in collaborative work and research ventures across various disciplinary and international boundaries. But, in spite of this sense of optimism, feminism has never sat easily in the IR discipline. IR feminists have devoted quite a bit of time trying to converse with the wider discipline on these issues. Peterson's radical goal—reconstructing theory by recognizing gender as an analytical and structural category—has never been acknowledged by non-feminists. Feminist work is not regularly cited either by mainstream or critical scholars, and gender is rarely recognized as a legitimate category of analysis by non-feminists.[6] Whereas the subject matter that feminists address is frequently deemed important and interesting, nevertheless it is often thought to be outside the subject matter of disciplinary IR. The methods that feminists use to answer the questions they ask are often dismissed as not being "scientific." These misunderstandings and lack of recognition have led some IR feminists to leave the IR discipline and migrate to women's studies programs. Many who do choose to stay find more hospitable homes outside the United States where tolerance for a broader range of issues and methodologies is more evident.

Looking back at my own writings and teachings, I am aware of both the successes and frustrations. On the positive side, some of the articles reproduced in this book are regularly used in IR classes, and some have been reprinted in IR readers. However, the biggest frustration for me has been over issues of methodology—a series of my articles, some of which I include in Part Two,

---

6. This is changing somewhat with respect to critical scholars. Today many introductory IR textbooks include a chapter on feminist international relations.

address the continuing challenge issued to IR feminists, that they are not doing legitimate "scientific" research unless they use conventional methodologies. This has been a continuing hurdle for those trying to publish in mainstream US journals.[7]

Thanks to the ideas of so many creative feminist scholars, one of the greatest rewards for me in my journey through feminism has been not only to look for women but also for other marginalized people who have also been "hidden from international relations." My recent articles, on religion and retelling IR's foundational stories (Part Three of this book) mark the beginnings of my efforts to look at religion, imperialism, and race, issues hitherto neglected by IR. While I realize that there has been more attention recently to religion, very little of it comes out of a feminist perspective. Apart from the work of postcolonial scholars and feminists, IR has almost completely ignored race.

However, as I look back at my work, I realize that I too have been guilty of ethnocentrism and what many have suggested is an excessive focus on the US mainstream. I have learned so much from scholars in other parts of the world: at the University of Uppsala, where I was introduced to Swedish peace research, an important formative framework for my definition of comprehensive security (Tickner 1992, 2001); multiple visits to Australia and New Zealand, which, besides introducing me to the lively feminist IR communities there, exposed me to feminist international law and, in New Zealand, to Maori scholarship. I have appreciated my many visits to the United Kingdom to celebrate the success of the rich array of feminist scholarship there. Time and space, the theme of the 2006 Russian International Studies Association meeting, afforded me my first opportunity to try out ideas about postcolonialism. I intend to explore these very diverse multidisciplinary literatures that feminist scholars have been producing over the past twenty years more fully in my future work. But when I first started on my feminist journey, my intention was to attempt to speak to the US mainstream of IR, my first intellectual home. While such a strategy has placed constraints on my writings, I hope that, in some small measure, it has allowed me to speak to IR students who might not otherwise have encountered feminist perspectives in their traditional IR classes.

As I reflect on the writings included in this book, I see my intellectual development as a feminist scholar in terms of three phases—not necessarily time sequential: first, putting women and gender into the theoretical concepts of, and approaches to, IR; second, methodological interventions and attempts at "conversations" with the IR mainstream (mainly in the US) on the scientific

7. There is a large body of gender work that does use positivist, often quantitative, methodologies, which will be discussed in more detail in subsequent chapters. See, for example, Caprioli (2000), Caprioli and Boyer (2001), Carpenter (2006), and Hudson et al. (2008/2009).

validity of feminist research; third, investigations into areas, such as race, imperialism, and religion, that have traditionally been under-recognized in IR. For me, the third phase signals new beginnings—one that starts to look at IR from the perspective of those whose voices have never been heard in the field. As I have taken this feminist journey, I, like all feminists, have become increasingly aware of the issues of knowledge and power—whose knowledge gets validated and whose is forgotten or never heard. Thanks to all the innovative paths that IR feminists are now taking, many of these hidden voices are now coming to light.

A Feminist Voyage through
International Relations

PART ONE
Seeing Women and Gender in the Discipline of International Relations

Part One is a selection of my earlier work that introduces gender and women to the discipline of international relations (IR) in which, until the late 1980s, they had been notable for their absence. Most of the chapters are based on articles and book chapters written during the late 1980s and 1990s, a time, immediately after the Cold War, when a discipline that had been preoccupied with national security and efforts to promote "scientific" methodologies seemed to be opening up to a broader array of issues and epistemologies. Yosef Lapid's much-cited article "The Third Debate" (Lapid 1989) proclaimed the beginning of a post-positivist era in which he expected the discipline to become more receptive to different ways of accumulating knowledge, of which feminism was one.

I begin Part I with my reformulation of Hans Morgenthau's six principles of political realism. Published originally in 1988 in the journal *Millennium,* this was my first published piece using a feminist lens. I chose to focus on Morgenthau's work because he was (and still is) such an influential figure in the discipline. Morgenthau is often credited with being the founder of the post–World War II Realist School in the United States, but his influence spread well beyond the United States and even beyond realism.[1] He is also credited with putting IR on a more "scientific" footing, but his definition of science was one with which many IR feminists have problems, as will be discussed in more detail in Part Two.[2] Chapter 1 uses feminist analysis to challenge Realist

---

1. When I was teaching IR theory to graduate students in the 1990s, I would ask the international students which had been the most influential books that they had read in their own countries as undergraduates. Their responses almost always included Morgenthau's *Politics among Nations,* even when its relevance to their state's security issues seemed minimal.
2. It is the case that Morgenthau himself was ambivalent about using models from the natural sciences to talk about human behavior. I will address this in Chapter 10.

assumptions about unitary states in an anarchical world where security is defined as state security achieved through power. In this piece I first introduced my feminist redefinition of a more comprehensive notion of security, a definition that, for me, was influenced by Scandinavian peace research—one that includes not only state security but the security of individuals and the natural environment, a perspective that runs through all my subsequent work.

Chapter 2 focuses more directly on the fields of security studies and peace studies. Originally it was two separate articles written in 2004 and 1994, respectively. While security studies has always occupied a privileged position in IR, peace studies is a field that has struggled to earn the same degree of recognition. In this chapter, I begin to take up the theme of conversations across paradigms and disciplines, an important theme in all my subsequent work and one that is quite typical of feminism more generally. Much of my work has argued that the many communication problems between feminists and IR scholars are not only about what should be included in the subject matter of IR but also miscommunications about epistemological issues. I believe the latter are more constraining and have presented greater obstacles to bringing the two together. I discuss this in more detail in Part II. Since 2004, when the security section of this chapter was written, there has been a huge proliferation of IR feminist security studies. However, it remains the case that the field of security studies is still largely a male domain that remains quite resistant to introducing gender or women into its subject matter.[3]

Since women have traditionally been thought to have a special relationship with peace, peace studies is an approach that might be considered more hospitable to women and gender issues. However, peace studies has been just as resistant to feminism as have other IR approaches. And IR feminists have been ambivalent about peace studies as well. I believe this is due to what many feminists consider to be the problematic association of women with peace, an association that disempowers both women and peace. As in Chapter 1, I draw on a more robust definition of peace, introduced into the field by Scandinavian peace research scholars, that uses a more comprehensive definition of security involving the diminution, not only of physical violence, but of structural and ecological violence also. While this framework is not original to feminism, I suggest ways in which gender analysis enhances and deepens it. As feminist peace researcher Catia Confortini claims, there is not much evidence that peace studies has used gender analysis to any great extent in the intervening twenty years since this chapter was originally published (Confortini 2012, 6).

Using a gender lens, Chapters 3 through 5 investigate the field of international political economy (IPE) and its evolving focus on economic globalization. Each of these chapters elaborates once again on the theme of

---

3. For some of the recent feminist scholarship in security studies, see Cohn (2013); Sjoberg (2009); and Sjoberg (2013).

comprehensive security. Chapter 3, originally written in 1991, uses the framework developed by Robert Gilpin in his 1987 text, *The Political Economy of International Relations*, in which he conceptualizes IPE in terms of three constitutive ideologies: liberalism, nationalism (which he equates with realism), and Marxism (Gilpin 1987). Gilpin does not mention gender, but I claim that the units of analysis—the individual, the state, and class—that he associates with each ideology, respectively, are gendered and are gendered masculine. Individuals are assumed to be instrumentally rational beings exhibiting competitive behavior typical of the marketplace, while states, in the nationalist approach, are assumed to be exhibiting similarly economic competitive behavior in their efforts to be secure and self-sufficient in a dangerous international system. I argue that these behaviors are built on the behavior of (traditionally) men in the marketplace and that they ignore a great deal of economic activity having to do with caring and reproductive labor, most of which is performed by women. Marxism, which claims the standpoint of the weak and powerless, appears to be more compatible with feminist approaches; yet it, too, has typically ignored the role of women in the household and as caregivers. I conclude by offering a feminist perspective on IPE that would start at the bottom, looking at how to ensure individuals' basic needs. Although it is now twenty-five years since Gilpin's book was published, I believe my gendered reading has relevance today, since Gilpin's three defining ideologies are still foundational for the way in which we think about security and political economy. While Marxism is often ignored in political economy, at least in the United States, Marxism has provided a foundation for feminist socialist and standpoint theories that will be discussed later. Standpoint feminism claims that women's position, on the peripheries of the system, gives them an epistemological standpoint that provides a more comprehensive picture of reality.

Chapter 4 offers environmental and ecological perspectives on political economy, areas that have been neglected by IPE and feminist scholars alike. It examines the way in which interactions between states and markets have depended on the exploitation of nature since the seventeenth century. Certain ecofeminists believe that this attitude toward nature has also been associated with the exploitation of women and other cultures. Since much of ecofeminism assumes women's special relationship with nature—an assumption that many feminists see as disempowering for women—it is not a position that has been embraced by many IR feminists. Nevertheless, as we face environmental problems that seem even more immediate and pressing than when this chapter was written in 1993, revisiting these issues seems important.

Chapter 5, written in 2004, thirteen years after my initial intervention into the field, focuses on economic globalization, a term that is now widely used in IPE, and its consequences for the economic security of women. The chapter investigates what I call the invisible gendered frontiers of globalization and how they affect women. While few women can be found among the global citizens of the international business world, women are also on the move—crossing frontiers to take up work as domestic servants, sweatshop workers, and sex workers. I suggest some ways in which women's organizing at the grassroots, national, and international levels, in social movements and in nongovernmental organizations (NGOs), is attempting to mitigate what feminists have called the global gendered division of labor, and I discuss ways in which these groups are working toward creating a global economy that is less hierarchical and more just for everyone.

CHAPTER 1

Hans Morgenthau's Principles of Political Realism: A Feminist Reformulation

1988

It is not in giving life but in risking life that man is raised above the animal: that is why superiority has been accorded in humanity not to the sex that brings forth but to that which kills.

Simone de Beauvoir[1]

International politics is a man's world, a world of power and conflict in which warfare is a privileged activity. Traditionally, diplomacy, military service, and the science of international politics have been largely male domains. In the past, women have rarely been included in the ranks of professional diplomats or the military: of the relatively few women who specialize in the academic discipline of international relations, few are security specialists. Women political scientists who do international relations tend to focus on areas such as international political economy, North-South relations, and matters of distributive justice.[2]

In the United States, where women are entering the military and the foreign service in greater numbers than ever before, rarely are they to be found in positions of military leadership or at the top of the foreign policy

---

1. Quoted in Harding (1986, 148).
2. This has changed somewhat in the last twenty-five years, although security studies is still a male-dominated field, the exception being the very rich field of feminist security studies.

establishment.[3] One notable exception, Jeane Kirkpatrick, who was US ambassador to the United Nations in the early 1980s, described herself as "a mouse in a man's world." For in spite of her authoritative and forceful public style and strong conservative credentials, Kirkpatrick maintained that she failed to win the respect or attention of her male colleagues on matters of foreign policy (Crapol 1987, 167).

Kirkpatrick's story could serve to illustrate the discrimination that women often encounter when they rise to high political office. However, the doubts as to whether a woman would be strong enough to press the nuclear button (an issue raised when a tearful Patricia Schroeder was pictured sobbing on her husband's shoulder as she bowed out of the 1988 US presidential race) suggest that there may be an even more fundamental barrier to women's entry into the highest ranks of the military or of foreign policy-making. Nuclear strategy, with its vocabulary of power, threat, force, and deterrence, has a distinctly masculine ring;[4] moreover, women are stereotypically judged to be lacking in qualities that these terms evoke. It has also been suggested that, although more women are entering the world of public policy, they are more comfortable dealing with domestic issues such as social welfare that are more compatible with their nurturing skills. Yet the large number of women in the ranks of the peace movement suggests that women are not uninterested in issues of war and peace, although their frequent dissent from national security policy has often branded them as naive, uninformed, or even unpatriotic.

In this chapter I explore the question why international politics is perceived as a man's world and why women are so under-represented in the higher echelons of the foreign policy establishment, the military, and the academic discipline of international relations. Since I believe that there is something about this field that renders it particularly inhospitable and unattractive to women, I intend to focus on the nature of the discipline itself, rather than on possible strategies to remove barriers to women's access to high policy positions. As I have already suggested, the issues that are prioritized in foreign policy are issues with which men have had a special affinity. Moreover, if it is primarily men who are describing these issues and constructing theories to explain the workings of the international system, might we not expect to find a masculine perspective in the academic discipline also? If this were so, then it could

3. In 1987 only 4.8 percent of the top career foreign service employees were women. Statement of Patricia Schroeder before the Committee on Foreign Affairs, US House of Representatives, *Women's Perspectives on US Foreign Policy: A Compilation of Views.* (Washington, DC: US Government Printing Office, 1988), p. 4. This has changed in the last twenty years. The US has had three female secretaries of state and, in 2010, women made up 22 percent of senior foreign service officers (Statement of John M. Robinson for "Wanted: Qualified While Males," *State Magazine,* May 2010, 9). For an analysis of women's roles in the American military, see Enloe (1983).

4. For an analysis of the role of masculine language in shaping strategic thinking, see Cohn (1987).

be argued that the exclusion of women has operated not only at the level of discrimination but also through a process of self-selection, which begins with the way in which we are taught about international relations.

In order to investigate this claim that the discipline of international relations—traditionally defined by realism, the predominant approach during the post–World War II period (at least in the US)—is based on a masculine worldview, I propose to examine Hans Morgenthau's six principles of political realism. I shall use some ideas from feminist theory to show that the way in which Morgenthau describes and explains international politics, and the prescriptions that ensue, are embedded in a masculine perspective. Then I shall suggest some ways in which feminist theory might help us begin to conceptualize a worldview from a feminine perspective and to formulate a feminist epistemology of international relations. Drawing on these observations, I shall conclude with a reformulation of Morgenthau's six principles. Male critics of contemporary realism have already raised many of the same questions about realism that I shall address. However, in undertaking this exercise, I hope to link the growing critical perspective on international relations theory and feminist writers interested in global issues. Adding a feminist perspective to its discourse could also help to make the field of international relations more accessible to women scholars and practitioners.

HANS MORGENTHAU'S PRINCIPLES OF POLITICAL REALISM: A MASCULINE PERSPECTIVE?

I have chosen to focus on Hans Morgenthau's six principles of political realism because they represent one of the most important statements of post–World War II realism from which several generations of scholars and practitioners of international relations have been nourished. Although Morgenthau has frequently been criticized for his lack of scientific rigor and ambiguous use of language, these six principles have significantly framed the way in which the majority of international relations scholars and practitioners in the West have thought about international politics since 1945.[5]

Morgenthau's principles of political realism can be summarized as follows:

1. Politics, like society in general, is governed by objective laws that have their roots in human nature, which is unchanging: therefore it is possible to develop a rational theory that reflects these objective laws.

---

5. The claim for the dominance of the realist paradigm is supported by Vasquez (1979, 210–228). For a critique of Morgenthau's ambiguous use of language, see Claude (1962, 25–37).

2. The main signpost of political realism is the concept of interest defined in terms of power, which infuses rational order into the subject matter of politics, and thus makes the theoretical understanding of politics possible. Political realism stresses the rational, objective, and unemotional.
3. Realism assumes that interest defined as power is an objective category that is universally valid but not with a meaning that is fixed once and for all. Power is the control of man over man.
4. Political realism is aware of the moral significance of political action. It is also aware of the tension between the moral command and the requirements of successful political action.
5. Political realism refuses to identify the moral aspirations of a particular nation with the moral laws that govern the universe. It is the concept of interest defined in terms of power that saves us from moral excess and political folly.
6. The political realist maintains the autonomy of the political sphere. He asks "How does this policy affect the power of the nation?" Political realism is based on a pluralistic conception of human nature. A man who was nothing but "political man" would be a beast, for he would be completely lacking in moral restraints. But, in order to develop an autonomous theory of political behavior, "political man" must be abstracted from other aspects of human nature.[6]

I am not going to argue that Morgenthau is incorrect in his portrayal of the international system. I do believe, however, that it is a partial description of international politics because it is based on assumptions about human nature that are partial and that privilege masculinity. First, it is necessary to define gender. According to almost all feminist theorists, masculinity and femininity refer to a set of socially constructed categories that vary in time and place, rather than to biological determinants. Gender is a relational concept: masculinity and femininity depend on each other for the way each is defined. It is also important to note that gender is a relationship of unequal power. In the West, conceptual dichotomies such as objectivity versus subjectivity, reason versus emotion, mind versus body, culture versus nature, self versus other (or autonomy versus relatedness), knowing versus being, and public versus private have typically been used to describe male/female differences by feminists and non-feminists alike (Keller 1985; Harding 1986). In the United States, psychological tests conducted across different socioeconomic groups confirm

6. These are drawn from the six principles of political realism in Morgenthau (1973, 4–15). I am aware that these principles embody only a partial statement of Morgenthau's very rich study of international politics, a study which deserves a much more detailed analysis than I can give it here.

that individuals perceive these dichotomies as masculine and feminine and also that the characteristics associated with masculinity are more highly valued by both men and women alike (Broverman et al. 1972).[7] It is important to stress, however, that these characteristics are stereotypical; they do not necessarily describe individual men or women, who can exhibit characteristics and modes of thought associated with the opposite sex. Although feminists have tended to be suspicious of biological determinants that have generally been used for purposes of demeaning women, more recent work is beginning to investigate interactions between social construction and biology.

Using a vocabulary that contains many of the words associated with masculinity as I have defined it, Morgenthau asserts that it is possible to develop a rational (and unemotional) theory of international politics based on objective laws that have their roots in human nature. Since Morgenthau wrote the first edition of *Politics Among Nations* in 1948, this search for an objective science of international politics, based on the model of the natural sciences, has been an important part of the realist and neo-realist agendas, as well as that of the more recent liberal neo-institutionalists. In her feminist critique of the natural sciences, Evelyn Fox Keller points out that most scientific communities share the "assumption that the universe they study is directly accessible, represented by concepts shaped not by language but only by the demands of logic and experiment" (Keller 1985, 130). The laws of nature, according to this view of science, are "beyond the relativity of language." Like most feminists, Keller rejects this view of science that, she asserts, imposes a coercive, hierarchical, and conformist pattern on scientific inquiry. Feminists in general are skeptical about the possibility of finding a universal and objective foundation for knowledge that Morgenthau claims is possible. Most share the belief that knowledge is socially constructed: since it is language that transmits knowledge, the use of language and its claims of objectivity must continually be questioned.

Keller argues that objectivity, as it is usually defined in our culture, is associated with masculinity. She identifies it as "a network of interactions between gender development, a belief system that equates objectivity with masculinity, and a set of cultural values that simultaneously (and co-jointly) elevates what is defined as scientific and what is defined as masculine" (Keller 1985, 89). Keller links the separation of self from other, an important stage of masculine gender development, with this notion of objectivity. Translated into scientific inquiry, this becomes the striving for the separation of subject and object, an important goal of modern science and one, which Keller asserts, is based on the need for control: hence objectivity becomes associated with power and domination.

7. Replication of this research in the 1980s confirms that these perceptions still held in the 1980s when this piece was written.

The need for control has been an important motivating force for modern realism. To begin his search for an objective, rational theory of international politics, which could impose order on a chaotic and conflictual world, Morgenthau constructs an abstraction that he calls political man, a beast completely lacking in moral restraints. Morgenthau is deeply aware that real man, like real states, is both moral and bestial but, because states do not live up to the universal moral laws that govern the universe, those who behave morally in international politics are doomed to failure because of the immoral actions of others. To solve this tension, Morgenthau postulates a realm of international politics in which the amoral behavior of political man is not only permissible but prudent. It is a Hobbesian world, separate and distinct from the world of domestic order, in which states may act like beasts, for survival depends on a maximization of power and a willingness to fight.

Having long argued that the personal is political, most feminist theory would reject the validity of constructing an autonomous political sphere around which boundaries of permissible modes of conduct have been drawn. As Keller maintains, "the demarcation between public and private not only defines and defends the boundaries of the political but also helps form its content and style" (Keller 1985, 9). Morgenthau's political man is a social construct that is based on a partial representation of human nature. One might well ask where the women were in Hobbes's state of nature; presumably they must have been involved in reproduction and child rearing, rather than warfare, if life was to go on for more than one generation (Ketchum 1980). Morgenthau's emphasis on the conflictual aspects of the international system contributes to a tendency, shared by other realists, to de-emphasize elements of cooperation and regeneration which are also aspects of international relations.[8]

Morgenthau's construction of an amoral realm of international power politics is an attempt to resolve what he sees as a fundamental tension between the moral laws that govern the universe and the requirements of successful political action in a world where states use morality as a cloak to justify the pursuit of their own national interests. Morgenthau's universalistic morality postulates the highest form of morality as an abstract ideal, similar to the Golden Rule, to which states seldom adhere: the morality of states is an instrumental morality that is guided by self-interest. Morgenthau's hierarchical ordering of morality contains parallels with the work of psychologist Lawrence Kohlberg. Based on a study of the moral development of eighty-four American boys, Kohlberg concludes that the highest stage of human moral

8. Others have questioned whether Hobbes's state of nature provides an accurate description of the international system. See, for example, Beitz (1979, 35–50) and Hoffmann (1981, ch. 1).

development (which he calls stage six) is the ability to recognize abstract universal principles of justice; lower on the scale (stage two) is an instrumental morality concerned with serving one's own interests while recognizing that others have interests, too. Between these two is an interpersonal morality that is contextual and characterized by sensitivity to the needs of others (stage three).[9]

In her critique of Kohlberg's stages of moral development, Carol Gilligan argues that they are based on a masculine conception of morality. On Kohlberg's scale, women rarely rise above the third or contextual stage, but Gilligan claims that this is not a sign of inferiority, but of difference. Since women are socialized into a mode of thinking that is contextual and narrative, rather than formal and abstract, they tend to see issues in contextual rather than in abstract terms (Gilligan 1982, ch. 1). In international relations, the tendency to think about morality either in terms of abstract, universal, and unattainable standards or as purely instrumental, as Morgenthau does, detracts from our ability to tolerate cultural differences and to seek potential for building community in spite of these differences.

Using examples from the feminist literature, I have suggested that Morgenthau's attempt to construct an objective, universal theory of international politics is rooted in assumptions about human nature and morality that, in modern Western culture, are associated with masculinity. Further evidence that Morgenthau's principles are not the basis for a universalistic and objective theory is contained in his frequent references to the failure of what he calls the "legalistic-moralistic" or idealist approach to world politics that he claims was largely responsible for both the World Wars. Having laid the blame for World War II on the misguided morality of appeasement, Morgenthau's *realpolitik* prescriptions for successful political action appear as prescriptions for avoiding the mistakes of the 1930s, rather than as prescriptions with timeless applicability.

If Morgenthau's worldview is embedded in the traumas of World War II, are his prescriptions still valid as we move further away from this event? I share with other critics of realism the view that, in a rapidly changing world, we must begin to search for modes of behavior different from those prescribed by Morgenthau. Given that any war between the major powers is likely to be nuclear, increasing security by increasing power could be suicidal.[10] Moreover,

---

9. Kohlberg's stages of moral development are described and discussed in Kegan (1982, ch. 2).

10. There is evidence that, toward the end of his life, Morgenthau himself was aware that his own prescriptions were becoming anachronistic. In a seminar presentation in 1978, he suggested that power politics as the guiding principle for the conduct of international relations had become fatally defective. For a description of this seminar presentation, see Boyle (1985, 70–74). When this article was written in the late 1980s, nuclear war between the great powers still seemed like the greatest security threat to the United States.

the nation-state, the primary constitutive element of the international system for Morgenthau and other realists, is no longer able to deal with an increasingly pluralistic array of problems ranging from economic interdependence to environmental degradation. Could feminist theory make a contribution to international relations theory by constructing an alternative, feminist perspective on international politics that might help us search for more appropriate solutions?

A FEMINIST PERSPECTIVE ON INTERNATIONAL RELATIONS

If the way in which we describe reality has an effect on the ways we perceive and act upon our environment, new perspectives might lead us to consider alternative courses of action. With this in mind, I shall first examine two important concepts in international relations, power and security, from a feminist perspective and then discuss some feminist approaches to conflict resolution.

Morgenthau's definition of power, the control of man over man, is typical of the way that power is usually defined in international relations. Nancy Hartsock argues that this type of power as domination has always been associated with masculinity since the exercise of power has generally been a masculine activity; rarely have women exercised legitimized power in the public domain. When women write about power they stress energy, capacity, and potential, says Hartsock, and she notes that women theorists, even when they have little else in common, offer similar definitions of power that differ substantially from the understanding of power as domination (Hartsock 1983, 210).

Hannah Arendt, frequently cited by feminists writing about power, defines power as the human ability to act in concert, or action that is taken in connection with others who share similar concerns (Arendt 1969, 44).[11] This definition of power is similar to that of psychologist David McClelland's portrayal of female power, which he describes as shared rather than assertive (McClelland 1975, ch. 3). Jane Jaquette argues that, since women have had less access to the instruments of coercion, women have been more apt to rely on power as persuasion; she compares women's domestic activities to coalition-building (Jaquette 1984, ch. 2).

All of these writers are portraying power as a relationship of mutual enablement. Tying her definition of female power to international relations, Jaquette sees similarities between female strategies of persuasion and strategies of small states operating from a position of weakness in the international

11. Arendt's definition of power, as it relates to international relations, is discussed more extensively in Elshtain (1985).

system. There are also examples of states' behavior that contain elements of the female strategy of coalition-building. One such example is the Southern African Development Co-ordination Conference (SADCC) that is designed to build regional infrastructures based on mutual cooperation and collective self-reliance in order to decrease dependence on the South African economy. Another is the European Community, which has had considerable success in building mutual cooperation in an area of the world whose history would not predict such a course of events (Sylvester 1990). It is rare, however, that cooperative outcomes in international relations are described in these terms, though Karl Deutsch's notion of pluralistic security communities might be one such example where power is associated with building community (Deutsch 1957). I am not denying that power as domination is a pervasive reality in international relations, but sometimes there are also elements of cooperation in interstate relations that tend to be obscured when power is seen solely as domination. Thinking about power in this multidimensional sense may help us to think constructively about the potential for cooperation as well as conflict, an aspect of international relations generally downplayed by realism.

Redefining national security is another way in which feminist theory could contribute to new thinking about international relations.[12] Traditionally in the West, the concept of national security has been tied to military strength and its role in the physical protection of the nation-state from external threats. Morgenthau's notion of defending the national interest in terms of power is consistent with this definition. But this traditional definition of national security is partial at best in today's world (Azar and Moon 1984). When advanced states are highly interdependent, and rely on weapons whose effects would be equally devastating to winners and losers alike, defending national security by relying on war as the last resort no longer appears very useful. Moreover, if one thinks of security in North-South rather than East-West terms, for a large portion of the world's population, security has as much to do with the satisfaction of basic material needs as with military threats, According to Johan Galtung's notion of structural violence, the lowering of life expectancy by virtue of where one happens to be born is a form of violence whose effects can be as devastating as war (Galtung 1969). Basic needs satisfaction has a great deal to do with women, but only recently have women's roles as providers of basic needs, and in development more generally, become visible as important components in devising development strategies.[13] Traditionally,

12. "New thinking" is a term that was also used in the last years of the Soviet Union to describe foreign policy reformulations under Gorbachev. There were indications that the Soviets at that time were beginning to conceptualize security in the multidimensional terms described here. See Light (1988, ch. 10).

13. See, for example, Sen and Grown (1987). This is an example of a growing literature on women and development that deserves more attention from the international relations community.

the development literature has focused on aspects of the development process that are in the public sphere, are technologically complex, and are usually undertaken by men. Thinking about the role of women in development and the way in which we can define development and basic needs satisfaction to be inclusive of women's roles and needs are topics that deserve higher priority on the international agenda. Typically, however, this is an area about which traditional international relations theory, with its prioritizing of order over justice, has had very little to say.

A further threat to national security, more broadly defined, which also has not been on the agenda of traditional international relations, concerns the environment. Carolyn Merchant argues that a mechanistic view of nature, contained in modern science, has helped to guide an industrial and technological development that has resulted in the environmental damage that is now becoming a matter of global concern. In the introduction to her book *The Death of Nature,* Merchant suggests that "women and nature have an age-old association—an affiliation that has persisted throughout culture, language, and history" (Merchant 1980, xv). Hence she maintains that the ecology movement, which is growing up in response to these environmental threats, and the women's movement are deeply interconnected. Both stress living in equilibrium with nature rather than dominating it; both see nature as a living non-hierarchical entity in which each part is mutually dependent on the whole. Ecologists, as well as many feminists, are now suggesting that only with such a fundamental change in the way we view the world could we devise solutions that would allow the human species to survive the damage that we are inflicting on the environment.

Thinking about military, economic, and environmental security in interdependent terms suggests the need for new methods of conflict resolution that seek to achieve mutually beneficial, rather than zero-sum, outcomes. One such method comes from Sara Ruddick's work on "maternal thinking" (Ruddick 1984). Ruddick describes "maternal thinking" as focused on the preservation of life and the growth of children; to foster a domestic environment conducive to these goals, tranquillity must be preserved by avoiding conflict where possible, engaging in it nonviolently and restoring community when it is over. In such an environment, the ends for which disputes are fought are subordinated to the means by which they are resolved. This method of conflict resolution involves making contextual judgments, rather than appealing to absolute standards, and thus has much in common with Gilligan's definition of female morality.

While nonviolent resolution of conflict in the domestic sphere is a widely accepted norm, passive resistance in the public realm is regarded as deviant. But, as Ruddick argues, the peaceful resolution of conflict by mothers does not usually extend to the children of one's enemies, an important reason that women have been ready to support men's wars.[14] The question for Ruddick

14. For a more extensive analysis of this issue, see Elshtain (1987).

then becomes how to get "maternal thinking," a mode of thinking which she believes can be found in men as well as women, out into the public realm. Ruddick believes that finding a common humanity among one's opponents has become a condition of survival in the nuclear age, when the notion of winners and losers has become questionable.[15] Portraying the adversary as less than human has all too often been a technique of the nation-state to command loyalty and increase its legitimacy in the eyes of its citizens, but such behavior in the nuclear age may eventually be self-defeating.

We might also look to Gilligan's work for a feminist perspective on conflict resolution. Reporting on a study of playground behavior of American boys and girls, Gilligan argues that girls are less able to tolerate high levels of conflict, more likely than boys to play games that involve taking turns and in which the success of one does not depend on the failure of another (Gilligan 1982, 9–10). While Gilligan's study does not take into account attitudes toward other groups (racial, ethnic, economic, or national), it does suggest the validity of investigating whether girls are socialized to use different modes of problem-solving when dealing with conflict, and whether such behavior might be useful to us in thinking about international conflict resolution.

TOWARD A FEMINIST EPISTEMOLOGY OF INTERNATIONAL RELATIONS

I am deeply aware that there is no one feminist approach but many, which come out of various disciplines and intellectual traditions. Yet there are common themes in these different feminist literatures that I have reviewed, which could help us to begin to formulate a feminist epistemology of international relations. Morgenthau encourages us to try to stand back from the world and to think about theory building in terms of constructing a rational outline or map that has universal applications. In contrast, the feminist literature reviewed here emphasizes connection and contingency. Keller argues for a form of knowledge, which she calls "dynamic objectivity," "that grants to the world around us its independent integrity, but does so in a way that remains cognizant of, indeed relies on, our connectivity with that world" (Keller 1985, 117). Keller illustrates this mode of thinking in her study of Barbara McClintock, whose work on genetic transposition won her a Nobel Prize after many years of marginalization by the scientific community (Keller 1983). McClintock, Keller argues, was a scientist with a respect for complexity, diversity, and individual difference, whose methodology allowed her data to speak rather than imposing explanations on it.

15. This type of conflict resolution bears similarities to the problem-solving approach of Edward Azar, John Burton, and Herbert Kelman. See, for example, Azar and Burton (1986) and Kelman (1986).

Keller's portrayal of McClintock's science contains parallels with what Sandra Harding calls an African worldview (Harding 1986, ch. 7). Harding tells us that the Western liberal notion of rational economic man, an individualist and a welfare maximizer—similar to rational political man upon which realism has based its theoretical investigations—does not make any sense in the African worldview, where the individual is seen as part of the social order, acting within that order rather than upon it. Harding believes that this view of human behavior has much in common with a feminist perspective. If we combine this view of human behavior with Merchant's holistic perspective, which stresses the interconnectedness of all things including nature, it may help us to begin to think from a more global perspective, which appreciates cultural diversity but at the same time recognizes a growing interdependence that makes anachronistic the exclusionary thinking fostered by the nation-state system.

Keller's "dynamic objectivity," Harding's African worldview, and Merchant's ecological thinking all point us in the direction of an appreciation of the "other" as a subject whose views are as legitimate as our own, a way of thinking that has been sadly lacking in the history of international relations. Just as Keller cautions us against the construction of a feminist science, which could perpetuate these same exclusionary attitudes, Harding warns us against schema that contrast people by race, gender, or class and which originate within projects of social domination. Feminist thinkers generally dislike dichotomization and the distancing of subject from object that goes with abstract thinking, both of which, they believe, encourage a we/they attitude so characteristic of international relations. Instead, this literature points us toward constructing epistemologies which value ambiguity and difference, qualities that could stand us in good stead as we begin to build a human or ungendered theory of international relations containing elements of both masculine and feminine modes of thought.

MORGENTHAU'S PRINCIPLES OF POLITICAL REALISM: A FEMINIST REFORMULATION

In the first part of this chapter, I used feminist theory to develop a critique of Morgenthau's principles of political realism in order to demonstrate how the theory and practice of international relations may exhibit a masculine bias. I then suggested some contributions that feminist theory might make to reconceptualizing some important concepts in international relations and to thinking about a feminist epistemology. Drawing on these observations, I will now conclude with a feminist reformulation of Morgenthau's six principles of political realism, outlined earlier in this chapter, which might help us to begin to think differently about international relations. I shall not use the term "realism," since feminists believe that there are multiple realities: a truly

realistic picture of international politics must recognize elements of cooperation as well as conflict, morality as well as *realpolitik,* and the strivings for justice as well as order.[16] This reformulation may help us begin to think in these
multidimensional terms:

1. A feminist perspective believes that objectivity, as it is culturally defined,
   is associated with masculinity. Therefore, supposedly "objective" laws of
   human nature are based on a partial masculine view of human nature.
   Human nature is both masculine and feminine: it contains elements of
   social reproduction and development as well as political domination.
   Dynamic objectivity offers us a more connected view of objectivity with
   less potential for domination.
2. A feminist perspective believes that the national interest is multidimensional and contextually contingent. Therefore it cannot be defined solely in
   terms of power. In the contemporary world, the national interest demands
   cooperative rather than zero-sum solutions to a set of interdependent
   global problems that include nuclear war, economic well-being, and environmental degradation.
3. Power cannot be infused with meaning that is universally valid. Power as
   domination and control privileges masculinity and ignores the possibility
   of collective empowerment, another aspect of power often associated with
   femininity.
4. A feminist perspective rejects the possibility of separating moral command
   from political action. All political action has moral significance. The realist agenda for maximizing order through power and control prioritizes the
   moral command of order over those of justice and the satisfaction of basic
   needs necessary to ensure social reproduction.
5. While recognizing that the moral aspirations of particular nations cannot
   be equated with universal moral principles, a feminist perspective seeks
   to find common moral elements in human aspirations that could become
   the basis for de-escalating international conflict and building international
   community.
6. A feminist perspective denies the validity of the autonomy of the political.
   Since autonomy is associated with masculinity in Western culture, disciplinary efforts to construct a worldview that does not rest on a pluralistic
   conception of human nature, are partial and masculine. Building boundaries around a narrowly defined political realm defines political in a way that
   excludes the concerns and contributions of women.

---

16. "Utopia and reality are...the two facets of political science. Sound political
thought and sound political life will be found only where both have their place" (Carr
1964, 10).

In constructing this feminist alternative, I am not denying the validity of Morgenthau's work. Adding a feminist perspective to the epistemology of international relations, however, is a stage through which we must pass if we are to begin to think about constructing an ungendered or human science of international politics which is sensitive to, but goes beyond, both masculine and feminine perspectives. Such inclusionary thinking, which, as Simone de Beauvoir tells us, values the bringing forth of life as much as the risking of life, is becoming imperative in a world where the technology of war and a fragile natural environment are threatening human existence. This ungendered or human discourse becomes possible only when women are adequately represented in the discipline and when there is equal respect for the contributions of both women and men alike.

CHAPTER 2
Gendering Security Studies and Peace Studies

1994 and 2004

The fields of security studies and peace studies have both resisted recognizing that gender is relevant to their investigations.[1] It is also the case that gender studies have not always been hospitable terrain for studying war and conflict. And feminists have been rightly suspicious of the problems of associating women with peace. In this first part of this chapter, I discuss some of the IR feminist responses to security studies, an important field in international relations, generally associated with the realist approach discussed in Chapter 1: IR feminists have rightly claimed that we cannot fully understand war and conflict without gender analysis. First, I demonstrate how war, the state, and citizenship—central concepts in the field of security studies—are gendered. Then I say something about gender studies and its silences with respect to war and international security. I suggest some reasons why these two fields—security studies and gender studies—have a hard time communicating with each other. I then describe some of the recent feminist scholarship in IR that has begun to bridge this divide and some contributions that IR feminists have made to our understanding of war, peace, and international security.[2] In terms of its methodological sensibilities, which I discuss later in the chapter, most feminist work in security studies is closer to the field of critical security studies than to more conventional IR security scholarship,

---

1. This chapter has been compiled from shortened and edited versions of two separate articles, (Tickner 2004) and (Tickner 1994).
2. When I say silences I am referring to the field of gender studies more broadly. I am aware that feminist IR has contributed a great deal to the field of security studies, particularly in the last ten years since this article was originally written.

even though only a few critical security studies scholars have incorporated gender into their analyses.[3] I then offer some thoughts on possible convergences between IR feminist scholarship and critical security studies.

Whereas national security and military strategy are perceived as masculine domains—perceptions that contribute to their resistance to gender analysis—peace and conflict resolution are issues that we stereotypically associate with the feminine. Yet, as feminist peace researcher Betty Reardon claimed in 1985, the peace research establishment has been as heavily populated by men as has the discipline of national security studies (Reardon 1985; Murray and Mack 1985). Gender analysis is rarely included in the subject matter of peace studies, and there has been little attention to women's issues or women's experiences in spite of the field's avowed commitment to broad-based empirical investigations (Wallensteen 1988, 8).[4] Although women have frequently played leadership roles in various peace movements, the peace heroes whose lives we study are more likely to be men than women. The second part of this chapter will examine the reasons for this lack of feminist analysis in peace research and will suggest how introducing gender analysis could broaden and deepen the field of peace studies.

GENDERING SECURITY STUDIES

In his book *Beyond Left and Right: The Future of Radical Politics*, sociologist Anthony Giddens asked what we should make of the fact that "propagation of military violence has always been a resolutely male affair"(Giddens 1994). While acknowledging that there is a relation between war, military power, and masculinity, Giddens claimed that war is not a manifestation of male aggression; rather, it is associated with the rise of the state. In a rather different book, *War and Gender,* international relations scholar Joshua Goldstein asked why we have not been more curious about the fact that, while virtually all societies throughout history have engaged in war, overwhelmingly they have been fought by men (Goldstein 2001). Although Goldstein reaches a conclusion somewhat similar to Giddens, that war is not due to males' inherent aggression, he devotes his entire book to examining evidence about the association of war with men and masculinity.

3. In his later work Ken Booth, the founder of the Welsh School of critical security studies, cites a number of feminist works (Booth 2007). For a critical study that notes the lack of gender analysis in the Copenhagen School see Hansen (2000).
4. It is interesting to note that there were no female authors in Wallensteen's edited book. However, the Department of Peace and Conflict Research at Uppsala University in Sweden, an important center for peace research directed by Wallensteen, has subsequently published several important feminist research projects. See, for example, Olsson and Tryggestad (2001).

Giddens is undoubtedly correct in faulting the state system rather than the individual for international wars. Most IR scholars, as well as most IR feminists, have criticized reductionist arguments that attribute warfare to male aggression. But, to paraphrase Goldstein, should we not be more curious about the fact that state decision makers charged with constructing and implementing military and security policies have generally been men? In today's world of almost 200 states, less than 1 percent of presidents or prime ministers are women, a percentage that has remained remarkably consistent. The Greek model of the heroic citizen-warrior, which equated manliness with citizenship, has been replicated in many polities since. To die for one's country in battle is a patriotic duty that, until recently and in only a very few states, has been denied to virtually all women due to their nearly universal exclusion from combat positions. In the United States, military service has been a mark of first class citizenship and was an important rationale for the National Organization for Women's support, in 1990, for allowing women into combat positions in the military.[5]

But it is not only state decision making and militaries that have been mostly populated by men. The discipline of international relations, which was founded at the beginning of the twentieth century by scholars searching for explanations for the causes of war, has also been a field largely populated by men—although this is changing today. In the last thirty years, in the United States at least, IR has been heavily influenced by rational choice theory, which is modeled on the behavior of individuals in the market, behavior that, historically, is more typical of men than women. As I discussed in Chapter 1, power, autonomy, self-reliance, and rationality are all attributes that realism—the approach in IR that has had the most influence on security studies—deems desirable for state behavior if states are going to survive and prosper in a dangerous "anarchical" international system. All of these attributes are ones we associate with a socially constructed "ideal-type" masculinity.

As described in Chapter 1, the goal of theory building for conventional IR, which includes most realists, has been to generate propositions that are testable and that can help explain the security-seeking behavior of states in the international system. Neo-realism, the devolution of realism committed to scientific methods, believes that theory should be explanatory and separated, to the greatest extent possible, from norms and political practice. Though to feminists this view of theory appears thoroughly gendered—and gendered masculine—most international theorists would deny that their theories have anything to do with gender, since gender is usually assumed to be synonymous with women.

5. In January 2013, the US military opened all combat positions to women.

Conversely, and in spite of the presence of some women in foreign and defense policy leadership positions, the term "woman" is still antithetical to our stereotypical image of a "national security specialist." War and national security are areas where it has been presumed that women have little important to say. And it may also be that women are complicit in perpetuating this stereotype. According to feminist political scientist Judith Stiehm, since men (and she is talking specifically about the United States) have been given a near monopoly on the application of state violence, and most women have been exempt from firsthand experience of war, women tend to exhibit what Stiehm calls "a civilian mind," a certain ostrich-like obliviousness when it comes to matters of national security and war (Stiehm 1996). This can also be said for gender studies in the United States. I have sometimes found that in women's studies departments, audiences tend to be small when military or national security matters are on the agenda.

The distance and lack of understanding between international theory and feminist theory is something about which I have become increasingly concerned in my efforts to introduce a feminist perspective into international relations. I am convinced that the difficulties these two bodies of knowledge have in conversing with one another stem as much from epistemological differences as they do from the incompatibility of subject matter. Whereas conventional international theory builds on an ontology of interstate relations that sees states as unitary rational actors operating in an asocial international environment, feminist theory is sociological. It comes out of an ontology of social relations, particularly gender relations, which starts at the level of the individual embedded in hierarchical social, political, and economic structures.

Feminist theories seek to better understand women's subordination in order to prescribe strategies for ending it.[6] Unlike IR theory, feminist theory is explicitly normative and often emancipatory. Believing that claims of objectivity and universality that rest on knowledge primarily about men must be questioned, feminists seek to develop what they call "practical knowledge," or knowledge developed out of the everyday practices of peoples' lives. Preferring bottom-up rather than top-down knowledge, feminists believe that theory cannot be separated from political practice.

Feminist IR has questioned IR's assumptions and concepts and asked new questions, such as the questions about states and citizens that I mentioned earlier. While much of the early work was in areas such as the global economy, development, and human rights, there is also a growing literature on gender,

6. Feminism encompasses a rich array of theoretical literatures that come out of a variety of disciplines and paradigms including liberal, socialist, radical, critical, postmodern, and postcolonial traditions. Most are united by their common goals of describing and explaining gender inequality and subordination and seeking strategies to end it. For an overview, see Tong (1998).

war, and international security. Whereas conventional security studies have generally looked at conflict from a top-down or structural perspective, feminists have often taken a bottom-up approach, analyzing the impact of war at the micro level. Feminists have been particularly concerned with what goes on during wars, especially the impact of war on women and civilians more generally. They have challenged the myth that wars are fought to protect women, children, and others stereotypically viewed as "vulnerable."

In the 1980s, when nuclear strategy was high on the US security agenda, feminist scholar Carol Cohn analyzed the strategic language of national security planners involved in planning high-tech warfare (Cohn 1987). High-tech weapons that kill from great distances increase the impersonality of warfare and decrease the sense of personal responsibility among soldiers—this is one way the military deals with the problem that most men do not like to kill. On the other hand, we are also seeing patterns of increased intimacy of war, especially prevalent in today's ethno-national and religious conflicts. The targeting of victims' identity is an integral part of this type of war; the destruction of viable economies and civil societies, and the suffering this inflicts on entire populations, defies the rationalist explanations typical of IR theory. Feminism, with its focus on identity and social relations, has been shedding new light on today's ethno-national wars.

For example, feminists have shown that wartime rape, as witnessed in the former Yugoslavia from 1992 to 1995 and Rwanda in 1994, is now being used as a strategy of war; it not only terrorizes women but also contributes to male humiliation when men fail to protect "their women." Feminists have brought issues such as wartime rape and military prostitution onto the security agenda. They have questioned the role of the state as a security provider, suggesting that, in many of today's wars, states may actually be threatening to their own populations, either through direct violence or through trade-offs that tend to get made between warfare and welfare. And feminists are investigating whether there is a link between domestic violence and highly militarized societies. Feminists seek to understand how the security of individuals and groups is compromised by violence, both physical and structural, at all levels. Hierarchical social, political, and economic structures of inequality can contribute to the oppression of certain groups of people: how these structures are legitimated and maintained is also a subject of feminist research.

Feminist research on security has employed quite different methods from conventional IR security studies. Consistent with feminist approaches more generally, IR feminist Katharine Moon used ethnographic methods to examine prostitution camps around US military bases in South Korea in the 1970s (Moon 1997). Moon linked these women's life stories to US–Korean security relations at the highest level. She demonstrates how the security of the South Korean state translated into insecurity for these women. Carol Cohn used discourse analysis to help us understand the limitations placed on the ability to think fully and well about security when defense intellectuals are constrained in what they say by masculine discourse. From her ethnographic research among defense intellectuals engaged in strategic nuclear planning during the Cold War, Cohn concluded that the fear of sounding like a woman constrained the options that could be raised (Cohn 1993).

These methods, ethnography and discourse analysis, are not often used in conventional security studies. Feminists' focus on issues such as prostitution is sometimes dismissed as not relevant or important to the "real business" of national security and war. And there is always the fear, linked to the question of male aggression, that feminists are raising the specter of good women and bad men. Yet, most feminists are very reluctant to embrace essentialist and reductive notions of peaceful women and aggressive men. Many believe that the unproblematic association of women with an idealized and passive definition of peace has worked to devalue both women and peace, an issue I shall take up in more detail later in this chapter.

Different questions, different assumptions, and threats to gender identity are all issues that contribute to the gulf between conventional IR and feminist approaches to conflict and security. But the deeper divides are epistemological. International relations theorists expect that research programs will generate testable hypotheses about war and international security. Feminists counter that their research comes out of very different epistemological positions, which question claims about human intention built on models from the natural sciences and the claim to universality of a knowledge tradition built largely on the experiences of men, usually elite men. The judging of quite different epistemological traditions according to the scientific standards of one body of literature, in this case the dominant one, is problematic. It becomes even more so when issues of power are involved. Therefore, bridging this divide may prove difficult. But feminism and critical security studies—an approach that has gained increasing influence in IR, particularly outside the United States—have more in common.[7]

Like feminists, critical security studies scholars have suggested that issues they consider important for understanding security cannot be raised within a rationalist framework that depends on an ontology based on rational actors in a state-centric world. Their belief that state and other actors cannot be understood without examining their identities, as well as the identities they attribute to others, demands more interpretive modes of analysis that can investigate how these identities, which may lead to conflict, are constructed

---

7. There are several universities that are credited with producing foundational work in critical security studies. They include the University of Wales at Aberystwyth, the University of Copenhagen, and the University of Minnesota. Leading scholars associated with each of these schools include Ken Booth, Ole Waever, and Robert Duvall, respectively.

and maintained. Similarly, feminist theorists investigate how oppressive gender hierarchies that, they believe, decrease the security of individuals are constructed and maintained. More radical versions of critical security studies claim that when knowledge about security is constructed in terms of the binary metaphysics of Western culture—such as inside versus outside, us versus them, and community versus anarchy—security can be understood only within the confines of a domestic community whose identity is constructed in antithesis to external threat. Feminists have pointed to similar binaries that, they claim, are gendered; frequently, those living on the outside of one's own state's boundaries are seen as feminized, less rational, and more unpredictable than those on the inside.

Like much of feminism, critical security studies are also emancipatory. For example, critical security scholar Ken Booth has defined security as freeing individuals and groups from the social, physical, economic, and political constraints that prevent them from carrying out what they would freely choose to do (Booth 1991).[8] Perspectives on security that begin with the security of the individual provide an entry point for feminist theorizing. Claiming, as they do, that gender hierarchies are socially constructed allows feminists, like critical security scholars, to pursue an emancipatory agenda and to postulate a world that could be otherwise.

For example, Joshua Goldstein concludes his study by suggesting that the socialization practices of boys and girls motivates men's participation in combat and women's exclusion from it (Goldstein 2001). And practices can be changed. Feminist IR scholar Charlotte Hooper (1998) sees in the West some softening of what she terms "hegemonic masculinity," as we move away from warrior heroes to a masculinity linked to processes of globalization and capitalist restructuring, a shift that has been somewhat compromised by the post–9/11 security agenda.[9] The 1990s emphasis on the caring, humanitarian side of military duties, found in certain peacekeeping operations, and the increasing visibility of women and gay men in US and European militaries lend support to the idea that the military may be becoming detached from hegemonic masculinity.

Recent research has also suggested that those who oppose military solutions to conflict—women and men—are among those most likely to support feminist goals. Mark Tessler and Ina Warriner's article in *World Politics,* which described a study of Israeli, Egyptian, Palestinian, and Kuwaiti attitudes toward the Arab/Israeli conflict, reported that men and women in these societies did not have significantly different attitudes toward the conflict, and

---

8. For a feminist elaboration on Booth's concept of security as emancipation, see Basu (2011)

9. For an analysis of the remasculinization of US national security discourse after 9/11, see Chapter 9, which is an abbreviated version of Tickner (2002).

there was no evidence of women being less militaristic than men. There was a strong positive correlation, however, between those who supported equality of women and those who supported diplomacy and compromise (Tessler and Warriner 1997).

If women become warriors, it reinforces the war system. If women are seen only as peacemakers, it reinforces both militarized masculinity and women's marginality with respect to the national security functions of the state. Since the way we construct knowledge cannot be separated from the way we act in the world, perhaps these feminist attempts to move beyond gendered dichotomies that support militarism and war can help us all to construct more robust definitions of peace and security. With this goal in mind, I shall now turn to an analysis of some feminist contributions to peace studies.

GENDERING PEACE STUDIES

As is the case with security studies, peace studies and feminist studies have also proceeded on separate tracks. Like much of the theoretical literature in security studies, the peace studies discipline has assumed gender neutrality; in other words, gender issues are generally thought to be irrelevant to its theoretical assumptions and explanations. Peace studies rarely investigate how women are differentially affected by war, structural violence, and environmental degradation. Women's lives and the consequences of gender inequality may even seem like distractions from the more "important" issues in the field.

What accounts for this silence with respect to gender issues? One possible explanation might be the field's efforts to maintain academic respectability. The age-old association of women with pacifism and romanticized domestic values of caring and nurturance suggest dangers that peace researchers face when dealing with gender issues. Gaining respectability, or the ability to challenge "realist" concepts without being dismissed as "idealist," inhibits the consideration of what, in the academic mainstream, are perceived as marginal or radical issues (Reardon 1985, chap. 5; Murray and Mack 1985, 91–202).[10]

However, as discussed in Chapter 1, this stereotypical view of women as innately more peaceful than men is troubling to many feminists as well (Burguières 1990, 16). For this reason, certain feminists, in the 1980s, also cautioned against merging peace studies with feminist studies (Sylvester 1987). Jean Elshtain argued that feminists should be suspicious of definitions of peace that eschew difference and envision an unattainable world of harmony and abiding order (Elshtain 1988). Such visions relegate women's voices to

10. More recently, feminist peace researcher Catia Confortini has claimed that feminist IR has rarely engaged in theoretical questions about peace and gender for similar reasons (Confortini 2012, 9).

utopian and idealistic musings, thus permitting women's various struggles for justice and equality to be ignored. Adrienne Harris claimed that the opposition between aggressive war-making men and nurturing peaceful women is deeply problematic (Harris and King 1989). Such myths tend to devalue women, reinforce militarism, and consequently delegitimate peace experiments.

In reality, most feminist perspectives on peace and security are not searching for what Jane Addams called a "goody-goody" peace (Elshtain 1988); rather, they are seeking a more robust definition of peace as freedom from all sources of oppression. Therefore, in spite of the reservations of both feminists and peace researchers, peace studies has much to gain by incorporating gender analysis and feminist perspectives into its subject matter. Peace studies and feminism have much in common, both in terms of similar normative orientations toward issues of conflict resolution and socioeconomic justice and a shared commitment to an interdisciplinary methodology (Burguières 1990, 15). Having moved beyond romanticized images that link women with an idealized peace, feminist theories have the potential for extending and even transforming our understanding of the sources of conflict and the potential for long-term security.

Asserting that it is practice that informs theory, Adrienne Harris and Ynestra King have argued for constructing feminist perspectives on peace and world security out of ideas that have emerged from the intersection of women's practice in peace movements and the analysis of gender in feminist studies (Harris and King 1989, 1–2). Although their voices have not been part of the mainstream literature of peace studies, women in various peace movements worldwide have been writing and speaking about peace and security for a long time. Addressing the International Congress of Women at the Hague during World War I, Jane Addams spoke of the need for a new internationalism to replace the self-destructive nationalism that contributed so centrally to the outbreak of that war (Adams et al. 1916). At the Women's International Peace Conference in Halifax, Canada, in 1985, participants defined security broadly, in terms of safe working conditions and freedom from the threat of war or unemployment (Runyan 1988). The final document of the 1985 World Conference to Review and Appraise the Achievements of the UN Decade for Women, in Nairobi, offered a similar multidimensional definition of security that included economic as well as military concerns (Pietila and Vickers 1990).

These various definitions of peace and global security are not the idealized vision of peace that stereotypically is associated with women. These women, and others who have written or spoken about peace and security in very different contexts and over different time periods, define security in terms quite similar to contemporary analyses of structural violence (Galtung 1969).[11]

11. For a feminist critique of Galtung's concept of structural violence, see Confortini (2006). In this article Confortini calls for an alliance between feminism and peace studies.

Asserting that security cannot be built on others' insecurity, they offer multidimensional definitions of peace that are not zero-sum. Jane Addams's views, dismissed at the time as impractical, are quite compatible with recent attempts to redefine security—efforts that have had an important influence on broadening the curriculum of peace and conflict studies (Wallensteen 1988).

While these multiple dimensions of insecurity became more visible in the post–Cold War era, many peace researchers had already shifted, after the Vietnam War, from state-centric models that focused on military conflict to broader definitions of security, sometimes referred to as "common" or "comprehensive" security (Independent Commission on Disarmament and Security 1982). Proponents of comprehensive security claimed that examining only traditional security issues, such as the causes, outcomes, and consequences of international wars, arms control, and disarmament, seemed inadequate given the dramatic events that ended the Cold War—events that diminished the threat of nuclear war between two superpowers but focused attention on the large number of ethnic conflicts and economic disputes, as well as on a growing awareness of potential environmental disasters. In an international system wherein conflict has tended, over the past forty years, to have internal rather than international roots (albeit exacerbated by outside intervention), war between great powers across international boundaries has not been the dominant mode of conflict.

Moreover, economic competition between advanced capitalist states, as well as the enormous inequalities of wealth between these states and the rest of the world, brought concerns about justice and structural violence—similar to those expressed by women in Nairobi and Halifax—to the center of the peace studies agenda. Fears of the depletion of natural resources and the attention to air and water pollution further broadened the field to include ecological as well as economic concerns.

Peace researchers working in the framework of comprehensive security defined insecurity in terms of various types of violence: direct (or physical), structural, and, violence against nature. This comprehensive approach also looked at insecurity from a multilevel perspective. Whereas direct violence focuses on the state and its international conflicts, structural violence emphasizes the insecurity of individuals and social groups, and ecological threats draw attention to the insecurity of the entire planet.

This multidimensional, multilevel definition of security—which depends on the reduction of all these types of violence—is quite similar to the way in which certain women activists and feminist peace researchers have been thinking about human security for some time.[12] For this reason, peace studies

12. As feminist peace researcher Elise Boulding reminded us, new ideas in any discipline do not receive widespread attention unless they are adopted by significant numbers of men. See Boulding's contribution in Kramerae and Spender (1991).

have much to gain from the inclusion of women's voices and feminist theories. To this end, I shall now introduce a gendered perspective on the three dimensions of security outlined above. Drawing on a variety of feminist theories, I show that gender inequality is itself a form of violence that contributes to the insecurity of all individuals. Then, in response to Peter Wallensteen's (1988, 9) urging that peace studies include both criticism and utopianism, I offer some suggestions as to how feminist perspectives and women's experiences in working for peace can help us to rethink conventional analyses in ways that can transform our understanding of the meaning of peace and security in the post–Cold War era.

If we are to conceptualize peace studies from the comprehensive perspective that contemporary realities demand, we should surely include the experiences of people who constitute half the world's population. To avoid the dangers of essentializing women, a tendency that generally comes from speaking out of the experiences of white Western women, feminist perspectives on peace and security should include the voices of women worldwide. However, adding women's experiences to the subject matter of our investigations is not enough; feminist perspectives must also expose previously hidden gender relations in order to demonstrate how gender inequalities can themselves be a source of insecurity that contributes to both direct and structural violence as well as to violence against nature.

GENDER AND DIRECT VIOLENCE

The analysis of the connections between war and masculinity that I introduced in Chapter 1 points to some new ideas about how the national security functions of the state are legitimized. War and military issues have been deeply gendered activities throughout history. Although feminists caution that it is as simplistic to state that all men are innately aggressive as it is to assert that all women are naturally peaceful, aggressive behavior—necessary for soldiering and the conduct of war—is encouraged through appeals to masculinity. Military recruits are taught that to be a soldier, one must first be a "man."

Sheila Tobias declares that this association between soldiering and masculinity, which has been evident throughout most of history, extends into civilian life as well, where being a war veteran is a special mark of good citizenship. Being a war veteran is, therefore, an asset in running for most political offices—an advantage that is denied to women by virtue of their exclusion (until recently) from military combat (Tobias 1990). The association of citizenship with masculinity and military service makes it hard for women to be perceived as first-class citizens capable of holding positions of power. Moreover, this intimate connection between soldiering, citizenship, and masculinity gives special validation to the national security functions of the state: patriotism and service to one's country are associated with war-fighting rather than with other types of activities that are equally valuable contributions to the political and economic life of the state and its citizens.

However, as I discussed earlier in this chapter, it would be simplistic and reductionist to say that these appeals to masculinity can explain the causes of war. Therefore, what does exposing the masculinity of soldiering and citizenship contribute to our understanding of conflict and the politics of national security? To provide some answers to this question, Carol Cohn takes us inside the world of strategic planners, mostly men, and examines their modes of discourse, which she describes as loaded with masculine imagery. Although Cohn is not saying that this masculine language determines national security policy, she does suggest that it limits the options that leaders may consider when making decisions about military strategy and shapes their expectations regarding other states' behavior. Gendered discourses, which demand military planners and the states they represent to "act like men," legitimate certain options in strategic planning and ensure that others get left out. Cohn believes that this diminishes the possibility of thinking comprehensively about national security policy; it shapes and limits the possible outcomes of debates, for it is difficult for people involved in national security planning to express ideas marked as "feminine"—for example, a preference for negotiations over coercive threatening—if they are to maintain their credibility (Cohn 1990).

In contrast to images of men as legitimate and efficacious actors in matters of war and national security, images of women in this context are quite different. In an article in the *Village Voice* of September 25, 1990, Cynthia Enloe reminded us of media coverage of the communication between the United States and Iraq over the release of what she termed US "womenandchildren." Television pictures of families trying to leave Iraq in 1990 after its invasion of Kuwait depicted women as helpless dependents rather than as independent persons capable of coping with the complex world of realpolitik. Such a view denies the contributions made by women soldiers and diplomats in war and contributes to the legitimation of war as a manly activity necessary for the protection of women, children, and the "motherland."

The masculinity of war depends, therefore, on the myth that women are being protected (Stiehm 1983). Spike Peterson has argued that rethinking the meaning of protection is a crucial component of efforts to address problems of world security (Peterson 1992a). By exposing the protector/protected myth, we can deepen our understanding of the real victims of direct violence. The National Organization for Women has estimated that up to 90 percent of total casualties in conflicts since 1945 have been civilians, the majority of them women and children.[13] Moreover, as Judith Stiehm pointed out, if we are to

13. "Resolution on Women in Combat," September 16, 1990.

think of men as protectors we must remember that they are usually protecting women from other men (Stiehm, 1983).

Feminist theory also draws our attention to the issue of domestic violence, which is prevalent but generally underreported and not legislated against in most societies. By pointing to the high incidence of domestic violence in military families and in militarized societies, feminist perspectives can deepen our understanding of the connection between militarism and sexism. Peterson also asserts that the way notions of protection have traditionally been constructed by the state contributes to the reproduction of hierarchies, including gender hierarchies, and hence to the structural violence against which states say they offer protection (Peterson 1992a).

GENDER AND STRUCTURAL VIOLENCE

In the wake of the Vietnam War and the questions it raised about the asymmetric power relations between the major protagonists, peace research in the 1970s broadened its agenda to include issues concerned with economic development and economic justice (Wallersteen 1988). This focus on economic issues led to the introduction of the concept of "structural violence" into the literature of peace studies: according to Johan Galtung, structural violence exists when economic and social conditions are such that people die or suffer as a consequence of the unequal distribution of resources, not as a result of physical violence (Galtung 1969).

Evidence suggests that women are disproportionately victims of structural violence, and that it is gender inequalities that are often responsible for women's particular vulnerability. In most countries, women's wage rates fall below 75 percent of men's, and in some they average about half that of men (United Nations 2010, 207–210). Women work longer hours because much of their labor is performed outside the wage sector—in families or in the subsistence sector, particularly in the Global South. In some parts of Africa, women are responsible for up to 90 percent of agricultural production, but most of this production takes place on family plots outside the market, where technology is at its most primitive and economic returns are minimal.

Increasingly, young women are providing a docile, under-remunerated, and hard-working labor force for multinational corporations that relocate in states in the Global South to avoid minimum-wage requirements and other labor standards in their home countries, as well as constraints imposed by environmental legislation. The notion of the family wage has perpetuated the concept of "breadwinner," a role traditionally assigned to male heads of households. However, young women employed by light industry in the Global South are not thought of as "breadwinners" but as future housewives earning "pin money" (Enloe 1990, 162–163). As Maria Mies has suggested, the concept of "housewife" began coincidentally with the birth of capitalism, and has provided vast quantities of free labor for an ever-expanding global capitalist economy (Mies 1986).

All this evidence suggests that it is structures of gender inequality that are responsible for women's disproportionate representation at the bottom of the socioeconomic scale. Therefore, if the field of peace studies is to examine the causes and consequences of structural violence thoroughly, it must pay attention to the particular plight of women. A feminist perspective enables us to see that unequal gender roles, reinforced by historical cultural practices and patterns of economic production, often perpetuate women's victimization (Bunch and Carrillo 1994).

To establish links between direct and indirect violence, feminist perspectives have also investigated the apparent correlation between female poverty and defense spending. There is evidence that women's poverty is particularly sensitive to increases in defense spending. Because military spending is capital intensive, and tends to divert funds from labor-intensive activities, both men and women suffer when military spending rises, although it has been suggested that women may lose more jobs in relation to men. Women's jobs tend to be heavily concentrated in light manufacturing, services, and local governments—categories that are usually hardest hit when military spending is high. Moreover, women and children suffer when social welfare is traded for military spending; high military budgets typically mean decreases in domestic social programs, which result in particularly harsh effects on female heads of households who are disproportionately poor (Benería and Blank 1989). All of these issues should be raised if a comprehensive examination of structural violence is to be included in the subject matter of peace and security studies.

GENDER AND VIOLENCE AGAINST NATURE

Environmental issues offer the newest challenge to conventional thinking on peace and security. Images of a fragile and polluted earth underscore the futility of state boundaries as protection against environmental disasters; depletion of the ozone layer and pollution of rivers and oceans affect poor and rich alike. Scholars concerned with environmental security suggest that collective action to deal with these threats is hard to achieve in the contemporary international system, composed as it is of self-interested sovereign states. To the extent that war, weapons testing, and military maneuvers are among the most severe causes of environmental pollution and the biggest consumers of resources, traditional methods of protecting the state are, paradoxically, the greatest threats to environmental security.

Scholars concerned with the environment suggest that the international system may require major restructuring, with state-centric solutions giving way to global agreements if environmental security is to be achieved. The introduction of feminist perspectives on environmental security offers us a radically new way of thinking about these issues. Going beyond environmental management, certain feminists are suggesting that we must also reconsider humans' relationship with nature. Ecofeminists assert that the instrumental attitude toward nature, which they believe is responsible for contemporary environmental insecurities, arose in the seventeenth century (coincidentally with the birth of the modern state system), when nature began to be viewed as a resource to be exploited for the benefit of human progress (Merchant 1980).

The drive to impose human mastery over nature was a product of European Enlightenment thinking, which held that the taming and transformation of wild and "virgin" lands was a measure of human progress—a process that native peoples, often characterized in terms associated with women, were incapable of effecting for themselves (Merchant 1989). Ecofeminists assert, therefore, that gender hierarchies and the domination of nature are inter-related; only when both are eliminated can we move to a less instrumental view of nature that is needed to solve our present environmental insecurities. I take up this issue in greater detail in Chapter 4.

Because they arise out of the experiences of those on the margins, feminist perspectives can also deepen our understanding of linkages between poverty, structural violence, and environmental insecurities. Our tendency, in the West, to focus on global issues of air and water pollution can obscure the fact that, in all societies, it is the poor who suffer most from environmental degradation. The affluent are concerned with the potential hazards of a thinning ozone layer, but the poor are confronted with more immediate threats of contaminated water, soil erosion, and energy shortages that threaten their daily existence.

It is often women who are the worst victims of environmental degradation; as gatherers of firewood and drinking water in rural areas of the Global South, women are facing ever-greater constraints on providing these resources for their families (Dankelman and Davidson 1988). Moreover, toxic pollution and environmental disasters impact on women's reproductive systems. It is often women who organize local communities to fight such calamities. These protest movements, which often go unnoticed in the mainstream literature, are an important source of information on the politics of environmental security at the local level.

A FEMINIST PERSPECTIVE ON GLOBAL SECURITY

As well as examining sources of conflict and insecurity, peace and security studies should also include suggestions as to how a more secure world might be achieved. In this section I offer some thoughts on how the gendered analysis of the multidimensional view of security presented above can contribute to thinking about constructing a more peaceful world.

Uncovering hidden gender relations in each of the dimensions of security that I have discussed gives us some new perspectives on their interconnections. By more clearly illuminating aspects of gender inequality that contribute to militarism, structural violence, and violence against nature, feminist perspectives can enrich our understanding of the interrelationships between these various forms of insecurity. However, because feminists believe that gender systems of domination and subordination are not fixed but, rather, are constructed through socialization and perpetuated through unjust political and economic structures, our analysis also permits us to envisage more secure societies where these various forms of domination can be mitigated or even eliminated. As Betty Reardon says, just as the conduct of warfare and the practice of aggression are learned behaviors, their transcendence can also be learned (Reardon 1985, 9). By understanding the interrelationship between the various forms of domination, we can seek new ways to change the structures of oppression within which these behaviors are situated.

New thinking on comprehensive security encourages us to focus our attention on structures and individuals other than the state and national security policy-makers as potential providers of security. *Global citizenship* is a catchphrase that attempts to link the individual with global threats to security, many of which are not amenable to statist solutions. Feminist perspectives can help us to think about more global, less statist perspectives on security. Women have always been less identified with the state and its institutions than have men because they have generally been situated far from the seats of power. Likewise, the sort of citizenship and patriotism that have legitimized war and traditional concepts of national security have not valorized the contributions to society typically made by women. Feminist perspectives can help us to think about new definitions of citizenship that would validate activities associated with caring for the earth and its inhabitants. Exposing the myth of the protector/protected relationship permits us to envisage a different kind of citizenship whereby both women and men can become what Judith Stiehm has called "citizen defenders"—people whose roles would be compatible with less offensive military strategies (Stiehm 1983).

Traditional thinking about international security has posited a dangerous international environment against which the state must accumulate power to protect itself and its citizens. Because feminist perspectives are concerned with breaking down gender dichotomies, they can also help us to question the dichotomous "we/they" thinking that has contributed to so many international conflicts where the "other," or those on the outside, are perceived as dangerous or inferior. Furthermore, ecofeminists suggest ways of breaking down other barriers, notably those between humans and nature. Rather than viewing nature as "other," as a resource to be exploited for the benefit of (certain) human beings, ecofeminists suggest models for living in harmony with our natural environment.

In conclusion, the perspectives presented here are intended to suggest ways in which gender analysis can be introduced throughout the fields of peace and security studies. A deeper analysis can expose previously hidden gender inequalities and allow us to see how the militaristic practices of states are legitimated in the name of masculinity, and how structural violence—whose consequences are borne disproportionately by women—is often the result of unequal gendered practices. The association of women with nature helps us to understand how both have been dominated and exploited for the benefit of modern society. Moreover, if we are to understand the particular insecurities faced by women, we can do so only if they are analyzed not in isolation but in terms of women's relations to men. Including gender analysis in the way we think and write about peace and security not only deepens its empirical base but also transforms it in ways that can help us conceptualize a world that is more secure for all of us.

CHAPTER 3
On The Fringes of the World Economy: A Feminist Perspective

1991

International Political Economy (IPE) began to receive more attention in international relations (IR) in the 1970s and 1980s after the collapse of the Bretton Woods System in 1971. One of its foundational texts was Robert Gilpin's *The Political Economy of International Relations*. In this text, Gilpin described what he called the three constituting ideologies of international political economy: liberalism, nationalism, and Marxism (Gilpin 1987, chap. 2). Gilpin defined an ideology as a belief system that includes both scientific explanations and normative prescriptions. Because none of these ideologies discussed *gender,* we must presume that they are to be considered gender neutral, meaning that they claim that the interactions between states and markets (which is the limited way that Gilpin defined political economy) can be understood without reference to gender distinctions. Feminists would disagree with this claim; just as Marxists have argued that the world economy cannot be understood without reference to class, feminists make similar claims about gender. Ignoring gender distinctions hides a set of social and economic relations characterized by inequality between men and women. Feminists would argue that in order to understand how these unequal relationships affect the workings of the world economy and their consequences for both women and men, an approach that makes gender relations explicit must be constructed.

In this chapter, I investigate whether liberalism, nationalism, and Marxism are indeed gender neutral, with respect to their explanations and their normative prescriptions. I examine the individual, state, and class, the central unit of analysis for each of these perspectives, to see whether they evidence a masculine bias both in the way they are described and the interests they represent.

If this is the case, then it is legitimate to ask whether and how gender has circumscribed each perspective's understanding of the workings of the world economy. If there is evidence of a masculine bias in these representations, we must ask whether the normative preferences and policy prescriptions of each of these perspectives serve the interests of men more than those of women.

Having critiqued each ideology from a feminist perspective, I construct a feminist understanding of international political economy that takes us out of Gilpin's oppositional tricotomy. I do so by specifying a wider set of fundamental concepts and by employing a feminist perspective to redefine some of the core concepts central to Gilpin's three perspectives. I draw on feminist literature from different disciplines and approaches. As I said in Chapter 2, it is impossible to speak of one feminist approach—feminist theory is interdisciplinary and encompasses a broad ideological spectrum. Nevertheless, there are common themes in much of the feminist literature suggesting that any feminist perspective on international political economy would start with very different assumptions about the individual, the state, and class from those at the foundations of Gilpin's three ideologies. Whereas different feminist literatures respond to the needs and concerns of different groups of women—middle class or poor, Western or Third World[1]—feminism shares a common opposition to gender inequality and the oppression of women and a commitment to building a world in which women and men are equal participants in all aspects of society.

A FEMINIST CRITIQUE OF IPE LIBERALISM

I begin with a feminist critique of liberalism, the dominant view in Western international political economy. Although its proponents present it as a scientific theory with universal and timeless applications, liberalism, which arose together with modern capitalism in the eighteenth century, has generally been the ideology preferred by theorists from rich and powerful states. Liberal theory takes the individual as the basic unit of analysis. According to liberals, human beings are by nature economic animals driven by rational self-interest. They assume that rational economic man is motivated by the laws of profit maximization. He is highly individualistic, pursuing his own economic goals in the market without any social obligation to the community of which he is a part. Liberals believe that this instrumentally rational market behavior, even though it is driven by selfish profit motives, produces outcomes that are

---

1. I realize that the term "Third World" is used less frequently today than when this chapter was written, usually replaced by the term "Global South." However, some feminists still prefer to talk about the Third World, in which they include the disadvantaged from rich and poor states alike. Since this chapter deals primarily with how IPE developed in the 1970s and 1980s, as well as the women and development literature from the same period, I shall retain the term "Third World."

efficient or beneficial for everyone, even though they acknowledge that not everyone will benefit to the same extent. The detrimental effects of economic growth and market behavior, such as dwindling resources and environmental damage, are generally not considered.

A feminist critique of liberalism should begin with an examination of rational economic man, a construct that, although it extrapolates from roles and behaviors associated with Western men and assumes characteristics that I have described as masculine, has been used by liberal economics to represent the behavior of humanity as a whole. Nancy Hartsock, a feminist theorist who comes out of the Marxist tradition, suggests that rational economic man, appearing coincidentally with the birth of modern capitalism, is a social construct based on the reduction of a variety of human passions to a desire for economic gain (Hartsock 1983, 47). For Hartsock, as well as other non-liberal feminists, the highly individualistic, competitive market behavior of rational economic man could not be assumed as a norm if women's experiences were taken as the prototype for human behavior. Women in their reproductive and maternal roles do not conform to the behavior of individual instrumental rationality. Much of women's work in the provision of basic needs takes place outside the market, in households or in the subsistence sector, prevalent in agrarian economies. When women enter the market economy, they are disproportionately represented in the caring professions as teachers, nurses, or social workers—choices that are generally not made on the basis of profit maximization but on the basis of values that are emphasized in female socialization. If this is the case, we must conclude that most women's, as well as some men's, motivations and behavior cannot be explained using this model of rationality.

Rational economic man is extrapolated from assumptions about human nature that have their origins in Western liberal political theory. Rational economic man is a Hobbesian man whose passions have been tamed by the rational pursuit of profit. Liberal contract theories about men's origins depict a state of nature where individuals existed prior to and apart from the community; they came together not out of any desire for community but out of the need for a protected environment in which they could conduct their economic transactions more securely. Hartsock argues that, given its dependence solely on economic exchange, any notion of community in liberal theory is fragile and instrumental. She claims, however, that this liberal assumption that the behavior of individuals can be explained apart from society is unrealistic because individuals have always inhabited and been a part of society (Hartsock 1983).

Even though early liberal theorists were explicit in their assertion that their theories about human behavior applied to the behavior of men and not women, this distinction has since been lost as contemporary liberals assume this type of behavior for humanity as a whole. Feminists take issue with this theory of human behavior, claiming that it is biased toward a masculine representation. Feminist philosopher Sandra Harding claims that for women, the self is defined through relationship with others, rather than apart from others (Harding 1986). Alison Jaggar argues that liberalism's individualistic portrayal of human nature has placed excessive value on the mind at the expense of the body. Because, in our sexual division of labor, men have dominated the intellectual fields whereas women have been assigned the tasks necessary for physical survival, Jaggar concludes that given this sexual division of labor, women would be unlikely to develop a theory of human nature that ignored human interdependence or to formulate a conception of rationality that stressed individual autonomy. If the need for interdependence were taken as the starting point, community and cooperation would not be seen as puzzling and problematic (Jaggar 1983, 40–48).

Generalizing from rational economic man to the world economy, liberals believe that world welfare is maximized by allowing market forces to operate unimpeded and goods and investment to flow as freely as possible across national boundaries according to the laws of comparative advantage. Critics of liberalism question this liberal belief in openness and interdependence, claiming that it falsely depoliticizes exchange relationships and masks hidden power structures. They challenge the notion of mutual gains from exchange by focusing on the unequal distribution of gains across states, classes, and factors of production, arguing that gains accrue disproportionately to the most powerful states or economic actors. For example, Marxist critics argue that liberal economic theory obscures the unequal power relations between capital and labor. Because capital is mobile across interstate boundaries and controls strategic decisions about investment and production, it is being rewarded disproportionately to labor, a trend that took off in the 1980s when labor was becoming increasingly marginalized in matters of economic policy, a trend that is still very much in evidence today (Gill and Law 1988, 364).

If capital is being rewarded disproportionately to labor in the world economy, then men are being rewarded disproportionately to women. Much of women's work is performed outside the formal economy, but even when they enter the market economy, women are not being rewarded to the same extent as men; earning lower wages and owning an insignificant proportion of the world's capital puts women at an enormous disadvantage in terms of power and wealth.

This problem has been examined in some detail in studies of Third World women and development. The UN Decade for the Advancement of Women (1975–1985) assumed that women's problems in the Third World were related to insufficient participation in the process of modernization and development. But later studies of women and development suggested that, in many parts of the Third World, the position of rural women may actually decline as they become assimilated into a global market economy and that development aid can actually reduce the status of women relative to men. It is often the case that women's access to land and technology decreases as land reform is instituted and agriculture is modernized. Land reform, traditionally thought to be a vital prerequisite for raising agricultural productivity, often reduces women's control over traditional use rights and gives titles to male heads of households. Agricultural mechanization has also reduced women's control over agricultural production as men take over the mechanized part of the production process. The modernization of agriculture, which often leads to a dualism in agricultural production, tends to leave women behind in the traditional sector (Sen and Grown, 1987).

Liberals have generally supported export-led strategies of development. But, because states that have opted for export-led strategies have often experienced increased income inequalities and because women are disproportionately clustered at the bottom of the economic scale, such strategies may have a negative effect on women. The harsh effects of structural adjustment policies imposed by the International Monetary Fund (IMF) fall disproportionately on women as providers of basic needs as social welfare programs in areas of health, nutrition, and housing are cut. When government subsidies or funds are no longer available, women in their roles as unpaid homemakers and care providers must often take up the provision of these basic welfare needs.

Studies of Third World development and its effects on women have documented evidence that demonstrates that liberal strategies to promote economic growth and improve world welfare may have a differential impact on men and women. Because women's work more generally often takes place outside the market economy, a model based on instrumentally rational market behavior does not capture all the economic activities of women. Nor can we assume that prescriptions generated by such a model will be as beneficial to women as they are to men.

A FEMINIST CRITIQUE OF IPE NATIONALISM

The intellectual roots of the nationalist approach date back to the mercantilist school of sixteenth-, seventeenth-, and eighteenth-century Europe—the period coincidental with the rise of the nation-state. The contemporary version of nationalism, associated with the realist school of international relations, discussed in more detail in Chapter 1, became popular in the United States in the 1970s at the same time as its proponents became concerned with what they perceived as US hegemonic decline (Gilpin 1987; Krasner 1982). The nationalist approach takes the state and its behavior in the international system as its basic unit of analysis. All nationalists ascribe to the primacy of the state, of national security, and of military power in the organization and functioning of the international system (Gilpin 1987, 31).

Nationalism in orthodox IPE emerged as a critique of liberalism, but its explanation of state behavior is quite close to liberals' explanation of the behavior of rational economic man. States are assumed to be behaving as rational profit maximizers pursuing wealth, power, and autonomy in an anarchic international system devoid of any sense of community. In a conflictual world, states are striving to be economically self-sufficient. Their participation in the world economy is an attempt to create an international division of labor and resource allocation favorable to their own interests and those of groups within their national boundaries. Arguments against extensive economic interdependence are justified in the name of national security. Strategic domestic industries are to be given protection, especially when they produce military-related goods. National security and national interest are, therefore, the overriding goals of policy (Gill and Law 1988, 367).

A feminist critique of the nationalist approach must begin by asking whether the state, the central unit of analysis, is a gendered construct with respect to both its historical origins and its contemporary manifestations. In spite of advances in the legal rights of women in many states, none of the known forms of state politicizes women's roles in such a way as to give them de facto equality with men (Moore 1988, 150). In all states, institutions of state power are dominated by men, particularly in the realm of foreign policy and the military. Because most foreign-policy–makers and theorists who have explained the origins of states and state behavior in the international arena have been men, we might assume that this could influence not only the behavior of states and the prioritizing of certain statist goals, such as power and autonomy, but also the theoretical explanations of that behavior. We might also assume that prescriptions for maximizing state power might work more to the advantage of men than women.

The consolidation of the modern state system and the rise of modern science, from which the Western social sciences trace their origins, both occurred in the seventeenth century, a time of dramatic social, economic, and political upheaval well documented in Western history. Less well documented is the fact that the seventeenth century is also associated with the intellectual origins of Western feminism. According to Juliet Mitchell, this is not coincidental; women in the seventeenth century saw themselves as a distinct sociological group completely excluded from the new society rising out of the medieval order (Mitchell 1987, 31). Seventeenth-century feminists, such as Mary Astell, lamented that the new spirit of equality did not apply to women. In the seventeenth century, concepts of gender were shifting; coincidentally with the expansion of markets, definitions of male and female were becoming polarized in ways that were suited to the growing division between work and home required by early capitalism. The notion of housewife began to place women's work in the private domestic sphere, as opposed to the public world of the state and the market occupied by men. The needs of early industrial capitalism stimulated this growing division of labor between home and workplace that began the process by which the economic, political, and social options available to women were severely curtailed (Keller 1985, 61).

Although these new economic arrangements were synonymous with the birth of the Enlightenment, "female" became associated with what Enlightenment knowledge had left behind. The persecution of witches, who were defending the female crafts and medical skills of a pre-capitalist era against a growing male professionalism, reached new heights in the sixteenth and seventeenth centuries. Jean Bodin (1530–1596), a French mercantilist and founder of the quantitative theory of money as well as the modern concept of national sovereignty, was one of the most vocal proponents of the persecution of witches. According to Bodin's mercantilist philosophy, the modern state must be invested with absolute sovereignty for the development of new wealth necessary for war-fighting; to this end the state needs more workers and thus must eliminate witches held responsible for abortion and other forms of birth control (Mies 1986, 83).

Sovereignty and rationality were part of an Enlightenment epistemology, committed to the discovery of universal objective or "scientific" laws—an epistemology bent on discrediting superstition, often portrayed as "old wives tales." As mentioned earlier, notions such as objectivity and rationality, central to the definition of the modern natural and social sciences in the West, have typically been associated with masculine thinking. Beginning in the seventeenth century, the economy was placed in the public domain of men and of rational scientific knowledge.

The nationalist approach, particularly its contemporary neo-realist version, has taken the liberal concept of rational economic man, which grew out of this Enlightenment knowledge, and used it to explain the behavior of states in the international system (Waltz 1979). Using game theoretic models, such explanations of states' behavior draw on the instrumentally rational market behavior of individuals. Because international economic interactions rarely result in winner-take-all situations, neo-realists have focused on Prisoners Dilemma games to explain states' behavior in the international system. Where international cooperation is seen to exist, it is explained not in terms of international community but rather in terms of enlightened self-interest in an environment that is essentially anarchic (Axelrod 1984; Keohane 1984, 67–84).

Using game theoretic models to explain states' behavior in the international system, nationalists portray states as unitary actors: concentrating at the interstate level, nationalists do not generally focus their attention on the internal distribution of gains. But, if, as I have argued, women have been peripheral to the institutions of state power and are less rewarded economically than men, the validity of the unitary actor assumption should be examined from the perspective of gender. If, as I have shown, women tend to be clustered at the bottom of the socioeconomic scale, we must question whether women are gaining equally to men from nationalist prescriptions to pursue wealth and power.

A FEMINIST CRITIQUE OF IPE MARXISM

Unlike the liberal and nationalist approaches, which center on explaining the behavior of, and prescribing for, the interests of advanced capitalist states, the contemporary Marxist approach to international political economy comes out of a perspective of the weak and powerless in the world economy. Writers in the dependency and world systems schools—Marxist approaches that gained some recognition in the West in the 1970s—argued that the world economy operates, through trade and investment, in a way that distorts the economies of underdeveloped states in the Third World and condemns them to permanent marginalization. Their participation in the world capitalist economy was seen as detrimental to their development and as exacerbating domestic inequalities between the rich and poor (Gill and Law 1988, 54–69). Concepts of core and periphery, which exist both in the world economy and within the domestic economies of states themselves, were used to explain these inequalities: class alliances between capitalists in the Third World and transnational capital contribute to the further marginalization of Third World peripheries (Chase-Dunn 1982; Galtung 1971). Therefore, according to Marxists, both the domestic and international political and economic relations of Third World capitalist states are embedded in exploitative structures of a capitalist world economy. Authentic, autonomous development that satisfies the needs of all people can be achieved only by a socialist revolution and by delinking from the world economy.[2]

Because it speaks for the interests of the least powerful in the international system, Marxist theory would appear to be more compatible with a feminist perspective. In fact, feminist theory owes a strong intellectual debt to Marxism. Like Marxists, radical, socialist, and postmodern feminists see knowledge as historically and socially constructed. Marxists and feminists would agree that knowledge is embedded in human activity. Like much of feminist theory, Marxism rejects the notion of a universal and abstract rationality and objectivity upon which both the liberal and nationalist approaches are built. Class analysis has parallels with gender analysis. However, feminists criticize Marxists

2. The dependency approach has been somewhat discredited by evidence that has shown that certain countries that have opened up to the global economy have done relatively well in terms of overall growth. But even in these countries, internal inequalities have often increased, also a claim of the dependency literature.

for ignoring women's role in the family and also for ignoring the particular problems faced by women when they enter the labor market that are attributable to their sex. As discussed in the previous chapters, women do not have the same opportunities as men when they enter the workforce. Even in the United States, where considerable advances have been made in the economic position of women, full-time working women in 1987 earned an average of 71 percent of the earnings of full-time working men[3] (Okin 1989, 144). Women frequently experience harassment and intimidation in the workplace, and taking time off for bearing and raising children may impede opportunities for promotion. In many other parts of the world, the position of working women is more critical. As discussed in Chapter 2, multinational corporations in the Third World prefer to hire young women because they are willing to work for low wages and are more docile than men and therefore easier to control.

Feminists are most critical, however, of Marxism's tendency to ignore women in their reproductive roles. For classical Marxists, procreation was seen as a natural female process fixed by human biology. Therefore a division of labor, whereby women are primarily responsible for the rearing of children, was also seen as relatively fixed (Jaggar 1983, 75). Because Marxism assumed that women's roles as caretakers of children was "natural," an assumption questioned by many feminists, classical Marxism omitted women's roles in the family from its analysis. Feminists argue that ignoring women in their reproductive and childrearing roles, an omission common to all approaches to political economy, leaves all the unpaid labor that women perform in the family outside economic analysis. By ignoring women in their domestic roles, Marxists and non-Marxists alike neglect certain issues that are peculiar to women, regardless of their class position. In most cases, when married women move into the labor force, they continue to be responsible for most of the housework and childrearing (Okin 1989, 153). Besides the lack of respect for unpaid housework and the dependence of full-time housewives on the income of their husbands, women, including those in the workforce, usually suffer a severe decline in income should their marriage end in divorce. Economic dependence may force women to stay in marriages in spite of violent and abusive treatment.

Marxist theory has paid insufficient attention to women's private roles in households, and feminist writers also claim that contemporary Marxist analyses do not adequately deal with the position of marginalized women in the Third World. Although they often play a crucial role in subsistence production, increasingly women in the Third World are being defined as dependents

3. More recent data obtained, from the Institute for Women's Policy Research, reveals that in 2011, full-time working women in the United States were earning an average of 82.2 percent of full-time working men, with median weekly earnings of $684 compared to $832 for men.

(Mies 1986, 115). Although dependency theory recognizes this type of marginalization as a structural consequence of capitalist development, it does not acknowledge the special position of women among the marginalized nor the fact that the status of women relative to men has been declining in many parts of the Third World.

TOWARD A FEMINIST PERSPECTIVE ON IPE

I have shown that the individual, the state, and class, which are the basic units of analysis for the liberal, nationalist, and Marxist approaches to international political economy, respectively, tend to present a narrowly masculine representation. I have also suggested that the prescriptions that each of these perspectives offers for maximizing economic welfare and security may work to the advantage of men more than women. I shall now suggest how we might think about constructing a feminist perspective that could offer us a less gender-biased representation of international political economy and could represent the particular interests of women. Such a perspective, coming from the position of those on the fringes of the state and the market, might also help us to think about solutions to contemporary global problems such as militarism, economic injustice, and environmental degradation, which, although they have not traditionally been central to the field of international political economy, are problems with which the state and the market seem increasingly unable to cope.[4]

A feminist perspective on international political economy must be wary of discourses that generalize and universalize from theories based on assumptions taken from characteristics associated with Western men. Because, as I have shown, a masculine perspective is embedded in the epistemological foundations of all three approaches, the construction of a feminist perspective should include efforts to develop a feminist epistemology. Only by so doing can hidden gender relations be brought to light and an approach that takes gender into account both in its scientific explanations and normative prescriptions be constructed. A feminist perspective on international political economy might begin, therefore, by constructing some alternative definitions of concepts, such as rationality, security, and power—concepts that have been central to our understanding of the field but have been embedded in a masculine epistemology.

Both the liberal and nationalist perspectives rely on a depersonalized definition of rationality that equates the rationality of individuals and the state

---

4. I realize that since this was written in 1991, there has been a huge proliferation of feminist literature both in economics and in international political economy. It still remains the case, however, that mainstream approaches have generally not included gender in their analyses.

with a type of instrumental behavior that maximizes self-interest. Both of these approaches assume that rational action can be defined objectively, regardless of time and place. Most feminists take issue with this definition of rationality; agreeing with Marxists, they would argue that individuals and states are socially constituted and what counts as rational action is embodied within a particular society. In capitalist societies, rationality is associated with profit maximization; thus, the notion of rationality has been placed in the public sphere of the market and has been distinguished from the private sphere of emotion and the household. Feminists argue that because it is men who have primarily occupied this public sphere, rationality, as we understand it, is tied to a masculine type of reasoning that is abstract and conceptual. Women, whose lived experiences have been more closely bound to the private sphere of caretaking and childrearing, would define rationality as contextual and personal rather than as abstract. In their caring roles, women are engaged in activities associated with serving others—activities that are rational from the perspective of reproduction rather than production. A feminist definition of rationality would, therefore, be tied to an ethic of care and responsibility. Such a definition would be compatible with behavior more typical of women's lived experiences and would allow us to assume rational behavior that is embedded in social activities that are not necessarily tied to profit maximization.

The concept of security is central to the nationalist perspective. For nationalists, security has generally been subsumed under the rubric of power, particularly military power, and is usually associated with the security of the nation-state. As discussed in more detail in Chapter 2, national security is a concept that is particularly problematic for women. Betty Reardon has argued that, far from protecting women, national security, with its military connotations, can offer particular dangers for women. According to Reardon, sexism and militarism are two interdependent manifestations of social violence (Reardon 1985, 5). Largely excluded from the patriotic duty of defending the state, women have traditionally been defined as the protected rather than the protectors, although they have had little control over the conditions of their protection. Moreover, women experience special vulnerabilities within the state as frequent victims of family violence, which often takes place outside the protection of the law. As mentioned above, women are also subject to special economic vulnerabilities in households, in the workforce, and in the subsistence economy. Given these special vulnerabilities of women inside society and households, as well as with respect to the international system, security for women is not necessarily synonymous with national security. As discussed in previous chapters, a more adequate definition of security would be multilevel and multidimensional and would include both physical and economic security. A feminist perspective would therefore define security as the absence of violence, whether it be military, economic, or sexual.

Power in international relations, whether it is used to explain the behavior of states or classes, has generally been defined in terms of domination and coercion. While feminists would agree that this type of power is very real, feminists would argue that there are also other ways of seeing power as more collective and less zero-sum, such as those discussed in Chapter 1. Power can be seen, not only as domination, but also as a relationship of mutual enablement.

If we were to agree with Marxists that the way we describe reality has an effect on the way we perceive and act, and that autonomy and self-sufficiency are unrealistic in many situations, then a feminist perspective would assume a connected, interdependent individual whose behavior includes activities related to reproduction as well as production. In order to capture these productive and reproductive activities, the artificial boundaries between the world of rational economic man in the public sphere of production and the activities that women perform outside the economy as mothers, caregivers, and subsistence producers of basic needs must be broken down.[5] Breaking down these barriers would help to reduce the differential value attached to the rational or "efficient" world of production and the private world of reproduction. Were childbearing and childrearing to be seen as more valued activities, it could help to reduce the excessive focus on the productive efficiency of an ever-expanding commodity production—a focus whose utility in a world of shrinking resources, vast inequalities, and increasing environmental damage is becoming questionable. A perspective that takes this redefined individual as its basic unit of analysis could help to create an alternative model of political economy that respects human relationships as well as their relation to nature (Kaldor 1986, 454).

If a substantial portion of women's productive and reproductive activities takes place on the peripheries of the world economy, in households or in subsistence sectors, a feminist perspective must be concerned with achieving economic justice in these particular contexts. Although agreeing that women's domestic labor should be recognized as work, feminists caution that economic justice for women in households cannot be guaranteed in the family, as it is presently constituted. Although the family has been designated as the private sphere of women, the concept of male head of household has ensured that male power has traditionally been exercised in the private as well as the public realm. Feminist political philosopher Susan Okin has argued that families are unjust to women or children as long as women continue to bear a disproportionate share of childrearing, have lower expected incomes than men, and are left with primary responsibility for supporting and caring for children if families break up. Only when paid and unpaid work, associated with both

---

5. Of course, I realize that it is not only men who are actors in the public sphere and that many men operate in the private sphere, too. Nevertheless, the stereotypical gendered division between public and private does have real and tangible effects on the way we prioritize and value our various economic activities.

productive and reproductive labor, is shared equally by men and women can the family be a just institution and one that can provide the basis for a just society (Okin 1989, 171).

As discussed above, Third World development strategies have tended to ignore the subsistence sector, where much of women's labor is being performed, with the result that economic modernization has had a differential impact on men and women and has, in certain instances, actually reduced the position of women. Due to the absence of women from local and national power structures, development programs have tended to support projects in areas of production that are dominated by men. To achieve economic justice for rural women in the Third World, development must target projects that benefit women, particularly in the subsistence sector.[6] Improvements in agriculture should focus on consumption as well as production; in many parts of Africa, gathering water and fuel, under conditions of increasing scarcity and environmental degradation, are taking up larger portions of women's time and energy.

Because women are so centrally involved in basic needs satisfaction in households and in the subsistence economy of the Third World, a feminist approach to international political economy must be supportive of a basic needs approach where basic needs are defined in terms of both material needs and the need for autonomy and participation. Because, as I have argued, Third World development strategies that are export oriented have tended to contribute to domestic inequality and, in times of recession and increasing international indebtedness, have had a particularly detrimental impact on women, a strategy that seeks to satisfy basic needs within the domestic economy may be the best type of strategy to improve the welfare of Third World women. Local satisfaction of basic needs requires more attention to subsistence or domestic food production than to growing crops for export markets. A more self-reliant economy would also be less vulnerable to the decisions of foreign investment whose employment policies can be particularly exploitative of women. A basic needs strategy is compatible with values of nurturance and caring; such a strategy is dependency reducing and can empower women to take charge of their own lives and create conditions that increase their own security.

Women have generally been peripheral to the institutions of the nation-state and transnational capital; therefore, a feminist perspective on international political economy should take a critical stance with respect to these institutions, questioning whether they are effectively able to deal with global problems of militarism, poverty, and the environment—problems that

---

6. Since the original version of this chapter was written, there has been much more recognition by development agencies of the need to target women's development. Generally, this has been justified by evidence that shows that economies where there is greater gender equality experience higher economic growth, rather than for the purpose of aiding women per se.

have a particularly negative impact on women. Building a model of political economy that starts at the bottom, with the individual and the local satisfaction of the individual's basic needs, envisages a type of state that is more self-reliant with respect to the international system and more able to live within its own resource limits. Such a state would be less militaristic and give priority to welfare over military considerations.[7] Looking at the world economy from the perspective of those on the fringes of capitalism can help us to think about constructing a model that would be concerned with the production of life rather than the production of things and wealth. Maria Mies argues that the different conception of labor upon which such a model depends could help us to adapt our lifestyle at a time when we are becoming increasingly conscious of the finiteness of the earth and its resources (Mies 1986, 211 ff.). Such a model would depend on an extended definition of security, which goes beyond a nationalist, militarist focus and begins to speak to the economic and environmental security of individuals and states alike.

In their conclusion to *The Global Political Economy*, written one year after Glipin's text, Stephen Gill and David Law (1988) called for the formation of a counterhegemonic perspective on IPE, one based on an alternative set of concepts and concerns, which could deal with a series of problems associated with militarism, environmental crises, and the excesses and inequalities of the marketplace that are becoming more acute as we enter the twenty-first century. They suggest that such a perspective might emerge out of transnational linkages between grassroots social movements concerned with peace, ecology, and economic justice (Gill and Law 1988; see also Gill and Law 1989). Because women are represented in much larger numbers in these new social movements than they are in institutions of state power and transnational capital, women would be in a position to make a significant contribution to the formation of this counterhegemonic perspective. Some feminists have argued that women's position outside the structures of power, on the peripheries of the system, gives them a special epistemological standpoint, which can provide a more comprehensive view of reality. At a time when existing political and economic institutions seem increasingly incapable of solving many global problems, a feminist perspective, by going beyond an investigation of market relations, state behavior, and capitalism, could help us to understand how the global economy affects those on the fringes of the market, the state, or in households as we attempt to build a more secure world where inequalities based on gender and other forms of discrimination are eliminated.

7. Although I did not use a gender perspective, I elaborated on what such a strategy might look like in Tickner (1987), where I compared agrarian models of self-reliant development, articulated by Gandhi and Thomas Jefferson, to the national power-building strategies adopted by post-independence India and the early United States.

CHAPTER 4

States and Markets: An Ecofeminist Perspective on International Political Economy

1993

As mentioned in the conclusion to the last chapter, building a more sustainable global economy must be concerned with the production of life rather than with the production of commodities and wealth. This chapter looks in more detail at an ecofeminist perspective on global political economy that could help us envisage a more sustainable global economy that is less exploitative of the natural environment.

The evolution of the European state system and the capitalist world economy share a common history in their exploitative attitude toward the natural environment, an attitude that, for the most part, has been ignored by scholars of international political economy. Mercantilism, the intellectual precursor of Robert Gilpin's economic nationalist approach, discussed in Chapter 3 (Gilpin 1987), viewed natural resources as crucial elements of national power to be increased through overseas expansion if possible. Neoclassical economics' prescriptions for the expansion of the market also depend on the exploitation of the earth's resources: pollution control is seen as a cost rather than a benefit. National accounting data attach no economic value to policy measures designed to preserve natural resources and the health of the natural environment (Waring 1988).

Environmentalists in the field of international relations have begun to question these attitudes toward the natural environment common to both economic nationalism and neoclassical economics. Recent reconceptualizations of the meaning of security suggest that the pursuit of wealth and power may be self-defeating in the long run if physical limits on natural resources and the earth's toleration of pollution are assumed. Given these ecological threats, certain environmentalists are questioning whether states in the Global South can ever achieve a standard of living equivalent to that of states whose industrial take-off occurred in previous centuries (North 1990, ch. 10). While environmentalists suggest the need for international regulations to prevent future ecological catastrophes, scholars of international political economy point out the difficulties of achieving the cooperation necessary for such agreements in an anarchical international system (Keohane 1984).

The rapidity with which new ecological threats are appearing suggests that the investigations of scholars of international political economy into the historical interactions between states and markets should also include an examination of the attitudes of both of these institutions toward nature. Feminist theory has revealed important connections between states and markets and the exploitative attitude toward nature that both required. Positing an interrelationship between the evolution of the modern state and the market, and the exploitation of nature and women, feminist perspectives can make an important contribution to our understanding of the ecological constraints on the accumulation of power and wealth with which the field of international political economy should be concerned.

I begin this chapter with an ecofeminist account of the way in which nature has been viewed by western Enlightenment science. The changed perception of nature, from living organism to inert machine, began in the seventeenth century coincidentally with the birth of the modern state system and the capitalist world economy. This change, supported by Enlightenment philosophy, can be linked to the competitive wealth-seeking behavior of an expansionary Eurocentric state system whose colonizing activities caused ecological changes worldwide. Next I examine the thinking of some contemporary environmentalists who are questioning rejuvenative assumptions about nature's ability to provide unlimited resources for the expansionary activities of states and markets: while this environmental approach posits physical limits on the continued pursuit of wealth and power, it remains rooted in an Enlightenment view of nature as machine. Ecologists and ecofeminists have taken an even more radical step, which challenges modern science's mechanistic view of nature. I conclude by examining the views of some ecologists and ecofeminists who believe that solutions to our contemporary dilemmas demand a revolution, not only in our political and economic thinking, but also in the way we view nature—in other words, a revolution as fundamental as that which took place in seventeenth-century Europe.

THE STATE, THE MARKET, AND NATURE IN EARLY MODERN EUROPE

The view that natural resources are to be exploited to advance the power and wealth of the state is reflected in the shift toward a mechanistic view of nature that began in seventeenth-century Europe around the time of the birth of the modern state system. Feminist scholar Carolyn Merchant claims that, in medieval Europe, nature had been viewed as an organism or living system in which human beings and their natural environments were highly interdependent. Nature was generally depicted as female, the earth as a nurturing mother who provided for the needs of humankind; but nature could also be dangerous, a force whose wild and uncontrollable behavior could produce chaos (Merchant 1980). Merchant describes a process, which began in the seventeenth century, whereby the concept of nature was gradually transformed so that rather than being seen as a living organism, it was viewed as an inert, lifeless machine, thereby permitting its exploitation and use for purposes of human progress. This evolving view of nature as machine was vital for the project of the scientific revolution, which sought to tame nature's wild behavior through the discovery of predictable regularities within a rationally determined system of laws. According to Merchant, a central concern of the scientific revolution was order and power, to be achieved through the discovery and application of mathematical laws and human beings' active intervention in a secularized world (Merchant 1980, 216).

The taming of nature was often described in gendered terms that reflected the social order. Feminist scholars more generally have drawn attention to the sexual metaphors employed by Francis Bacon and other Enlightenment scientists. Central to Francis Bacon's scientific investigations was a natural world, frequently described as a woman, who required taming, shaping, and subduing by the scientific mind (Keller 1985, 36). As seventeenth-century science associated nature and the body with women, so the mind or rational thought came to be associated with men. According to Merchant, this nature/culture dichotomy was used as a justification for devaluing women. As discussed in Chapter 3, the Enlightenment period was not a progressive time for women: at such moments of great historical change, usually identified with progress, feminist historians claim that women are often left behind both politically and economically.

The transition to a market economy and to early capitalism required a greater exploitation of natural resources than did the subsistence economy of feudal Europe. For example, changes in seventeenth-century English agriculture began an encroachment on woods and fenlands in the pursuit of the higher yields required for production for the market (Merchant 1980). Seventeenth-century scientists justified their goals of "mastering" and "managing" the earth in the name of human progress and increasing material wealth. The demands of a market economy, and the increases in productivity that it generated, required the use of nonrenewable energy resources such as timber and coal. The rendering of nature as a dead, inert object was essential if fears of violating nature's inner resources through the mining of metals and fuels crucial for the coming industrial revolution were to be eliminated.

Feminist scholars, who have written about the origins of these Enlightenment views on nature, claim that the domination of certain men over other human beings, other cultures, and nature, which the process of accumulating wealth and power involved, cannot be fully understood unless gender is taken as a central category of analysis. These feminists believe that seventeenth-century gender metaphors were fundamental to developing attitudes toward nature and women, as well as attitudes toward non-Western peoples—attitudes that were both racist and consistent with the practices of a capitalist world economy and an expansive Eurocentric state system.

THE DOMINATION OF NATURE GLOBALIZED

A nascent market economy and its need for an ever-expanding resource base, together with a new vision of scientific progress, were important motivating forces as the early modern state system began to expand beyond its European boundaries. Europeans started venturing overseas in search of the additional wealth and natural resources required by an expanding market. Merchant describes an ecological crisis as early as the sixteenth century caused by Europe's shipbuilding industry, an industry that was one of the most critical for subsequent commercial expansion and national supremacy. Ship-building, which depended on mature oaks for masts and hulls, caused a severe wood shortage in many parts of Europe, stimulating the rise of coal mining as an alternate source of fuel (Merchant 1980, 65–66). As Europeans began to sail beyond their shores, the exploitation of natural resources took on wider dimensions, beginning a process that culminated in today's highly interdependent global resource base (North 1990, chap. 8).

In an international system consisting of independent sovereign political units, the notion of the world as a single resource base led inevitably to economic competition and political conflict. European expansion extended the seventeenth century's instrumental view of nature beyond the boundaries of Europe, as scientific progress became a justification for imperialist projects (Choucri and North 1975). Enlightenment beliefs about the transformation of the environment as a measure of human progress were used as a justification for colonialism where native populations were not deemed capable of effecting this transformation for themselves (Leiss 1972, ch. 4). The lower position assigned to women and nature in early modern Europe was extended to members of other cultures and races. "Empty" or "virgin" lands became sites for European conquest and settlement: "wastelands," a category loaded with the biases of colonial rule, were seen as spaces to be cultivated for the generation of revenue and resources for the mother country (Shiva 1989, 85). In reality, these spaces were not empty at all but were occupied by people with very different relationships with their natural environment. The expansion of the European state system meant that the scientific revolution's mechanistic attitude toward nature began to take on global dimensions with far-reaching implications for non-Western ecological traditions that were not able to withstand assimilation by the global economy.

Merchant's account of changing attitudes toward nature in seventeenth- and eighteenth-century New England provides a case study of one such ecological revolution caused by European expansion. Before European colonization, Native American populations, living in subsistence communities, regarded natural resources as gifts given by nature to take care of human needs: humans and animals lived in interlacing cyclical time and space. As European settlers moved into these spaces, they saw these new lands very differently, as "wastes" or wildernesses to be tamed and "improved," projects that required the expertise of a "superior" culture. Gradually this taming process set humans—European and native alike—apart from nature. Although the Indians continued to be associated with animals in the minds of European settlers, and were thus placed below Europeans in the social and political hierarchy, Indians began to see themselves as distanced from natural resources and apart from nature (Merchant 1989).

Merchant's account of the next phase of this ecological revolution in early New England parallels her earlier work on seventeenth-century Europe. As agricultural production was transformed from subsistence to market, farming was gradually changed into a manufacturing industry: production and reproduction were split into separate spheres with women defined by their reproductive function within the private sphere. Commercial farming, conducted mostly by men, required management of nature as an abstract mechanical force: nature as mother retreated into the private sphere, along with women, who were expected to be the upholders of moral values that had no place in a market economy (Merchant 1989, chap. 7).

Merchant's conclusion is an ironic one when framed in a global perspective. She argues that, since contemporary New England depends on outside sources for most of its energy, food, and clothing, some of its own environment has recovered, as evidenced by the regeneration of its natural forests. However, with the colonial legacy as supplier of raw materials to the "civilized" world, areas of the Global South today suffer some of the harshest effects of environmental degradation. The resource demands of the Eurocentric state system and the capitalist world economy have imposed and continue to impose heavy burdens on the natural environment and its human inhabitants worldwide.[1]

---

1. Since the original article was written in 1993, the burden is increasing as countries outside the West also become "developed" and have ever-greater need for resources to fuel their industrialization. It is also the case that states rich in natural resources and minerals frequently experience high degrees of conflict.

This mechanistic attitude toward nature, which began in seventeenth-century Europe and which was subsequently globalized through imperialism, led to a fundamental shift in the conceptualization of geographical space. In the case of early America, a breakdown of the Indian way of life began with the mapping of their homeland onto geometric space by European explorers and mapmakers. As space was reorganized, fixed boundaries between wild and civilized appeared, boundaries unknown to Native American cultures. Mapping the world by European explorers led to similar processes of reconceptualizing and organizing geographical space on a global basis, a process that has lent itself to projects of management, control, and domination of the natural environment (Merchant 1989).

The history of spatial changes is also the history of power changes. The interrelation between geographical space and power politics, an important influence on economic nationalism, was developed by the Western geopolitical tradition of the nineteenth and early twentieth centuries. In his study of Western geopolitical thought, Geoffrey Parker defines geopolitics as the study of international relations from a spatial viewpoint; geopolitics views the world as an interlocking mechanism, an assumption that links it to the Enlightenment's view of nature as a machine (Parker 1985, 2). While looking at the globe as a totality, geopolitics, like mercantilism, sees a world divided into bounded political entities competing for control over their environment. The German school of *Geopolitik* was founded on environmental determinism: the power that any state could command depended on its geographical circumstances. In geopolitical terms, spaces are contested areas populated by colonists, soldiers, navies, and traders. As geopolitical thinkers, along with mapmakers, were effecting this transformation in our perception of the global environment, the native inhabitants of these spaces were being marginalized, just as women were increasingly being confined to the private space of the family.[2]

While geopolitics made explicit the domination that states, striving for wealth and power, have attempted to impose on their natural environments, modern science's mechanistic view of nature provided some of the framing assumptions of political realism upon which economic nationalism bases its analysis. State of nature myths, fundamental to realist explanations of the anarchy/order distinction, are based on Thomas Hobbes's portrayal of the state of nature (Waltz 1959, chap. 6). Consistent with seventeenth-century assumptions about nature and science, Hobbes's *Leviathan* is a mechanistic model of society in which order could only be guaranteed by an absolute

---

2. This is not to deny that most women have always worked outside the family also—at least in market economies—out of economic necessity. Nevertheless, their association with the private sphere of the household has had detrimental social and economic effects, as discussed in Chapter 3.

sovereign operating the machine from outside (Merchant 1980, 209–215). The lack of such a sovereign in the state of nature led to disorder owing to the unbridled competition for scarce resources. Used by realists as a metaphor to portray the international system, the wildness of nature beyond the boundaries of an orderly "domesticated" political space demands that states try to control and dominate this external environment and accumulate the natural resources necessary for increasing wealth and power.[3]

ENVIRONMENTAL PERSPECTIVES ON STATES AND MARKETS

The geopolitical tradition has drawn our attention to boundaries and spaces carved out by states to enhance their command over natural resources and national wealth. Environmental perspectives on international relations first drew attention to ecological threats by eliminating boundaries made by humans altogether. Pictures of the earth sent back from the Apollo II spacecraft in 1969 changed our spatial perception of the globe from a world divided into hierarchical, competitive states to "spaceship-earth," a fragile, interconnected whole whose inhabitants—women, men, as well as non-human forms of life—are all equally at risk.

Just as Merchant describes a reformulation of geopolitical space brought about by an ecological revolution in early New England, scholars concerned with environmental degradation challenge us to rethink once again our ideas about contemporary geopolitical space. In an era when modern ecological revolutions have had dramatic impacts on non-Western cultures and peoples worldwide, environmentalists encourage us to look at the world, not as a system of competitive states or an interdependent global economy, but as an ecosystem, a global unity of natural carriers composed of the atmosphere and seawater (Sprout and Sprout 1971, chap. 11). This fragile ecosystem cannot be protected by boundaries, traditional instruments for preserving wealth and power. Problems of the ozone layer, acid rain, river and ocean pollution are impervious to national boundaries.

While these universalizing images of "one world" and its fragility have served to alert people to the dangers of environmental degradation and resource constraints, they have seriously depoliticized issues associated with power and economic inequality, which remain embedded in the historical practices of the European state system and the evolution of the capitalist world economy. The image of "Mother Earth" tames and domesticates our perception of a world in which these historically expansive systems have been responsible for the erection of contemporary boundaries between North and

3. In Machiavelli's *The Prince*, another classical text on which realists rely, anarchy, or nature's wildness, was also gendered and depicted as female. See Pitkin (1984).

South, rich and poor, and men and women (Diamond and Orenstein 1990, 264–278). These boundaries are boundaries of inequality that affect the various ways in which environmental dangers impact upon people's lives. While the affluent are concerned with the potential hazards of a thinning ozone layer, the poor, in all parts of the world, are confronted by more immediate environmental degradation, such as contaminated water and soil erosion, which threatens their daily existence.[4]

A common theme running through much of the environmental literature is that the contemporary state system is not an adequate framework within which to solve ecological problems. Just as the modern state system was born at a time of scientific revolution, many contemporary environmentalists believe that another revolution, the technological revolution of the late twentieth century, is creating problems with which our present state system will be unable to cope (Pirages 1989). Resource interdependence and pollution demonstrate the permeability of traditional international boundaries and the impossibility of separating domestic from international issues: in a highly interdependent global ecosystem, many environmentalists believe that the state is becoming anachronistic (Sprout and Sprout 1971, chap. 1).

The nationalist approach to international political economy which assumes that states are self-seeking and conflict-prone as they pursue wealth and power in an anarchic international system, draws attention to the problem of the state as an environmental manager. Collective action for the common good is hard to achieve in anarchic realms with no sanctioned method of enforcement. Collective goods, which can be consumed by all members of the system, encourage states to act selfishly, hoping that others will pay. Paradoxically, the great powers, the traditional managers of the international system and, therefore, the most likely suppliers of collective goods, pose the greatest threat to the environment by virtue of their disproportionate consumption of resources, their high level of pollution, and their possession of large numbers of environmentally threatening weapons systems. Given the principle of national sovereignty, internal boundaries that contribute to environmental degradation are also hard to change when it is not in the interests of national political and economic elites to do so.

Given these obstacles, there is a sense among environmentalists that an international system, composed of sovereign states that have sought to ensure and enhance their wealth and power at the expense of the natural environment and its individual inhabitants, requires a fundamental restructuring if it is to overcome our contemporary environmental dilemmas. Yet few of these scholars have made similar inferences about the need to restructure the relationship between humans and nature that has evolved coincidentally with

---

4. Since this was written in 1993, there is greater awareness of the commonality of environmental problems for rich and poor states alike.

the globalization of the state system and the market economy. Ecologists and ecofeminists offer this more radical critique: they believe that only by changing our relationship with nature can real security, for both our natural environment and its human inhabitants, be assured.

AN ECOLOGICAL PERSPECTIVE ON INTERNATIONAL POLITICAL ECONOMY

An environmental perspective on international political economy (IPE) suggests that states' pursuit of wealth and power may be self-defeating in the long run. It emphasizes the need for global institutions to manage problems of environmental degradation with which the state is unable to cope. Ecologists, however, question whether environmental management can ever be adequate for the task of assuring an ecologically safe future. They claim that management techniques grow out of the reductionist methodology of modern science, which cannot cope with complex issues whose interdependencies are barely understood. A mechanistic view of nature leads to assumptions that it can be tinkered with and improved for human purposes. Such methodologies perpetuate a dominating, instrumental view of nature that attempts to render it more serviceable for the needs of the state and the market.

Ecologists believe that only with a fundamental change in human relationships with nature can we solve our contemporary dilemmas. The mechanistic view of nature, bequeathed to us by the scientific revolution, does not bode well for an ecologically secure future. Many ecologists are critical of modern society, given its dependence on a market economy fueled by an excessive appropriation of nature's resources. They suggest that the values of modern society are based on an incomplete model of human behavior that emphasizes instrumental rationality, production, and consumption, at the expense of traits such as humaneness, creativity and compassion.

Driven by social incentives that reward profit maximization, "economic man" is a compulsive producer and consumer with little thought for deeper needs or ecological constraints. Political and economic development, which together have legitimized these destructive behaviors, have led to a loss of control over science and technology, which today is causing severe environmental stress (Orr and Soroos 1979, chap. 4). Modernization, a project of the European Enlightenment, is now being reproduced in the Global South, where development projects often contribute to further strains on limited environmental resources, as well as to the reproduction of inequality.

Social ecologists, such as William Leiss, explicitly link man's domination of nature with man's domination over man. Defending the original goals of the scientific revolution as an attempt to liberate human beings from the constraints of their natural environment and increase their material well-being,

Leiss claims that the rationalism of modern science became caught in a web of social contradictions. The instruments through which humans have transformed the resources of nature into means for the satisfaction of material desires have increasingly come to be regarded as objects of political conflict both domestically and internationally (Leiss 1972, 22). According to Leiss, the real object of domination has not been nature but human beings: through enhanced technological capabilities, certain men have appropriated nature's resources and thereby dominated others. A more rational science would understand the world in a way that would produce harmony with the environment. But this can only be realized when the struggle for domination ends, along with the disparities in power among groups and nations fostered by the contemporary international system (Leiss 1972, 120–122).

Social ecologist Murray Bookchin also points to the hierarchical structuring of the contemporary world embodied in man's domination over man, over woman, and over nature. Bookchin believes that these modes of domination are historically constructed and, therefore, can be transcended. He stresses the emancipatory potential of ecology, a science that recognizes no hierarchy and is therefore in a position to combat domination at all levels (Bookchin 1980).

AN ECOFEMINIST PERSPECTIVE ON INTERNATIONAL POLITICAL ECONOMY

While calling for fundamental changes in both modern science and contemporary political, social, and economic structures as great as those that were set in motion in the seventeenth century, few ecologists have raised the issue of gender relations, which Merchant and many other feminists concerned with ecological issues see as fundamental to the hierarchical nature of these social structures, as well as to the projects of modern science. For this reason, these feminists maintain that, in order to live up to its claim as a holistic science, ecology must incorporate gender as a category of analysis.

The gender-sensitive ecological analysis that I have presented in this chapter suggests that the contemporary ecological crisis stems from a historically expansive state system and a growth-oriented capitalist world economy, and from an ideology that believes that both nature and women can be exploited for human progress. Certain socialist feminists claim that the rise of capitalism eroded subsistence-based agriculture and urban workshops in which production was oriented toward use-value—a mode of production in which men and women were economic partners—and replaced it with a system in which men dominated the market and women retreated into the home, where they provided unpaid labor. As certain ecofeminists suggest, the expansion of the market also required the ever-increasing exploitation of natural resources, which were needed to fuel subsequent industrial revolutions: these exploitative attitudes toward nature were frequently described in gendered terms. Coincidentally, the state system, which was expanding beyond its European origins in search of wealth and power, imposed its ideology of domination over nature onto very different cultures and civilizations worldwide.

Speaking out of the experiences of women, who have been on the margins of the state and the market throughout modern history, these various ecofeminist perspectives can offer us some important new insights as we begin to reexamine the evolution of the world political economy from an ecological perspective. By making explicit what they claim is an inherent connection between the domination of nature and the domination of women, ecofeminist perspectives suggest that both gender hierarchies and the hierarchical relationship between humans and nature must be overcome simultaneously if an ecologically secure future is to be achieved. Developing sustainable non-dominating relations with nature and assuring all peoples of an adequate quality of life require an ethic that rests, not on hierarchical relationships, but on the mutual interaction between women and men, as well as between humans and nature.

CHAPTER 5

The Gendered Frontiers of Globalization

2004

In his 1991 bestseller, *The Borderless World*, Kenichi Ohmae, a leading international business thinker, described himself as a global citizen, a resident of his community, and Japanese, in that order. For Ohmae the term "global citizen" meant a citizen of what he described as a "borderless world," an interlinked economy of one billion people where political maps indicating boundaries between countries are being replaced by "competitive maps" marked by flows of finance and industrial activity from which political boundaries have disappeared (Ohmae 1991, 18).[1] Ohmae used the analogy of the duty-free shop as a precursor to what life would be like in this borderless world. Quoting the ancient Chinese philosopher Sun Tzu, that the best strategy in war is one that allows you to win without having to fight, Ohmae's text reads like a military manual for business executives. Ohmae's self-defined identity as a citizen warrior on the frontier of this new borderless world (if frontier is the right term) did not include his gender identity. Yet, it is fair to say that the frontier he depicted is one populated mostly by men.

In her textual analysis of *The Economist*, a British weekly business news magazine, Charlotte Hooper portrayed an international corporate and financial world similar to Ohmae's—a world of Darwinian struggle rhetorically constructed around metaphors of war and sport (Hooper 2001, 151). According to Hooper, the dominant image of globalization in the pages of *The Economist* is a "frontier masculinity" in which capitalism meets science fiction and is

---

1. The term "global citizen," popular with environmentalists in the 1970s and 1980s as described in Chapter 4, is now widely used by the business community.

moving, metaphorically at least, toward the colonization of space (Hooper 2001, 160). Advertisements that feature images of planet earth seen from space abound; the corporate mission is often phrased as being at the forefront of a dynamic global marketplace where only the intrepid businessman dares to tread. Globalization belongs to an elite cosmopolitan culture of men.

This story of manly conquest is not the whole story, however. Hooper, writing in 2001, also recognized the introduction into the pages of *The Economist* of a more feminized cooperative style of management, more typical of Asian business, which has the potential to soften and feminize Western business practices. Nevertheless, Hooper does not see this change in style as translating into advances for women in the corporate world. Indeed, it would be fair to ask: Where *are* the women on these new frontiers of globalization? Looking for women in this elite corporate world yields dismal results. Throughout the 1980s and 1990s, women comprised less than one half of one percent of the 4,000 top executives of Fortune 500 companies (Goldstein 2001, 43).[2] And when women do rise to the top, they almost always earn less than men.

Even if women are not to be found on the extraterrestrial frontiers of the globalizing economy, they are also on the move. Women are crossing different frontiers—from countryside to city to take up jobs in the newly globalized industrial production. Indeed, industrialization in the context of globalization is as much female-led as it is export-led. Women are not only moving to cities, they are also moving across international borders. While, in general, the international mobility of labor is more restricted than it was a century ago, women are moving across international frontiers in larger numbers than ever before, as domestic servants, sweatshop workers, mail-order brides, and sex workers. Another boundary—that between home and workplace—is also being challenged by a growth in home-based production (Prügl 1999).

These women on the move have been described as the new proletariat of the global economy; with a growing feminization of poverty, some see a world of "gender apartheid" (Shiva 1995). Yet the picture is more complicated and the gender impact of globalization is quite variable. In the last fifty years, women almost everywhere have been gaining in terms of legal rights, education, job opportunities, and wages, while many men, particularly blue collar or non-white and especially in developed countries, have been losing in terms of wages and bargaining power. But even in an economy where men suffer, gender bias exists. Women continue to experience persistent discrimination and inequality by virtue of being women. The United Nations Human Development Report of 1995 reported that, of the 1.3 billion people living in poverty at that time, 70 percent

2. According to a 2013 study done by Catalyst, a nonprofit research group, the number of women in top executive positions of Fortune 500 companies is still low. The percentage of female executive officers at Fortune 500 companies was 14.3 percent in 2013, a percentage that remained constant over the previous three years (Fisher 2013).

were women (United Nations 1996, 36).[3] Female poverty was attributed to women's unequal situation in the labor market, their treatment under social welfare systems, and their status in the family.

My purpose in this chapter is to explore the frequently invisible gendered frontiers of globalization on which women are living and working. The term "globalization" is used to describe the intensification of economic, political, social, and cultural relations across borders. While I realize that it is not possible to separate economic aspects of globalization from social, cultural, and political phenomena, here I concentrate on the economic aspects.[4] I discuss how economic globalization is gendered and how this impacts women. I also outline some ways in which women's social movements and nongovernmental organizations (NGOs), as well as international governmental organizations (IGOs), are attempting to move the policy process toward creating a global economy that is less hierarchical and more just for everyone.

THE GENDERED EFFECTS OF ECONOMIC GLOBALIZATION

In her 1998 book, *Globalization and Its Discontents,* Saskia Sassen claimed that mainstream accounts of globalization emphasize technical and abstract economic dynamics and proceed as if they were gender neutral when they are not. These accounts operate according to what she termed a "narrative of eviction" because they exclude an entire range of workers, firms, and sectors that do not fit the prevalent masculinized images of globalization such as the one I described in the introduction to this chapter (Sassen 1998, 82). Even though the number of women in top-level global economic activities is growing, it is a world that is male gendered in that its cultural properties and power dynamics have historically been associated with powerful men.

Certainly, there are legal and economic barriers to women's integration into the global workforce and the global economy. Nevertheless, legal and economic barriers are not the only explanations for the disproportionate number of women in marginal, under-rewarded economic activities. In order to understand these gendered boundaries of economic activity, it is necessary to examine the social construction of gender hierarchies that have the effect of assigning women disproportionately to the margins of the global

---

3. The percentage of women in poverty has not changed significantly. The United Nations Human Development Report of 2010 reported that 1.75 billion people live in multidimensional poverty that consists of acute deprivation in health, education, and standard of living (United Nations 2010, 6). Data provided by UN Women stated that, in 2011, women still represented 70 percent of the world's poor (UN Women 2011).

4. For an analysis that links all of these features of globalization with their gendered effects, see Peterson (2003).

economy. Gender hierarchies directly affect specific women's economic situation; they also construct social structures in which women in general are disadvantaged.

In Chapter 3, I described the gendered division of labor that had its origins in seventeenth-century Europe and involved the division between work and home required by early capitalism. In Europe, it was not until the end of the eighteenth century that the concept of "family" became popular; at that time it had distinctly class connotations in that only those with property could afford to have a "family" (meaning a "non-working" wife). Nevertheless, the concepts of male "breadwinner" and female "housewife," which spread throughout the world through colonization, have affected women worldwide in terms of their classification as workers, welfare recipients, and refugees (Mies 1986, 104–110: see also Mohanty 2003, 150). Divisions between "public" and "private" marginalize those who are associated with "private" places like the home, a gender bias that Gillian Youngs has called a "patriarchal prism" through which women's identities and roles are perceived as being associated with the devalued private sphere, even after women move into the public space of the market (Youngs 2000, 45–46). Even though, today, the majority of women work outside the home, the association of women with female gendered roles, such as housewife, caregiver, and mother, has become institutionalized and even naturalized, decreasing women's economic security and autonomy. Indeed, the modern global economy could not operate without these traditional ideas about appropriate gender roles, which result in women assuming much of the unpaid reproductive and caring labor.

Because of these historically and culturally determined gender expectations, when women do enter the workforce, they are disproportionately represented in the caring professions or in "light" manufacturing industries, occupations that are chosen, not on the basis of market rationality, but because of values that are emphasized in female socialization. Societies' stereotypes about "who women are" affect which jobs they take, and how they are compensated for their labor. In many cases, when women do move into the waged sector they provide an optimal labor force because, since they are defined as housewives rather than workers, they can be paid lower wages on the assumption that their wages are supplemental to their family's income. In many places, companies favor hiring young unmarried women who can achieve a high level of productivity at a low wage; these women are frequently fired if they get married or become pregnant. Long hours, extremely strict supervision of work, and long travel time have often been the norm in many export industries—often worse in small local firms than in multinational corporations. And, because of expectations associated with traditional gender roles there is a belief that women possess "nimble fingers," have patience for tedious jobs, and sew "naturally"; thus, this kind of work is not seen as skilled and is remunerated accordingly (Enloe 1990, 162). Characterizing women as supplemental wage earners belies the fact that at least 20 percent of all households worldwide are headed by women (Seager 2003, 21).

There is also evidence to suggest that, in many middle-income countries, demand for women's labor has been weakening as production becomes more skilled and capital-intensive. This suggests that female gains in employment in global industries may be short-lived. Indeed, it has usually been the case that as jobs become more skilled and wages improve, women have tended to lose or be excluded from them. In Mexico, for example, the majority of factory jobs for women are in the Maquiladoras, or twin plants to American industries that operate at a lower cost in Mexico. Many of these jobs are low paying and detrimental to the personal health, physical safety, and social viability of women (Ver Beek 2001).

Gender consequences enter into another global labor issue—that of part-time and home-based work. As companies have moved to a more "flexible" labor force in all parts of the world, cost containment strategies have resulted in increased use of part-time and/or home-based workers who are easily hired and fired. Exempt from any national labor standards that may exist, "domesticated" workers are outside the working class and its regulations and are not paid when there is no work. They have no contracts and few rights. Home-based work is proliferating, especially in the developing world. Since women, often of necessity, prefer work that more easily accommodates to family responsibilities, the vast majority of home-based workers are women. Traditional notions of the division of labor that define women as housewives—a category associated with the expectation that labor is free—legitimizes wages at below subsistence levels. Home-workers generally have no networks or other organizational basis for bargaining for improved conditions and higher wages.

In an era when global cities, the newest challengers to traditional international boundaries, have become strategic sites for the coordination of global economic processes, Saskia Sassen claims that women and immigrants serve as the systemic equivalent of what she calls an "offshore proletariat" (Sassen 1998, 86). She sees the global labor system as one in which women and immigrants lose in terms of jobs, wages, and stability. Many of the jobs in leading services, dominated by finance, are, in actual fact, low paying and manual. Increasingly, immigrant women are filling these low-paying jobs and are also serving as domestic workers for wealthy urban elites, including elite women (Sassen 1998, 88).

Even in cases where women do benefit from entry into the workforce, they continue to perform most of the unremunerated household labor associated with reproductive and caregiving tasks. Although there is a sense that women are "not working" when they engage in this type of labor, they are actually playing a crucial role in the reproduction of labor necessary for waged work; moreover, these activities often constrain women's opportunities for paid work. Although housework is not seen as "work" when women do it in their own homes, without household maintenance, neither men nor women could work outside the home. The difficulties of household tasks increase substantially in bad economic times; this is evident in the effects of financial crises and structural adjustment policies on women.

Structural adjustment programs (SAPs), imposed by the International Monetary Fund (IMF) on countries that have sought help from international financial institutions for international debt repayment, involve budget rationalization, market liberalization, privatization, and price decontrol. The effects of adjustment have fallen disproportionately on the poor due to increased levels of unemployment and cuts in government spending on social services. These services are often taken up by women in the household, resulting in the intensification of women's unremunerated caring and reproductive work and the interruption of children's (particularly girls') education (Benería 2003, 49–50; Peterson 2003, 153).[5]

I have suggested some difficulties that women encounter at the less visible frontiers of economic globalization. However, this is not the only story and it is not true of all women. The female share of employment has steadily increased around the world, and falling fertility rates, rising educational levels, and increased urbanization have all had positive effects on women's lives. The percentage of women in the workforce increased about one percent between 1993 and 2003 (ILO 2004, 3). Accompanying this increase in work participation is a worldwide decrease in women's fertility rates. In every region of the world, fertility rates decreased markedly between 1995 and 2000 (ILO, 2004, 6). Though women's access to education decreased in some places in the 1990s, UNESCO estimated that the aggregate enrollment of women in educational programs increased 5% worldwide (UNESCO, 2004).

While acknowledging that women's entry into the labor force has put an undue burden on their lives in terms of triple roles associated with their disproportionate engagement in caring and reproductive work, Manuel Castells sees the incorporation of women into paid work as increasing their bargaining power vis-à-vis men and undermining the legitimacy of men's domination that occurs because of their traditional roles as providers for the family. What he calls the "end of patriarchialism" is, according to Castells, the most important revolution in the contemporary world because it goes to the roots of society and to the heart of who we are (Castells 1997, 242). Worldwide, about half of economically active women work in services and, according to

5. Today, structural adjustment is no longer only a problem for developing countries. After the global financial crisis that began in 2008, Western countries, particularly some of those in the European Union, have also felt the harsh effects of structural adjustment.

Castells, women are not being relegated to the lowest skilled service jobs; the growth of women's jobs is higher at the upper end of the occupational structure (Castells 1997, 168). However, Castells concedes that the reason for this is that women perform similarly qualified jobs at lower pay than men and with greater job insecurity and lower chances of getting to the top.[6] Nevertheless, entry into the labor force increases women's power within the household and gives them a greater sense of autonomy; having a job may be better than no work at all, and the extra cash flow can significantly enhance the income of very poor families. It also increases women's financial independence.

It is difficult to generalize, therefore, about the gender consequences of economic globalization. How well, or how poorly, women are doing can only be determined by careful empirical case studies. The United Nations' effort over the last thirty years to disaggregate data by sex is important in this regard. Nevertheless, the claim that we live in a world characterized by gendered as well as class and racial boundaries of inequality—boundaries that are far from breaking down—is undisputed. Perceptions about what it means to be a "woman" dominate the roles available to women in the global economy. Even if women have made strides over the past fifty years, much remains to be done. And the likelihood of a backlash against women's greater autonomy remains significant, as evidenced in culturally conservative, often religiously based movements in all parts of the world that aim at putting women back in their traditional domestic roles associated with "female respectability." This backlash may be fueled further by the perception of blue-collar men that they are losing jobs to women and immigrants. Male anger at losing power to women abounds in all parts of the world.[7]

SOME POLICY PRESCRIPTIONS

I conclude by discussing some of the efforts that have been made to diminish the negative gendered effects of economic globalization that I have outlined. The globalization of communications has resulted in the rapid growth of social movements. Electronic communications have vastly increased people's ability to organize across traditional boundaries and the women's movement is no exception (Keck and Sikkink 1998). Beginning with the first United Nations Conference on Women in Mexico City in 1975, which launched the UN Decade for Women (1976–1985), women worldwide have been organizing in increasing numbers around a variety of issues from human rights to the environment,

6. According to a 2011 report by the International Labour Organization, in spite of progress, women's average monthly wages still represent only 75 percent of men's (ILO 2011, 43).
7. This backlash appeared to intensify after the financial crisis of 2008.

labor issues, and the effects of SAPs. Organizing is taking place at the local, national, and transnational level.

At the beginning of the UN Decade, women from the North took the lead in organizing; economic issues having to do with employment and wages took precedence over development issues. By the end of the Decade, women from the South began to organize around the impact of economic crises on their lives. Their work resulted in the establishment of DAWN (Development Alternatives with Women for a New Era), a network of Southern women that, among other issues, has provided analysis of the consequences of structural adjustment policies on women's lives (Stienstra 2000, 212–213). Attendance at the NGO conferences that have paralleled each of the official UN Conferences on women grew from 5,000 in Mexico City in 1975 to an estimated 25,000 in Beijing in 1995 (Jaquette 2003, 336). Women's movements have been among the pioneers in extending the principles of networking to facilitate social change from the grassroots to the global level. They have shared "best practice" strategies for mobilizing societies and pressuring governments (True 2003, 378). The work of women's caucuses at various UN conferences, not only the women's conferences, has yielded strong feminist agendas, and states now recognize this work as an important contribution to all of these conferences. Women's activism has challenged the hierarchical political structures and masculinized traditions evident at the intergovernmental UN conferences, and NGO forums have practiced forms of participatory democracy and have moved feminist ideas into the policy mainstream of these organizations (West 1999, 192).

Pressure from women's groups was important in getting the United Nations to disaggregate its data by sex. The adoption of the gender-related development index (GDI) by the UN Human Development Programme in 1995, which has developed gender-differentiated quality of life indices using indicators such as literacy, life expectancy, income, and political participation, was an important step in helping to formulate policies to improve women's well-being. Often, the adoption of international legal conventions that promote gender equality begin with local grassroots organizing. For example, in 1996, the International Labor Organization adopted a convention that set international standards for individuals who work at home for pay. This was the result of organizing by the Self Employed Women's Association (SEWA), a trade union based in India that organized women engaged in small-scale trade and home-based work.

The adoption by the UN and other international intergovernmental organizations of "gender mainstreaming," a policy that aims to evaluate the gendered effects of all aspects of institutional decision-making at the national and international levels, is also an important step toward gender equality. Gender mainstreaming mandates that every policy or piece of legislation be evaluated as to whether or not it reduces or increases gender inequalities (True 2003, 371). Gender mainstreaming was established as a global strategy for achieving gender equality in the 1995 Beijing Platform for Action ratified by all UN member states. It has been adopted as the official policy of the United Nations, the European Union, the Organization of American States, and a number of other governmental and intergovernmental organizations.

While gender mainstreaming has made substantial progress in intergovernmental and governmental circles, many problems remain. A policy imposed from above, gender mainstreaming does not address the diversity of women's lives. The dominance of the neo-liberal economic paradigm in international financial and development institutions, such as the IMF and the World Bank, as well as institutional resistance and lack of funding, are significant barriers against the types of transformational changes that would be required to eliminate the kind of structural gender hierarchies that I have documented in this chapter. The issue remains whether women's groups should seek equality of women within existing frameworks or seek to challenge frameworks such as those upon which the gendered constructions of the meaning of labor that I described earlier are based.

Changing norms and rules at the international level can exert pressure on national governments to effect change. For, in spite of the challenges to our traditional understanding of boundaries and territoriality posed by the globalizing economy, it remains the case that states are still the only institutions in the international system that are, or have the potential to be, democratically accountable to their citizens. States are also the only institutions that have the power to implement international norms or effect significant redistribution of economic resources. Given the enormous distance between the extraterrestrial frontiers of global business where I began this chapter, and the marginalized, and often invisible, spaces in which many women can be found, feminists from all parts of the world have begun to rethink women's relationships to the state. Increasingly, states are being seen as potential buffers against the detrimental effects of neo-liberalism and global capitalism; it has often been the case that women have gained more power through the state than through the market. Jane Jaquette has claimed that, in order to be effective, women's organizations must work with governments and explore ways to make bureaucracies more responsive to women's concerns (Jaquette 2003, 343).

In conclusion, I do not believe that women will be able to travel in significant numbers to the extra terrestrial frontiers of globalization until traditional gender expectations about the differing roles of women and men are challenged and broken down. As I have documented, progress has been made, locally, nationally, and internationally, albeit at different levels in different places. Building on new opportunities of global communications, women's organizations and networks have been important vehicles for this progress. Nevertheless, much remains to be done before significant numbers of women (and of course many men) can experience the benefits that proponents of economic globalization believe exist.

PART TWO
Methodological Engagements

As I indicated in Part One, my explorations of the gendered dimensions of IR's theoretical and conceptual foundations led me to reflect further on the deep ontological and epistemological divides between feminism and IR, a topic I pursue in greater detail in this section. While I realize that these divides may be less severe outside the United States, my earlier methodological interventions were aimed largely at the US mainstream and at a US IR audience. Part Two begins with the first of these methodological engagements, or attempted conversations as I call them, which was published in *International Studies Quarterly (ISQ)* in 1997. During the next fifteen years I continued to engage with the issue of dialogue across methodological divides; Chapters 6 and 7 deal directly with the methodological challenges in bringing feminist perspectives to IR. Chapter 8, written six years later, attempts to engage more broadly with the discipline and suggests some new avenues for dialogue.

Chapter 6 recounts some conversational encounters between feminists and IR theorists and offers some hypotheses as to why misunderstandings result from these encounters so frequently. It develops a claim that has preoccupied me since I started working in the area of feminist IR—that feminist perspectives on international relations are often based on very different ontologies and epistemologies from those that inform the conventional discipline, a claim that I believe still has validity today. I suggest, in conclusion, how feminist/IR engagements might be pursued more constructively.

In the issue subsequent to the one in which my 1997 article appeared, *ISQ* published several responses. One of them, by Robert Keohane (1998), challenged feminists to come up with a research program that used what he termed the "scientific method." Chapter 7, originally published also in *ISQ* in 2005, offers a response to this challenge. As I discuss in Chapter 6, methodological issues have constituted some of the deepest sources of misunderstanding between IR feminists and IR theorists working in social scientific frameworks. Epistemological divisions about the construction and purpose of knowledge make bridging these methodological divides difficult. I suggest that feminists often ask very different questions from those typically asked in IR. To answer them, many feminists have drawn on ethnographic, narrative, cross-cultural, and other methods that are rarely taught to IR students. Drawing on a range of interdisciplinary scholarship on feminist methodologies and some IR feminist case studies, Chapter 7 analyzes and assesses how these methodological orientations are useful for understanding the gendering of international politics, the state and its security-seeking practices, and its effects on the lives of women and men.

Chapter 8 offers my thoughts on a possible way forward toward greater respect for different ways to conduct IR feminist research and suggests some avenues through which IR scholars, from a variety of methodological approaches and different geographical locations, might better dialogue with each other in mutually respectful ways. Since this piece was originally written as an address for the 2010 *Millennium* annual conference on conversations across IR paradigms, it is situated in a broader IR disciplinary context. I begin by briefly revisiting IR's great debates, since they represent the way the discipline has traditionally told its history. These debates have centered on challenging the predominance of a US-centered discipline and its commitment to neo-positivist methodologies. Drawing on postcolonial and feminist literatures, I then offer some suggestions as to how we might envisage an IR that is built on more global foundations and on a more pluralist understanding of what we define as scientific knowledge. I conclude with some thoughts on possible paths toward placing different scientific traditions on a more equal and mutually respectful footing. I see this chapter as a pathway to my current interest in moving beyond efforts to engage the discipline in conversation into new avenues in which I explore some untold stories about IR's disciplinary histories, different from the standard one I tell here. Coming out of feminist sensibilities about whose knowledge gets validated, my goal is to attempt to uncover voices that have not previously been heard in the discipline. These topics will be addressed in more detail in Part Three.

CHAPTER 6

You Just Don't Understand: Troubled Engagements Between Feminists and IR Theorists

1997

After feminist approaches to international relations first made their appearance in the late 1980s, courses on women and world politics and publications in this area proliferated rapidly, as did panels at professional meetings. Yet, the effect on the mainstream discipline, particularly in the United States, continued to be marginal, and the lack of attention paid to feminist perspectives by other critical approaches was also disappointing (Sylvester 1994b, chap. 4). While feminist scholars, as well as a few IR theorists, called for conversations and dialogue across paradigms (Keohane 1989; Peterson 1992b, 184), few public conversations or debates have occurred.[1] These continuing silences have led one scholar working in this area to conclude that most women are homeless as far as the canons of IR knowledge are concerned (Sylvester 1994a, 316).

Linguist Deborah Tannen, from whose widely read book the title of this chapter is taken, asserts that everyday conversations between women and men are

---

1. Since I wrote this chapter in 1995, there has been some engagement, particularly by critical scholars. Introductory texts have incorporated feminist approaches. See, for example, Goldstein (2012). Feminist articles in mainstream US IR journals are still rare unless they use conventional methodologies. See Caprioli and Boyer (2001) and Carpenter (2006) for examples. There has been more recognition of critical approaches other than feminism by the mainstream; however, they have often been dismissed or assessed quite negatively, particularly postmodernism. For two early more constructive engagements, see Keohane (1998) and the response by Walker (1989). For an observation that the field of IR in the United States remains relatively narrow, fifteen years later, see Biersteker (2009).

cross-cultural and are fraught with all the misunderstandings and talking at cross-purposes that cross-cultural communications frequently incur (Tannen 1990).[2] The lack of sustained dialogue or substantively focused debates between feminists and scholars of international relations is troubling. Could this reluctance to engage in similarly difficult cross-cultural conversations be due to the very different realities and epistemologies with which feminists and international relations scholars are working?

Although critical engagement is rare, evidence of awkward silences and miscommunications can be found in the oral questions and comments IR-trained feminists frequently encounter when presenting their work to IR audiences. Having articulated what seems to her (or him)[3] to be a reasoned feminist critique of international relations, or some suggestions as to the potential benefits of looking at IR through "gender-sensitive" lenses, a feminist scholar is often surprised to find that her audience does not engage with what, to her at least, are the main claims of her presentation. Questioners may assert that her presentation has little to do with the discipline of international relations or the practice of international politics.[4] Prefaced by affirmations that the material presented is genuinely interesting and important, questions such as the following are frequently asked: What does this talk have to do with solving "real-world" problems such as Bosnia, Northern Ireland, or nuclear proliferation?[5] Why does gender have anything to do with explaining the behavior of states in the international system? Isn't IR a gender-neutral discipline? More unsettling are comments suggesting that the presentation is personally insulting to the audience, or that the material is more suitable for bedside reading than for serious scholarly discussion.

Furthermore, to scholars trained in conventional scientific methodologies, feminist approaches appear to be a-theoretical—merely criticism, devoid of

2. While *You Just Don't Understand* is a popular, somewhat stereotypical book, I believe it is a useful entry point for offering insights into the problems of gendered cross-cultural communications. It comes out of a rich tradition of gender-sensitive discourse analysis, many of whose classics are cited in Tannen's bibliography.

3. I am not saying that men cannot engage in feminist or gender analysis; indeed, gender is not just about women but also about men and masculinity. However, it is usually women and feminists who write about gender issues. The main reason for this is that what it means to be human has generally been equated with (often Western elite) men. As feminists point out, women have often been rendered less than fully human, or even invisible, by this move.

4. I am drawing on fairly widely shared experiences that I and other feminist scholars have had when speaking to IR audiences. I cannot analyze these engagements more systematically since these types of comments rarely appear in print.

5. That this happens frequently is supported by the title of an article by Marysia Zalewski (1995), "Well, What Is the Feminist Perspective on Bosnia?" Zalewski suggested, in 1995, that the reason for the frequency of such questions is that feminist theory has only recently infiltrated the discipline. Since such questions still get asked, I believe that their frequency is the result of a much deeper level of misunderstanding.

potential for fruitful empirical research. Therefore, they ask: Where is your research program? or: Why can't women just as well be subsumed under established theoretical approaches? Assuming the idealist notion that women are more peaceful than men lurks somewhere behind the presenter's remarks, a questioner may challenge this unasserted claim by referring to former UK prime minister Margaret Thatcher, who was responsible for the Falklands War, or former Israeli prime minister Golda Meier, who was described as the "Iron Lady" of Israeli politics. Believing these questions to be indications of an audience unfamiliar with, or even threatened by, feminist subject matter, a frustrated presenter may well wish to declare: You just don't understand.

These, often unsatisfactory, oral engagements illustrate a gendered estrangement that inhibits more sustained conversations, both oral and written, between feminists and other international relations scholars. I am not saying that this is an estrangement that pits men against women. A majority of IR women scholars do not work with feminist approaches, and some men do use gender as a category of analysis in their research. Nevertheless, I do believe, and will argue below, that these theoretical divides evidence socially constructed gender differences. Understanding them as such may be a useful entry point for overcoming silences and miscommunications, thus beginning more constructive dialogues.

In this chapter I explore the implications and apparent presuppositions of some of these frequently asked questions. I will demonstrate that feminists and IR scholars are drawing on very different realities and are using different epistemologies when they engage in theorizing about international relations. It is my belief that these differences are gendered, with all the difficulties of cross-cultural communication that this implies.

While misunderstandings occur in both directions, I will focus on feminist responses to questions and comments from conventional IR scholars because these are less familiar to IR audiences. Because I believe it is where the greatest misunderstandings occur, I have chosen to engage with methodologically conventional IR scholars—whom I define as realists, neo-realists, neo-liberals, peace researchers, behavioralists, and empiricists committed to data-based methods of testing, rather than with critical approaches, associated with post-positivist methodologies as defined in the third debate (Lapid 1989). I realize there are significant differences between these conventional approaches. However, none of them has used gender as a category of analysis; it is in this sense, as well as in their shared commitment to a scientific methodology, that I have grouped them together.

There are three types of misunderstandings embedded in the questions outlined above: first, misunderstandings about the meaning of gender, as manifested in the more personal reactions; second, the different realities or ontologies that feminists and non-feminists see when they write about international politics, evident in comments that feminist scholars are not engaging the subject matter of IR; third, the epistemological divides that underlie questions as to whether feminists are doing theory at all.

SOURCES OF MISUNDERSTANDING

Gender: Is the Personal International?

Responding to a call to change the name of the International Brotherhood of Teamsters to include recognition of its 30 percent female membership, James Hoffa asserted that the name should remain because "the definition of brotherhood is that it's neutral" (Killborn 1996). While scholars of international relations, aware of the need to pay attention to gender-sensitive language, would probably want to claim some distance from this statement, it does indicate how, all too often, claims of gender neutrality mask deeply embedded masculinist assumptions that can naturalize or hide gender differences and gender inequalities. Even among the most sophisticated audiences, feminist challenges to these assumptions can often appear threatening, even when "male-bashing" is not intended.[6] Deborah Tannen has suggested that the reason gender differences are more troubling than other cross-cultural differences is that they occur where the home and hearth are: "[W]e enact and create our gender, and our inequality, with every move that we make" (Tannen 1990, 283). Feminist scholars claim that gender differences permeate all facets of public and private life, a socially constructed divide which they take to be problematic in itself; IR scholars, however, may believe that gender is about interpersonal relations between women and men, but not about international politics.

Given that most contemporary feminist scholarship takes gender—which embodies relationships of power inequality—as its central category of analysis, the fact that the meaning of gender is so often misunderstood is, I believe, central to problems of misunderstanding and miscommunication. Almost all feminists who write about international relations use gender in a social constructivist sense, as I defined it in Chapter 1, a move that many see not only as necessary for overcoming gender discrimination, but also as a way of opening avenues for communication by avoiding some of the threatened responses illustrated above.

As Sandra Harding (1986, 17–18) has suggested, gendered social life is produced through three distinct processes: assigning dualistic gender metaphors to various perceived dichotomies, described in Chapter 1, appealing to these gender dualisms to organize social activity, and dividing necessary

---

6. Conversely, dangers lurk in the uncritical switch to gender-neutral language when it is used even though the speaker is clearly not speaking for or about women. See Okin (1989, 10–13) for elaboration of this point.

social activities between different groups of humans. She refers to these three aspects of gender as gender symbolism, gender structure, and individual gender. As Tannen (1990, 43) claims, girls and boys grow up in different worlds of words, but gender goes beyond language: it is a symbolic system that shapes many aspects of our culture. And as Carol Cohn (1993, 229) has suggested, even if real men and women do not fit stereotypically gendered ideal types, the existence of this system of meaning affects us all—both our interpretations of the world and the way the world understands us.

As Joan Scott (1986, 1069) claims, while the forms that gender relations take across different cultures may vary, they are almost always unequal; therefore, gender, in the structural sense, is a primary way of signifying relationships of power. Although gender is frequently seen as belonging in the household and, therefore, antithetical to the "real" business of politics—a reason that it is often seen as irrelevant to IR—Scott argues that it is constructed in the economy and the polity through various institutional structures that have the effect of "naturalizing," and even legalizing, women's inferior status. Recent feminist writings that deal with issues of race and class problematize these power relationships still further.[7]

Individual gender relations enter into and are constituent elements in every aspect of human experience (Flax, 1987, 624). Jane Flax reminds us that, while feminism is about recovering women's activities, it must also be aware of how these activities are constituted through the social relations in which they are situated. Therefore, gender is not just about women; it is also about men and masculinity, a point that needs to be emphasized if scholars of international relations are to better understand why feminists claim that it is relevant to their discipline and why they believe that a gendered analysis of its basic assumptions and concepts can yield fruitful results.

Theorizing the International: Are Feminists Really "Doing" IR?

Deborah Tannen (1990, 97) claims that women are more comfortable than men with an ethnographic style of individually oriented storytelling typical of anthropology, a difference that is true of much of feminist IR scholarship as well. International relations, particularly after the move toward science in the post–World War II period in the United States, has generally shied away from

---

7. For example, as bell hooks (1984) claims, non-white women would not subscribe to the feminist goal of making women equal to men who are themselves victims of racist oppression. I am aware of the importance of including class and race differences when defining and analyzing gender and women's oppression. However, I do not believe this should prevent us from making testable, generalizable claims about the gendering of the discipline of international relations. For a useful discussion of this issue more generally, see Martin (1994).

level-one analysis, preferring a more systemic or state-oriented focus. Coming out of literatures that are centrally concerned with individuals and social relations, and that are more explicitly normative, feminist perspectives, on the other hand, demonstrate a preference for more humanistically oriented methodologies. Although their focus is different, their discomfort with structural IR is similar to that captured in Martin Wight's famous title, "Why Is There No International Theory?"

In "Why Is There No International Theory?" Martin Wight (1995) remarked on the absence of an international theoretical tradition comparable to the very rich historical tradition of Western political philosophy.[8] According to Wight, the reason for this absence can be found in the character of the international system. Theorizing the international would mean speculating about a society or community of states. Since he saw the international system as evidencing the absence of society, a "realm of necessity" characterized by "recurrence and repetition," Wight (1995, 32) claimed that there could be no "progressive" international theory, only a "theory of survival" marked by "an intellectual and moral poverty."[9] Wight is, of course, using theory in an explicitly normative sense, not fashionable among contemporary, more scientific theoretical approaches. He is postulating a "theory of the good life" (Wight 1995, 32), a progressive theory of social relations that calls for societal improvements—improvements, Wight claims, that can take place only within a political space such as the state.

While many contemporary feminist theorists would take issue with Wight's views on equating progressive theory with a tradition of Western political thought that has generally either excluded women altogether or treated them as less than fully human (Okin 1980),[10] his reasons for claiming the poverty of international theory have relevance for problems that feminists encounter when theorizing the international. With an ontology based on unitary states

8. It is interesting to note that certain IR feminists have expressed some affinity with classical realism and/or more sociological approaches associated with the English School of which Wight was a founder. Whitworth (1989, 268) claims that the classical realism of Morgenthau acknowledges that meaning is contingent and socially constructed, thus creating a space, in theory if not in practice, for the analysis of gender. The authors chosen by James Der Derian for his edited volume *International Theory* (1995), which includes Wight's piece, illustrate the link between the English School and some other contemporary critical perspectives. It also includes American scholars of the scientific tradition. I have chosen to cite from this volume, rather than going back to the original sources, for this reason.

9. Here Wight is presenting a realist worldview. However, it is difficult to place Wight exclusively within any one of the three theoretical traditions that he himself outlined. For further elaboration of this point, see Yost (1994).

10. Feminist perspectives on international relations have focused on the explicitly gendered writings of political philosophers, such as Hobbes and Machiavelli, whose works have served as foundational texts for the discipline. See, for example, Grant (1991), and Sylvester (1994a).

operating in an asocial, anarchical international environment, there is little in realist theory that provides an entry point for feminist theories, grounded as they are in an epistemology that takes social relations as its central category of analysis.[11]

Much of contemporary feminism is committed to progressive or emancipatory goals, particularly the goal of achieving equality for women through the elimination of unequal gender relations. Drawing on earlier literatures, such as those on women in the military and women and development, feminist writings on international relations have focused on individuals in their social, political, and economic settings, rather than on decontextualized unitary states and anarchical international structures. They investigate how military conflict and the behavior of states in the international system are constructed through, or embedded in, unequal gendered structural relations and how these affect the life chances of individuals, particularly women. These very different foci evoke the kind of questions introduced above about what is the legitimate subject matter of the discipline.

Returning to Martin Wight's discomfort with the realist tradition, with which feminists might find some common ground, could we find an entry point for feminist theorizing about the international system in approaches that start with different assumptions? Given a high level of economic interdependence, the growth of transnational non-state actors, and the proliferation of international institutions, many IR scholars, particularly liberals with progressive views of the international arena, prefer to work in the Grotian or Kantian traditions, which postulate not an anarchy, but an international society of states within which a discussion of social relations becomes possible. Writing in the Kantian tradition, Andrew Linklater (1982) offers a critique of Wight. While acknowledging the tension between man as a universal category and citizens bound by loyalties to their states, Linklater postulates a Kantian resolution: "[B]ecause modern citizens are more than mere members of their communities, since they are responsive to universalistic moral claims, it is within their power to transform international relations in a direction which realizes their capacity to lead free lives" (Linklater 1982, 18). "Kant held that all men were bound together by the necessary obligation to so arrange their social and political lives that they could gradually realize a condition of universal justice and perpetual peace.... [These] were essential or categorical ends which men were under an unconditional obligation to promote by virtue of their rational nature" (Linklater 1982, 97).

The Kantian ethic, a progressive interpretation of international relations, is one of the important foundations of the so-called idealist tradition, a tradition to which feminist writings in international relations are often mistakenly

11. For further elaboration on these ontological distinctions, as well as on the problems of articulating a world politics beyond the state, see Walker (1992).

assigned by international relations scholars.[12] In spite of its commitment to emancipatory goals of justice and peace that, in theory at least, could include the elimination of unjust social relations, this tradition is also problematic for feminists (Sylvester 1994b, 94). Western theories of universal justice, built on a rather abstract concept of rationality, have generally been constructed out of a definition of human nature that excludes or diminishes women. Feminists assert that the universalism they defend is defined by identifying the experience of a special group (elite men) as paradigmatic of human beings as a whole (Benhabib 1987, 81). Most Western political theorists were quite explicit in their claims that women either were not capable of, or should not be encouraged in, the attainment of enlightenment, autonomy, and rationality. For example, while Kant viewed the development of rationality as necessary for the formation of a moral character, he denied that women were capable of such achievements; he also recommended against the education of women because it would inhibit man's development (Tuana 1992, 52–53).[13]

While IR scholars might argue that Kant's views on women were a time-bound premise that can safely be discarded in today's more gender-sensitive climate, feminists believe that the Western philosophical tradition is too deeply implicated in masculinist assumptions to serve as a foundation for constructing a gender-sensitive IR. Therefore, the gender biases of this tradition, which are fundamental to its normative orientation, must be exposed and challenged. For this reason, feminists claim that works that have served as foundational texts for international relations must be reexamined for evidence of gender biases that call into question the gender neutrality frequently claimed in response to feminist critiques. In the words of one feminist theorist, "all forms of feminist theorizing are normative in the sense that they help us to question certain meanings and interpretations in IR theory" (Sylvester 1994a, 318). However, challenging the core assumptions, concepts, and ontological presuppositions of the field with claims of gender bias are bound to result in miscommunications and make conversations with international theorists difficult.

---

12. Feminists believe that labeling their work as idealism is a mistake. They claim they are describing a reality rarely acknowledged in the discipline. I use the term *so-called* when referring to idealism because the label was invented by realists and is one that has contributed to the delegitimation of the idealist tradition. It is interesting to note that the language of the realist/idealist debate has gendered connotations. Communitarian, liberal, or cosmopolitan might serve as better definitions of this rich tradition. However, women's voices and gender analysis have been absent also from international law from which the cosmopolitan and communitarian traditions have drawn inspiration (see Charlesworth, Chinkin, and Wright, 1991).

13. I am aware that the exclusion of women from traditions of universalist ethics and justice is quite a different issue from postulating a universalist ethic that could include women. Indeed, this is an important and contentious issue in feminist theories of justice. For positions on both sides of this debate, see various chapters in Nussbaum and Glover (1995).

International Theory

In his commentary on Wight's piece, discussed earlier, Hans Morgenthau (1995) asserted that international theory could be progressive but in a rather different sense: "[T]he ideal toward which these theories try to progress is ultimately international peace and order to be achieved through scientific precision and predictability in understanding and manipulating international affairs" (Morgenthau 1995, 40). For Morgenthau, the purpose of theory was "to bring order and meaning into a mass of unconnected material and to increase knowledge through the logical development of certain propositions empirically established" (Morgenthau 1995, 46). Unlike Wight, Morgenthau, motivated by countering German fascism of the 1930s, was making the case for a scientific international theory, a type of theory that has strongly influenced mainstream international relations, at least in the United States.[14]

As I shall discuss below, this view of the purposes of theory is one that feminists have found problematic. However, feminists often misunderstand or ignore the rationale for the search for more scientific theories offered by early realists such as Morgenthau. Most of the founding fathers of American realism in the post–World War II period were European intellectuals fleeing from Nazi persecution. Flagrant violations of international law and abuses of human rights in the name of German nationalism motivated Morgenthau, and other early realists, to dissociate the realm of morality and values from the realpolitik of international politics. As I discussed in more detail in Chapter 1, Morgenthau painted a gloomy picture of "political man" and the dangers of an anarchic international system where war is always a possibility. However, he did believe that the search for deeper explanations of the laws that govern human action could contribute to lessening the chances that such disasters would recur in the future. Defending science against ideologically charged claims, which he associated with European fascism of the 1930s, Morgenthau believed that only by a more "scientific" understanding of its causes could the likelihood of war be diminished.

According to Stanley Hoffmann (1977), Morgenthau shaped these truths as a guide to those in power; thus, the growth of the discipline cannot be separated from the growing American role in world affairs in the post–World War II era. Speaking to and moving among foreign policy elites, this "American discipline" was, and is, aimed at an audience very different from feminist

---

14. Just as he was not considered scientific enough by many subsequent international theorists, Morgenthau was himself ambivalent about the turn to science in American international theory. For evidence of this ambivalence, see Morgenthau (1946). For an analysis of the reasons for the preference for scientific methodologies in the United States, see Hoffmann (1977).

international relations. This difference—to which I return below—also causes misunderstandings.

The scientific turn in postwar realism was also adopted by behavioralists, neo-realists, liberal institutionalists, and some peace researchers, all of whom drew on models from the natural sciences and from economics to build their theories. Seeking scientific respectability, international theorists turned to the natural sciences for their methodologies; many of them were also defending the autonomy of rational inquiry against totalitarian ideologies, this time of postwar Communism. Theories were defined as sets of logically related, ideally causal propositions, to be empirically tested or falsified in the Popperian sense. Scientific research programs were developed from realist assumptions about the international system serving as the "hard core" (Lakatos and Musgrave 1970). While international theorists never sought the precision of Newton's grand schemes of deterministic laws and inescapable forces, they did claim that the international system is more than the constant and regular behavior of its parts (Hollis and Smith 1990, 50). Structural theories, popular in the discipline, account for behavior by searching for causes. These theorists believe that events are governed by the laws of nature; in other words, behavior is generated by structures external to the actors themselves (Hollis and Smith 1990, 3).[15] In all these endeavors, theorists have generally assumed the possibility as well as the desirability of conducting systematic and cumulative scientific research.

Borrowing from economics, game theory, and rational choice theory became popular for explaining the choices and optimizing behavior of self-interested states in an anarchical international system, as well as a means for interpreting the actions of their foreign policy decision-makers. Given the dangers and unpredictability of such a system, theory building was motivated by the desire to control and predict (Waltz 1979, 6).[16] The search for systematic inquiry could, hopefully, contribute to the effort of diminishing the likelihood of future conflict. Broadly defined as positivist, this turn to science represents a view of the creation of knowledge based on four assumptions: first, a belief in the unity of science—that is, the same methodologies can apply in the natural and social worlds; second, that there is a distinction between facts and values, with facts being neutral between theories; third, that the social world has regularities like the natural world; and fourth, that the way to determine the

15. Hollis and Smith (1990) identify two traditions in international theory, "inside" and "outside." Since "inside" theories are interpretive or hermeneutical, feminist theories would probably fit more comfortably into this tradition, although it too presents problems for feminists. A tradition constructed out of the beliefs and intentions of human actors has rarely included women as actors.

16. What level of prediction is desirable or possible is a matter of some contention among international theorists. Claims that international theorists failed to predict the end of the Cold War has added fuel to this debate. See Gaddis (1992–1993).

truth of statements is by appeal to neutral facts or an empiricist epistemology (Smith 1997, 168).[17]

Feminist Theory

Since it entered the field of international relations in the late 1980s, feminist theory has often, but not exclusively, been located within the critical voices of the "third debate," a term first articulated by Yosef Lapid in 1989 (Lapid 1989). Although they are not all postmodern, or even post-Enlightenment, in their normative orientation, an assumption sometimes implied by conventional scholars, many feminist international relations scholars would identify themselves as post-positivists in terms of Lapid's articulation of the term and in terms of the definition of positivism outlined above. While there is no necessary connection between feminist approaches and post-positivism, there is a strong resonance for a variety of reasons, including a commitment to epistemological pluralism as well as to certain ontological sensitivities. With a preference for hermeneutic, historically based, humanistic and philosophical traditions of knowledge cumulation, rather than those based on the natural sciences, feminist theorists are often skeptical of empiricist methodologies that claim neutrality of facts. While many feminists do see structural regularities, such as gender and patriarchy, they define them as socially constructed and variable across time, place, and cultures, rather than as universal and natural.

Agreeing with Robert Cox's assertion that theory is always for someone and for some purpose, the goal of feminist approaches is similar to that of critical theory as defined by Cox. Cox asserts that critical theory "stands apart from the prevailing order of the world and asks how that order came about": it can, therefore, be a guide to strategic action for bringing about an alternative order (Cox 1981, 129–130). Cox contrasts critical theory with conventional theory, which he labels "problem-solving"—a type of conversation that Tannen associates with men (1990, chap. 2). Problem-solving takes the world as it finds it and implicitly accepts the prevailing order as its framework (Cox 1981, 130). Since feminist theorists believe that the world is characterized by gender hierarchies that are detrimental to women, they would be unlikely to

17. Not all IR theorists who associate themselves with the scientific tradition would agree with all parts of this definition. Few social scientists believe that their work is value-free or that universally valid generalizations are possible; nevertheless, they would probably agree that these are useful standards to which to aspire. Most would believe, however, that systematic social scientific research is possible and desirable and that methodologies borrowed from the natural sciences can be useful, although some have recognized the problems of applying natural science methods to the social sciences.

take such an epistemological stance. In the words of one feminist scholar who defines herself as a post-positivist, "post-positivism compels our attention to context and historical process, to contingency and uncertainty, to how we construct, rather than dis-cover, our world(s)" (Peterson 1992a, 57).

In constructing their approaches to international theory, feminists draw on a variety of philosophical traditions and literatures outside international relations and political science, within which most IR scholars are trained. While IR feminists are seeking genuine knowledge that can help them to better understand the issues with which they are concerned, the IR training they receive rarely includes such knowledge. Hence, they, like scholars in other critical approaches, have gone outside the discipline to seek what they believe are more appropriate methodologies for understanding the social construction and maintenance of gender hierarchies. This deepens the level of misunderstanding and miscommunication and, unfortunately, often leads to negative stereotyping on all sides of these epistemological divides.

As mentioned in Chapter 2, feminist theories, variously identified as Marxist, radical, psychoanalytic, socialist, standpoint, existentialist, and postmodern, describe the causes and consequences of women's oppression and prescribe strategies for removing it;[18] thus, many of them are progressive in the sense in which Martin Wight was using the term. While psychoanalytic traditions look for causes of women's inequality in socialization practices of early childhood, radicals, Marxists, and socialists look for explanations in structures of patriarchy that "naturalize" women's oppression, or in the labor market with its gender discriminations and divisions between public (paid) and private (unpaid/domestic) work. As Carole Pateman (1994, 21) has emphasized, feminism is more than a derivation from other bodies of political and social theory because it is centered on an investigation of the forms of power that men exercise over women.

All these feminist theoretical approaches, upon which IR feminists have drawn, are grounded in social and political theory and sociological traditions, many of which lie outside the discipline of international relations. Therefore, while international theorists are often justifiably frustrated when feminists cannot provide a brief overview of feminist theory, feminists find communication on this issue with scholars trained in social scientific methodologies equally difficult because of the lack of agreement as to what counts as

---

18. One must be wary of putting feminist perspectives into boxes, however. There is considerable overlap among approaches, and many theorists draw on a variety of intellectual traditions. The interdisciplinarity of feminism compounds the difficulties and limitations of categorizations. I am also aware that, as with my definition of conventional theory, I am conflating divergent bodies of scholarship. The unifying theme upon which I draw is that most feminist approaches take gender as a central category of analysis and seek to understand the sources of women's oppression and how to end it. For a useful introductory overview of feminist theories, see Tong (1998).

legitimate scientific inquiry. Since all these feminist approaches question the claim that women can simply be added to existing theoretical frameworks, it is predictable that misunderstandings will compound when those working within the scientific tradition suggest that feminist approaches can be incorporated into conventional IR methodologies. Indeed, feminists have a legitimate fear of co-optation; so often women's knowledge has been forgotten or subsumed under more dominant discourses.[19]

Incorporation can also be a source of misunderstanding when international theorists, responding to challenges of gender blindness, have attempted to make women more visible in their texts. For, as Emily Rosenberg (1990) tells us, efforts to integrate women into existing theories and consider them equally with men can only lead to a theoretical cul-de-sac that further reinforces gender hierarchies. For example, in international relations, when we add exceptional women—the famous few such as Margaret Thatcher or Golda Meier who succeed in the tough world of international politics by acting like men—to existing frameworks, it tends to imply, without the claim being made overtly, that the problem of their absence lies with women themselves. Conversely, if we go looking for women working in "women's spheres," such as peace groups, it only reinforces the socially constructed boundaries between activities differentially deemed appropriate for women and for men; moreover, it contributes to the false claim that women are more peaceful than men, a claim that disempowers both women and peace. Although feminists are frequently told that they are implying that women are more peaceful than men, as I discussed in Chapter 2, many are quite suspicious of this association of women with peace. Besides being derivative of an essentialized position about women's "nature," to which most contemporary feminists do not subscribe, this association tends to brand women as naive and unrealistic, thereby further delegitimizing their voices in the world of foreign policy-making (Sylvester 1987; Elshtain 1990).

Feminists are arguing for moving beyond knowledge frameworks that construct international theory without attention to gender and for searching deeper to find ways in which gender hierarchies serve to reinforce socially constructed institutions and practices that perpetuate different and unequal role expectations, expectations that have contributed to fundamental inequalities between women and men in the world of international politics. Therefore, including gender as a central category of analysis transforms knowledge in ways that go beyond adding women; importantly, but frequently misunderstood, this means that women cannot be studied in isolation from men.

19. This issue of co-optation is evidenced in Weber's (1994) critique of Keohane (1989) that called for an alliance between neo-liberal institutionalism and standpoint feminism.

While most feminists are committed to the emancipatory goal of achieving a more just society, which, for them, includes ending the oppression of women, the Kantian project of achieving this goal through Enlightenment knowledge is problematic because of feminist claims that this type of knowledge is gendered. Feminists assert that dichotomies, such as rational/irrational, fact/value, universal/particular, and public/private, upon which Western Enlightenment knowledge has been built and which they see as gendered, separate the mind (rationality) from the body (nature) and, therefore, diminish the legitimacy of women as "knowers." Susan Hekman has claimed that, "since the Enlightenment, knowledge has been defined in terms of "man," the subject, and espouses an epistemology that is radically homocentric." Since Enlightenment epistemology places women in an inferior position, outside the realm of rationality, challenging the priority of "man" in the modern episteme must be fundamental to any feminist program (Hekman 1990, 2). Similarly, Patricia Hill Collins (1989) claims that Black women would be unlikely to subscribe to an epistemology that has, for the most part, excluded Blacks and other minorities. Black women, she claims, prefer, and consider more legitimate, knowledge construction based on concrete experience of everyday lives, stories, and dialogues. These subjective epistemological positions are unsettling for scholars trained in scientific methodologies based on more abstract knowledge claims.

Throughout most of the history of the modern West, men have been seen as the knowers; what has counted as legitimate knowledge, in both the natural and social sciences, has generally been knowledge based on the lives of men in the public sphere. The separation of the public and private spheres, reinforced by the scientific revolution of the seventeenth century, has resulted in the legitimation of what are perceived as the "rational" activities (such as politics, economics, and justice) in the former while devaluing the "natural" activities (such as household management, childrearing, and caregiving) of the latter (Peterson 1992b, 202).

As Carole Pateman (1988, 90) argues, in the seventeenth century women began to be deprived of the economic basis for independence by the separation of the workplace from the household and the consolidation of the patriarchal structures of capitalism. The separation of public and private spheres has also engendered a division between reason and feeling as the household, the "natural" site of women's existence, became associated with moral sentiments as opposed to self-interest, more characteristic of the public world (Tronto 1993, 52–56), a split that has been particularly evident in rationalist theories of international relations. Feminists believe that the legitimation of particular types of knowledge, intensified by this public/private divide, shapes and restricts the kinds of questions that get asked and how they get answered.

Stephen Toulmin (1990) analyzes the coincidence of the birth of the modern scientific method and the birth of the modern nation-state. He contrasts the scientific method with a "pre-modern" or "early modern" humanistic tradition, incorporating writers such as Erasmus and Montaigne, whose skeptical tolerance for ambiguity and diversity in knowledge accumulation seems more compatible with feminist thinking than with the rationalist universalism of the scientific revolution. Most feminists claim that knowledge is socially constructed, contingent, and shaped by context, culture, and history. According to Sandra Harding (1991, 59), the subject of knowledge is never simply an individual capable of transcending historical location: in other words, there is no impartial, value-neutral Archimedian perspective. Feminist analysis insists that the inquirer be placed in the same critical plane as the subject matter (Harding 1987, 9). Even the best forms of knowledge cannot be divorced from their political consequences, a claim that can only appear unsettling to proponents of scientific methodologies who frequently label such knowledge claims as relativist and lacking in objectivity.

Feminists argue, however, that broadening the base from which knowledge is constructed, that is, including the experiences of women, can actually enhance objectivity.[20] Arguing from a modified standpoint position,[21] Sandra Harding explores the question as to whether objectivity and socially situated knowledge are an impossible combination. She concludes that adopting a feminist standpoint actually strengthens standards of objectivity. While it requires acknowledging that all human beliefs are socially situated, it also requires critical evaluation to determine which social situations tend to generate the most objective knowledge claims. Harding argues for what she calls "strong objectivity," which extends the task of scientific research to include a systematic examination of powerful background beliefs and making strange what has hitherto appeared as familiar (Harding 1991, 142, 149).

Likewise, Donna Haraway argues for what she calls "embodied objectivity" or "situated knowledge." For Haraway, situated knowledge does not mean relativism but shared conversations leading to "better accounts of the world" (Haraway 1988, 580).[22] Indeed, feminists frequently use the metaphor of conversation both as a preferred methodology and in their calls for engagement

20. As Sandra Harding (1991, 123) emphasizes, women's experiences alone are not a reliable guide for deciding which knowledge claims are preferable because women tend to speak in socially acceptable ways. Nevertheless, Harding believes that women's lives are the place from which feminist research should begin.

21. I use the term *modified* to indicate that Harding takes into consideration postmodern critiques of an essentialized standpoint that, they say, speaks from the position of privileged Western women. Standpoint feminism comes out of Hegel's notion of the master/slave relationship and out of Marxist theory more generally. Hegel and Marxists claim that the slave (or the proletariat) has, by necessity, a more comprehensive understanding of the position of both the master (or the capitalist) *and* the slave.

22. Christine Sylvester's method of empathetic cooperation draws on this idea of shared conversations (see Sylvester 1994a, 1994b).

with IR scholars. Since conversational or dialogic methodologies come out of a hermeneutic tradition, conversation is not a metaphor that social scientists are likely to employ; indeed, it is one that would appear quite strange as a basis for theory construction.[23]

This brief overview of a variety of feminist epistemologies suggests that they are quite different from those prevailing in conventional international relations. Since all feminist approaches are concerned with social relations, particularly the investigation of the causes and consequences of unequal relationships between women and men, the questions they ask about international relations are likely to be quite different from those of international theorists primarily concerned with the interaction of states in the international system. While feminist theories might fit more comfortably into what Hollis and Smith (1990) term the "inside," or hermeneutical approach, feminists construct their knowledge about international relations not so much from the perspectives of "insiders" but from voices of the disempowered and marginalized not previously heard.[24] The sounds of these unfamiliar voices and the issues they raise sometimes cause conventional scholars to question whether feminists even belong within the same discipline.

As Sandra Harding (1991, 123) tells us, an important task of feminist theory is to make strange what has previously appeared familiar, or to challenge us to question what has hitherto appeared as "natural." In international relations, this has involved an examination of the basic assumptions and concepts of the field, taken as unproblematic—and gender-neutral—by conventional international theorists. While critical approaches more generally have often been accused of indulging in criticism rather than producing new research programs (Walt 1991, 223), feminists would argue that a critical examination is necessary because feminist research agendas cannot be built without first exposing and questioning the gender biases of the field. My critical re-evaluations of security studies, peace studies, and international political economy in Part One offered some possible avenues for exposing these gender biases.

23. Tannen's (1990, chap. 3) distinction between "report-talk" and "rapport talk" may be relevant to this discussion of the gendering of scientific methods. According to Tannen, for most men, talk is a means of preserving independence, whereas, for most women, it is a way of establishing connections.

24. It is important to stress that feminists recognize the multiplicity of women's voices mediated by class, race, and cultural positions. Debate on the problems of essentialism is one of the most vital in feminist theory today. For an elaboration of the issues at stake, see Martin (1994).

CONCLUSION

Feminist theorists have rarely achieved the serious engagement with other IR scholars for which they have frequently called. When they have occurred, conversations have often led to misunderstandings and other kinds of miscommunication, such as awkward silences and feminist resistances to suggestions for incorporation into more mainstream approaches. In this chapter I have tried to reconstruct some typical conversational encounters and to offer some hypotheses as to why estrangement seems so often to be the result. Although I realize that these encounters demonstrate misunderstandings on both sides, I have emphasized some feminist perspectives because they are less likely to be familiar to IR scholars. While it is all too easy to account for these troubled engagements between IR scholars and feminists solely in terms of differences in ontologies and epistemologies, it must be acknowledged that power differences also play an important role. Inequalities in power between mainstream and feminist IR allow for greater ignorance of feminist approaches on the part of the mainstream than is possible for feminists with respect to conventional IR, if they are to be accorded any legitimacy within the profession. Because of this power differential, feminists are suspicious of co-optation or attempts to label certain of their approaches as more compatible than others.

Understanding that all these problems are inherent in calling for conversation, I have tried to suggest and analyze reasons for the frequent failures or avoidance of such conversational efforts, comparing these failures to problems of cross-cultural communications. Lack of understanding and judgments of irrelevance are two major causes of the silence with which feminist approaches have generally been received by the discipline of international relations. Contemporary feminist perspectives on international relations are based on ontologies and epistemologies that are quite different from those that inform the conventional discipline. Since they grow out of ontologies that take individuals or groups embedded in and changed by social relations, such relationally defined feminist approaches do not fit comfortably within conventional levels of analysis theorizing or the state-centric and structural approaches which grow out of such theorizing. They are also informed by different normative concerns. Moreover, feminists claim that normative international theories, such as the Grotian and Kantian traditions, are based on literatures that have often diminished or excluded women.

Feminist epistemologies that inform these new ways of understanding international relations are also quite different from those of conventional international theory. But, as I have argued, feminists cannot be anything but skeptical of universal truth claims and explanations associated with a body of knowledge from which women have frequently been excluded as knowers and subjects. However, this does not mean that feminists are abandoning theory or the search for better knowledge. Although they draw on epistemologies quite different from conventional international relations, they also are seeking better understanding of the processes that inform international political, economic, and social relations. Building knowledge that does not start from the position of the detached universal subject involves being sensitive to difference while striving to be as objective as possible. By starting thought from women's lives, feminists claim that they are actually broadening the base from which knowledge is constructed. While feminist perspectives do not claim to tell us everything we need to know about the behavior of states or the workings of the global economy, they are telling us things that have too often remained invisible.

Feminists often draw on the notion of conversation when pursuing their goal of shareable understandings of the world. Skeptical of the possibility of arriving at one universal truth, they advocate seeking understanding through dialogues across boundaries and cultures in which the voices of others, particularly those on the margins, must be seen as equally valid as one's own.[25] This method of truth-seeking, motivated by the attempt to separate valid knowledge from what feminists see as power-induced distortions, is far removed from more scientific methodologies and from a discipline whose original goal was to better understand the behavior of states in order to offer advice to their policy-makers. Therefore, feminists must understand that their preferred methodologies and the issues they raise are alien to the traditional discipline; and IR scholars must realize that speaking from the perspective of the disempowered appears increasingly urgent in a world where the marginalized are the most likely victims of war and the negative effects of economic globalization.

Seeking greater understanding across theoretical divides, and the scientific and political cultures that sustain them, might be the best model if feminist international theory is to have a future within the discipline. Feminist theorists may claim that conventional IR has little to offer as to how to make cross-paradigm communications more effective and mutually successful. But feminists must understand that methodologies relevant to the investigations of their preferred issues are not normally part of a graduate curriculum in IR in the United States; therefore, they appear strange, unfamiliar, and often irrelevant to those so trained. However, feminists, along with other critical scholars, are pioneering the effort to look beyond conventional training and to investigate the relevance of other disciplines and literatures for these methodologies. Conversations will not be successful until the legitimacy of these

---

25. Jef Huysmans (1995, 486) suggests that this dialogic approach, typical of late-modern or postmodern approaches to IR, is inspired by the liberal idea of pluralism and a democratic ethos.

endeavors is more widely recognized and acknowledged as part of the discipline of international relations.

Asking the question as to how we open lines of communication, Deborah Tannen (1990, 120–121) suggests that men and women must try to take each other on their own terms rather than applying the standards of one group to the behavior of the other. Additionally, she claims that this is not an easy task because all of us tend to look for a single "right" way of doing things. Could this be a model for beginning more productive conversations between feminists and IR theorists?

CHAPTER 7

What Is Your Research Program? Some Feminist Answers to IR's Methodological Questions

2005

Responding to my call for conversation, the journal *International Studies Quarterly*, in which Chapter 6 originally appeared, published a symposium on my piece in the subsequent issue. In response to my article, one of the symposium authors, Robert Keohane, challenged feminists to come up with a research program using "scientific method in the broadest sense" (Keohane 1998). Keohane outlined a possible research program for international relations feminists focused on a variant of the democratic peace theory. He suggested that feminists investigate whether countries with highly unequal gendered hierarchies would behave differently internationally from those with less unequal social structures at home. In other words, are more gender-equal societies less inclined to fight each other? Keohane proposed that feminists investigate this question, or others, using the basic "method" of social science:[1]

1. What Keohane calls "method" I call "methodology," which I define below. Keohane refers to this methodology as *"the* (italics added) basic social science method." I would argue it is *one* such methodology and the one generally employed by US IR scholars working in the scientific tradition. In this chapter, I use the term "conventional social science" to refer to this particular type of work. While, for purposes of responding to Keohane's challenge, I engage with this type of work, which I refer to as "IR research," I am aware that there are many IR scholars outside this tradition who would also refer to their work as social science, as well as many who come out of more humanistic, interpretive traditions. I also realize that this is not necessarily the dominant methodology outside the United States. For further elaboration on a variety of scientific traditions that IR scholars use in their research, see Jackson (2011). Jackson defines the methodology to which Keohane refers as "neopositivism," one of four that Jackson describes. I shall elaborate further on the other three in Chapter 8.

make a conjecture about causality; formulate that conjecture as an hypothesis consistent with established theory; specify the observable implications of the hypothesis; test for whether those implications obtain in the real world; and report one's findings, ensuring that one's procedures are publicly known and hence replicable to other members of a particular scientific community, which he identified as the IR community of scholars. This, Keohane claimed, would be "the best way to convince nonbelievers of the validity of the message that feminists are seeking to deliver" (Keohane 1998, 196–197).

Keohane described himself as a "neopositivist" who acknowledges that "scientific success is not the attainment of objective truth, but the attainment of wider agreement on descriptive facts and causal relationships, based on transparent and replicable methods" (Keohane 1998, 195).[2] While recognizing that knowledge is socially constructed, since the questions we ask and the methods we use reflect our preoccupations as members of particular societies at particular times, Keohane urged scholars to seek to widen inter-subjective agreement about important issues. He insisted that researchers must strive to be as objective as possible. Keohane remained committed to an essentially positivist methodological framework, which assumes that the social world is amenable to the kinds of regularities that can be explained by using causal analysis with tools borrowed from the natural sciences and that the way to determine the truth of statements is by appealing to neutral facts.[3]

Keohane's suggestions for a feminist research program using this conventional social scientific methodology share some similarities with what Sandra Harding terms "feminist empiricism," an epistemology that argues that sexism and androcentricism in existing research are social biases correctable by stricter adherence to the existing methodological norms of scientific inquiry (Harding 1986, 24). While not an empiricist herself, Harding claims that feminist empiricism is appealing because it leaves unchallenged the existing methodological norms of science; this means that it would be more easily accepted in the broader social scientific community—or, as Keohane puts it, it would be the best route for convincing IR nonbelievers, using the social science methodology that he advocates, of the validity of feminist IR research.

---

2. In a communication with this author, Keohane said he prefers to describe himself as a "scientific realist" rather than a "neopositivist." Keohane claimed rightly that he has always favored multiple methods, especially qualitative and historically sensitive ones. However, here I focus on Keohane's (1998) reply to my article in which he proposed a causal, social scientific study of the democratic peace.

3. For a fuller elaboration on Keohane's articulation of social scientific methodology for IR, see King, Keohane and Verba (1994). This definition of a positivist methodological framework assumes no necessary difference between the methodologies of the natural sciences and the social sciences.

Since Keohane issued his challenge to feminists to build a research program using neo-positivist methods, IR feminist empirical research, which took off in the mid-1990s, continued to grow; yet the majority of it has not followed the path that Keohane suggested—formulating hypotheses and providing evidence that can be used to test, falsify, or validate them. With some exceptions that I will discuss below, IR feminists have employed a variety of methods, most of which would fall into methodological frameworks that have variously been described as post-positivist, reflectivist, or interpretivist.[4] Feminist empirical research has been situated in critical, constructivist, or postmodern rather than empiricist frameworks. Therefore, it is probably the case that IR feminists have not convinced those whom Keohane described as "IR nonbelievers" of the validity of their research.[5]

The first section of this chapter explains why I believe IR feminists have, for the most part, not followed the empiricist route. I elaborate on four distinctive features of feminist methodology, which I construct by drawing on the work of feminists in the disciplines of sociology, philosophy, history, political theory, and anthropology, disciplines in which feminism has had a longer history than in IR—a history that includes rich and diverse literatures on methodological issues. I distinguish between the term "methodology," a theory and analysis of how research does or should proceed, and "method," a technique for gathering and analyzing evidence (Harding 1987, 2–3).[6] I argue that there is no unique feminist research method; feminists have drawn upon a variety of methods, including ethnography, statistical research, survey research, cross-cultural research, philosophical argument, discourse analysis, and case study. What makes feminist research unique, however, is a distinctive methodological perspective that fundamentally challenges the (often unseen)

4. There is a body of IR research on gender and women that does use conventional social scientific methodology, although not all of these authors would necessarily define themselves as feminists in the epistemological sense in which I am using the term. There have been studies of the effect of gender equality on public opinion, on foreign policy, and on violence, as well as studies of the effect of the gender gap in voting on foreign policy and the use of force. See, for examples, Gallagher (1993); Brandes (1994); Tessler and Warriner (1997); Caprioli (2000); Caprioli and Boyer (2001); Eichenberg (2003).

5. Of course, I cannot (and should not) speak for all IR feminists. As in IR more generally, there is diversity in views on methodological preferences among feminist scholars. For purposes of this chapter, I define IR feminist research as research that uses gender as a category of analysis and, for the most part, follows the methodological guidelines that I develop below. IR feminists have also been defined as "a group of scholars who read and refer to each other's work" (Prügl 1999, 115). Following *The American Heritage Dictionary* (third edition, 1994), I define "empirical" as "guided by practical experience and not theory." I distinguish it from "empiricism," which the dictionary defines as "employment of empirical methods as in science." Feminists, whose methodological perspectives I am describing, generally reject empiricism.

6. Within what I have defined as "method," discussions of technique-specific methodological assumptions do take place.

androcentric or masculine biases in the way that knowledge has traditionally been constructed in all the disciplines.

In the second section, I discuss two examples of IR feminist empirical scholarship that exemplify these methodological perspectives. I chose them because each focuses on the state, a central unit of analysis in IR, and security, a central concept in the discipline. Each of the chosen authors makes use of methods not typical of conventional IR social scientific research. These IR feminists' methodological sensitivities parallel those of feminists in other disciplines—sensitivities that complicate efforts to construct the type of research program for which Keohane is calling. Drawing on the previous methodological discussion and my chosen case studies, the third section of the chapter offers some observations on the problems of and possibilities for the use of quantitative methods. While I am aware that conventional social scientific IR uses both quantitative and qualitative methods, I focus on quantitative methods of the type that would be required to answer the research question that Keohane illustratively posed to IR feminists.

FEMINIST PERSPECTIVES ON METHODOLOGY

In contrast to Keohane's commitment to a broadly defined scientific methodology, feminists claim no single standard of methodological correctness or "feminist way" to do research (Reinharz 1992, 243); nor do they see it as desirable to construct one. Many describe their research as a journey, or an archaeological dig, that draws on different methods or tools appropriate to the goals of the task at hand rather than to any prior methodological commitment that is more typical of IR conventional social science (Reinharz 1992, 211; Charlesworth 1994, 6; Jayaratne and Stewart 1991, 102; Sylvester, 2002).[7] In contrast to the social scientific method articulated by Keohane—initially specifying hypotheses that are open to subsequent testing—feminist knowledge-building is an ongoing process, tentative and emergent; feminists frequently describe knowledge-building as emerging through conversation with texts, research subjects, or data (Reinharz 1992, 230).[8] Many feminist scholars prefer to use the term "epistemological perspective" rather than

---

7. This stands in contrast to one of King, Keohane, and Verba's criteria for choosing a research question "explicitly locating a research design within the framework of the existing social scientific literature" (King, Keohane, and Verba 1994, 16).

8. In her biography of biologist Barbara McClintock, Evelyn Fox Keller describes McClintock's method for researching the transmutation of corn as letting the plants speak rather than trying to impose an answer. Keller talks about McClintock's "passion for difference" rather than looking for similarities in her data (Keller 1983). This tolerance and, indeed, preference for ambiguity is in contrast with conventional social science.

methodology to indicate the research goals and orientation of an ongoing project, the aim of which is to challenge and rethink what we mean by "knowledge." Rather than producing research that is likely to convince one's disciplinary colleagues, as Keohane urges, many feminist scholars emphasize the challenge to and estrangement from conventional knowledge-building due to the tension of being inside and outside one's discipline at the same time. Given that feminist knowledge has emerged from a deep skepticism about knowledge that claims to be universal and objective but which is, in reality, knowledge based on men's lives, such knowledge is constructed simultaneously out of disciplinary frameworks and feminist criticisms of these disciplines. Its goal is nothing less than to transform these disciplinary frameworks and the knowledge to which they contribute. Feminist inquiry is a dialectical process—listening to women and understanding how the subjective meaning they attach to their lived experiences are so often at variance with meanings internalized from society at large (Nielsen 1990, 26). Much of feminist scholarship is both transdisciplinary and avowedly political; it has explored and sought to understand the unequal gender hierarchies, as well as other hierarchies of power, which exist in all societies, to varying degrees, and their effects on the subordination of women and other disempowered people with the goal of changing them.[9]

Four methodological guidelines inform feminist research perspectives: a deep concern with which research questions get asked and why; the goal of designing research that is useful to women (and also to men) and is both less biased and more universal than conventional research; the centrality of questions of reflexivity and the subjectivity of the researcher; and a commitment to knowledge as emancipation.[10] I realize that not all these guidelines are unique to feminism. Reflexive and emancipatory knowledge-building has a long history in critical/hermeneutic traditions.[11] What is unique to feminism, however, is a commitment to asking feminist questions and building knowledge from women's lives—a commitment that, feminists believe, has

9. "Third-wave feminism," which began in the early 1990s and which was reacting against treating "woman" as an essentialized universal category, has emphasized the different positionality of women according to class, race, culture, and geographical location. IR feminists who emphasize difference and this type of intersectionality might reject attempts to generalize about knowledge from women's lives. While I agree with these cautions about generalization, I make the assumption that it is possible to construct some generalizable answers to the questions addressed in this chapter.

10. The following section relies heavily on Harding (1987), Fonow and Cook (1991), and Bloom (1998), but the extent to which much of the work on feminist methodology and feminist research implicitly or explicitly raises these same issues is striking.

11. Feminist knowledge-building is closer to what Habermas describes as the historical-hermeneutic sciences than to the empirical-analytic sciences. Whereas the goal of the empirical-analytic sciences is prediction, and hence control, hermeneutic sciences are geared toward producing self-reflective knowledge, the goal of which is emancipation. For an extended discussion of these issues see Habermas (1971, Appendix).

wider implications that have the potential to transform existing knowledge frameworks.

Feminists Ask Feminist Research Questions

A research project should pose a question that is "important" in the "real world" (King, Keohane, and Verba 1994, 15; Van Evera 1997, 97). Feminists and IR scholars would probably agree on this statement but disagree as to the definition of what is "important." They would also have conflicting views of what constitutes the "real world." However, Sandra Harding has claimed that conventional Western scientific progress is judged not on the merit of the questions that are asked but on how questions are answered. It is not in the origin of the scientific problem or hypothesis, but rather in the testing of hypotheses or the "logic of scientific inquiry" that we look to judge the success of science (Harding 1987, 7), a standard that is close to that articulated by Keohane. On the other hand, feminists counter that, from their perspective, *the questions that are asked*—or, more important, *those that are not asked*—are as determinative of the adequacy of the project as any answers that we can discover.

The questions that IR has asked since the discipline was founded have typically been about the behavior of states, particularly powerful states and their security-seeking behavior, given an anarchical international environment. Much of the scholarship in international political economy and international institutions has also focused on the behavior of the great powers and their potential, or lack thereof, for international cooperation. These questions are of particular importance for the foreign policy interests of the most powerful states.[12] A frequently asked IR research question has focused on the effects of political institutions and forms of governance on the prospects for international peace. Much of this research has supported or challenged the claim that democracies are less warlike, at least in their relations with other democracies (Russett 1993).[13] The question that Keohane poses—whether relative gender equality is likely to have an effect on states' security-seeking behavior—is a variant of this type of question. It is an important one that has already been addressed. For example, Mary Caprioli has demonstrated that, according to her measures, domestic gender equality has a pacifying effect on state behavior at the international level (Caprioli 2000; see also Caprioli and Boyer 2001).

12. I am aware that IR has asked other questions about different issues, such as human rights and social movements. Nevertheless, questions coming out of a statist ontology remain at the core of the discipline

13. Russett and other IR scholars' work on the democratic peace emerge out of Kant's ideas about the peacefulness of democracies. See Doyle (1983).

This line of research is an important addition to the IR literature that is seeking to understand how domestic democratic institutions shape states' foreign policies. The questions it asks are state-centric and are designed to provide answers about interstate behavior; the methods it uses emerge out of conventional empirical social science.

Many IR feminists have asked very different questions and have used different methodological perspectives within which to provide their answers. While they may seek to understand state behavior, they do so in the context of asking why, in so many parts of the world, women remain so fundamentally disempowered in matters of foreign and military policy. For example, rather than speculate on the hypothetical question as to whether women *might be* more peaceful than men as foreign policy-makers, IR feminists have focused on the more immediate problem as to why there *are so few* women in positions of power.[14] Why, predominantly, have wars been fought by men, and how do gendered structures of masculinity and femininity legitimate war and militarism for both women and men?[15] Feminists have also investigated the problematic essentialized association of women with peace, an association that disempowers both women and peace, questions that I investigated more fully in Chapter 2 (Sylvester 1987; Tickner 2001, 59). Rather than uncritically assume the state as a given unit of analysis, IR feminists have investigated the constitutive features of "gendered states" and their implications for the militarization of women's (and men's) lives (Peterson 1992; Enloe 2000). But the basic question that remains is why, in just about all societies, are women disadvantaged—politically, socially, and economically—relative to men, and to what extent is this due to international politics and the global economy? Conversely, in what ways do these hierarchical gendered structures of inequality support the international system of states and contribute to the unevenly distributed prosperity of the global capitalist economy? (I explored these questions more fully in Part One.) Although Marxists may be cited as the legitimate precursors concerning such issues, these are questions that, in this form, have rarely been asked in IR; while IR scholars would not deny that they are important questions, they would probably deem them at best tangential to the core subject matter of the discipline.

The "message that feminists are seeking to deliver" is, therefore, a more profound challenge to the discipline than Keohane implies; moreover, the questions that feminists deem important are typically not adequately answerable within a conventional social scientific framework. Feminist questions challenge the core assumptions of the discipline and deconstruct its central

14. Speculation on this issue was undertaken by Francis Fukuyama (1998). For a critique see Tickner (2002).
15. As Joshua Goldstein (2001) claims, it is remarkable how many books have been written on war and how few of them have asked the question as to why wars are fought predominantly by men.

concepts; many of them are constitutive rather than causal.[16] Working from the discovery of the gendered biases in state-centric security thinking feminists have redefined the meaning of (in)security to include the effects of structural inequalities of race, class, and gender. Similarly, on the bases of theoretical critiques of the gendered political uses of the public/private distinction, feminists have rearticulated the meaning of democracy and have tried to reconstitute its practice to include the participation of women and men in all the political and economic processes that affect their daily lives (Ackerly 2000, 178–203). While not rejecting in principle the use of quantitative data, feminists have recognized how past behavioral realities have been publicly constituted in state-generated indicators in biased, gendered ways, using data that do not adequately reflect the reality of women's lives and the unequal structures of power within which they are situated.[17] For this reason they rely on hermeneutic, historical, narrative, and case study methodological orientations rather than on causal analysis of unproblematically defined entities and social relations. Importantly, feminists use gender as a socially constructed and variable category of analysis to investigate these dynamics. They suggest that gender inequality as well as other social relations of domination and subordination have been among the fundamental building blocks on which, to varying extents, the publicly recognized features of states, their security relationships, and the global economy have been constructed and on which they continue to operate to varying degrees.

In contrast to an ontology that depicts states as individualistic autonomous actors—an ontology typical of conventional social science perspectives on IR and of liberal thinking more generally—feminist ontologies are based on social relations that are constituted by historically unequal political, economic, and social structures.[18] Unlike conventional social science IR, which draws on models from economics and the natural sciences to explain the behavior of states in the international system, IR feminists have used sociological analyses that begin with individuals and the hierarchical social relations in which their lives are situated. Whereas much of IR is focused on factors that explain the behavior of states, feminists are motivated by the goal

16. Causal questions, such as "does *x* cause *y*?" aim to explain changes in the state of some variable or system. Constitutive questions ask how the properties of a system are constituted. Constitutive questions ask "how possible?" or "what?" Wendt (1998, 105).

17. Since this piece was originally published, there have been important efforts by IR feminists to collect data on such issues. The WomenStats project is one such project. It is available at www.womanstats.org.

18. This is an important reason that a convergence between post-positivist feminisms and naturalistic social scientific methodologies is so problematic. There is, of course, a wide variety of IR scholarship that also draws on sociologically oriented methodologies, much of it published outside the United States. See, for example, Hobden and Hobson (2003).

of investigating the lives of women within states or international structures in order to change or reconstitute them. Given these different ontological pre-suppositions and emancipatory goals, evaluation of feminist research accord-ing to the scientific standards articulated by Keohane is problematic.

Use Women's Experiences to Design Research
That Is Useful to Women

A shared assumption of feminist research is that women's lives are important (Reinharz 1992, 241). "Making the invisible visible, bringing the margin to the center, rendering the trivial important, putting the spotlight on women as competent actors, understanding women as subjects in their own right rather than objects for men—all continue to be elements of feminist research" (Reinharz 1992, 248). Too often women's experiences have been deemed triv-ial or only important insofar as they relate to the experiences of men and the questions they typically ask.

An important commitment of feminist methodology is that knowledge must be built and analyzed in a way that can be used by women to change whatever oppressive conditions they face. When choosing a research topic, feminists frequently ask what potential it has to improve women's lives (Jayaratne and Stewart 1991, 101). Feminists study the routine aspects of everyday life that help sustain gender inequality; they acknowledge the perva-sive influence of gender and acknowledge that what has passed as knowledge about human behavior is, in fact, frequently knowledge about male behav-ior (Cook and Fonow 1990, 73). What is called "common sense" is, in real-ity, knowledge derived from the experiences of men's lives, usually privileged men. Importantly, "male behavior" and "men's lives" are highly dependent on women and other subordinate groups playing all kinds of supportive roles in these lives and behind this behavior: for if there were only (privileged) men, their lives would surely be different. Designing research useful to women involves first deconstructing previous knowledge based on these androcentric assumptions.

Feminist research represents a paradigm shift in the Kuhnian sense in that it sees women, rather than just men, as both the subject matter and cre-ators of knowledge. This leads to anomalies or observations that do not fit received theory. Joyce Nielsen outlines the way in which androcentric theo-ries have been used to explain the origins of human society. By focusing on "man the hunter" man's [sic] origins were associated with productive rather than reproductive tasks. Men were seen as responsible for organizing human life, and women's roles as gatherers and reproducers were completely ignored. These partial stories are not good science since they rely only on knowledge about men's lives. They negate the claim that science is a foolproof procedure that relies on observation to test theories and hypotheses about the world (Nielsen 1990, 16–18). A distinctive feature of feminist research is that it uses women's experiences as an indicator of the "reality" against which conventional hypotheses are tested and unconventional questions are formulated (Harding 1987, 7). Feminists also claim that knowledge based on the standpoint of women's lives, particularly marginalized women, leads to more robust objectivity, not only because it broadens the base from which we derive knowledge, but also because the perspectives of "outsiders" or marginalized people may reveal aspects of reality obscured by more orthodox approaches to knowledge-building.[19]

Designing IR research of special use to women involves considerable paradigm shifts. While the role of women as reproducers, caregivers, and unpaid workers has been largely ignored in conventional economic analysis, it is central to feminist concerns. Marilyn Waring has documented how national income data ignore reproductive and caring tasks. She describes the daily routine of a girl in Zimbabwe who works at household tasks from 4 a.m. to 9 p.m. but who is officially classified as "economically inactive" or "unoccupied" (Waring 1988, 15–16). Yet national income concepts, variables, and empirical data, which ignore these reproductive and caring tasks, are used by political elites to make public policy. Since the industrial revolution the home has been defined as a feminine space devoid of work, even though women in the home are engaged in various productive and reproductive tasks, such as domestic service, homework, and caring and reproductive labor. These paid and unpaid tasks are crucial to the maintenance of the global capitalist economy (Chin 1998; Prügl 1999).

Making visible that which was previously invisible has led IR feminists to investigate military prostitution and rape as tools of war and instruments of state policy (Moon 1997; Enloe 2000). This not only leads to redefinitions of the meaning of security but to an understanding of how the security of the state and the prosperity of the global economy are frequently dependent on the insecurity of certain individuals', often women's, lives. In bringing to light these multiple experiences of women's lives, feminist researchers also claim that the research they conduct cannot—and should not—be separated from their identities as researchers and their efforts to reconstitute their own identities and relationships in a more equitable fashion.

19. It is frequently the case that those who are subordinated or marginalized have a greater understanding of the lives of their oppressors than vice versa. For an elaboration on this idea from the standpoint of Black feminist thought, see Collins (1991, 36).

Reflexivity

Most feminist research insists that the inquirer be placed in the same critical plane as the subject matter. "Only in this way can we hope to produce understandings and explanations which are free of distortion from the unexamined beliefs of social scientists themselves" (Harding 1987, 9). In contrast to conventional social scientific methods, Harding believes that acknowledging the subjective element into one's analysis, which exists in all social science research, actually increases the objectivity of the research. Similarly, Mary Margaret Cook and Judith Fonow reject the assumption that maintaining a gap between the researcher and the research subject produces more valid knowledge; rather, they advocate a participatory research strategy that emphasizes a dialectic between the researcher and the researched throughout the project (Cook and Fonow 1990, 76). Feminists struggle with the issue of power differentials between the researcher and her subjects.

What Reinharz refers to as a "reflexive attitude" has developed in reaction to androcentric research with its claims to value neutrality. Personal experience is considered an asset for feminist research; in their texts, many feminist researchers describe how they have been motivated to conduct projects that stem from their own lives and personal experiences.[20] Often the researcher will reflect on what she has learned during the research process, on her "identification" with the research subjects, and on the personal traumas and difficulties that the research may have involved. For example, in her research on the (in)security of Mayan women in Guatemala, Maria Stern-Petterson reflects on her ethical obligation to her research subjects and her attempts to co-create a text in which the narrators can claim authorship of their own stories. This rewriting of (in)security using the voices of marginalized lives constitutes a political act that can challenge dominant and oppressive ways of documenting these lives (Stern-Petterson 1998, 75). Many feminists who conduct interview research acknowledge an intellectual debt to British sociologist Ann Oakley, who proposed "a feminist ethic of commitment and egalitarianism in contrast with the scientific ethic of detachment and role differentiation between researcher and subject" (Reinharz 1992, 27; see also Bloom 1998). Whereas personal experience is thought by conventional social science to contaminate a project's objectivity, feminists believe that one's own awareness of one's own personal position in the research process to be a corrective to "pseudo-objectivity." Rather than bias, they see it as a necessary explanation of the researcher's standpoint that serves to strengthen the standards of

---

20. This stands in contrast to King, Keohane, and Verba's statement that, "[P]ersonal reasons are neither necessary nor sufficient justifications for the choice of a topic. In most cases they should not appear in our scholarly writings" (King, Keohane, and Verba 1994, 15).

objectivity, resulting in "strong objectivity" or "robust reflexivity" (Reinharz 1992, 258; Harding 1991, 142; Harding 1998, 189). Many feminists also believe in the necessity of continual reflection on and critical scrutiny of one's own methods throughout the research project, allowing for the possibility that the researcher may make methodological adjustments along the way (Ackerly 2000). For feminists, one of the primary goals of this commitment to experiential and reflexive knowledge-building has been the hope that their research project might contribute to the improvement of women's lives, at least in part through the empowerment of their research subjects.

Knowledge as Emancipation

"Feminism supports the proposition that women should transform themselves and the world" (Soares, quoted in Ackerly 2000, 198). Since many feminists do not believe that it is possible to separate thought from action and knowledge from practice, they claim that feminist research cannot be separated from the historical movement for the improvement of women's lives out of which it emerged (Mies 1991, 64). If the aim of feminist research is to empower women, then the researcher must be actively engaged in political struggle and must be aware of the policy implications of her work.[21] Pursuing social change involves uncovering "practical knowledge" from people's everyday lives. This type of knowledge-building has parallels with participatory action research. Stephen Toulmin contrasts participatory action research, which he claims grows out of Aristotelian ethics and practical reasoning, with what he terms the High Science model with its Platonic origins, a model that is closer to conventional social scientific IR. The product of participatory action research is the creation of practical knowledge that emphasizes the improvement of practice rather than of theory. Toulmin sees the disciplines closest to this type of research as being history and anthropology, with their traditions of participant observation that grows out of local action, the goal of which is changing the situation (Toulmin 1996).

Feminists frequently engage in participant observation. They are generally suspicious of Cartesian ways of knowing, or the High Science model, which depicts human subjects as solitary and self-subsistent and where knowledge is obtained through measurement rather than sympathy. Feminists tend to believe that emotion and intellect are mutually constitutive and sustaining rather than oppositional forces in the construction of knowledge (Code 1991,

---

21. Of course, social scientific IR is also concerned that its research be prescriptive and useful for policy purposes. See Van Evera (1997, 17–21). But since feminism has been engaged in understanding and seeking to overthrow oppressive social hierarchies that subordinate women, the policy implications are typically more radical.

47). Maria Mies contrasts feminist research, which she claims takes place directly within life's processes, with what she calls an alienated concept of empiricism where "research objects" have been detached from their real-life surroundings and broken down into their constituent parts (Mies 1991, 66). She describes her research among rural women workers of Nalgonda, India as sharing as far as possible their living conditions and allowing them to carry out their own research on the researchers. Her findings were translated into Telugu so that they could be used for betterment of the society. Mies claims that this reciprocal exchange of experiences gave these women so much courage that they could tackle problems of sexual violence in new ways and come up with different solutions, thereby moving beyond their victim status (Mies 1991, 73; see also Ackerly 2000, ch.1). Conventional social science IR would rightly claim that its knowledge-building is also a contribution to the betterment of society; indeed, IR scholars from all methodological perspectives have been driven to ask research questions that can help to find ways to diminish violent conflict and enhance cooperation. Nevertheless, the goal of the research model to which conventional social science IR aspires to help answer such questions is to remain detached and, to the greatest extent possible, value-neutral and separate from political action.[22]

USING THESE METHODOLOGICAL GUIDELINES: SOME FEMINIST EXAMPLES

These four methodological guidelines, typical of feminist research, stand in contrast to the methodological criteria for social science research outlined by Keohane. Their emphasis on designing questions that are useful for women's lives, their insistence that objectivity can be strengthened through acknowledgment of the subjectivity of the researcher, and their explicit linking of theory with social action and social change, do not accord with the criteria for a successful research program as outlined by Keohane. While most of them are drawn from the work of scholars in disciplines, such as anthropology and sociology, whose subject matter is focused on studying human social

22. I use the term "value-neutral" to describe a social scientific tradition going back at least to Weber which, while it acknowledges that research is always motivated by a commitment to certain values, recognizes that "the investigator...should keep unconditionally separate the establishment of empirical facts and *his* [sic] own practical evaluations..." (Weber 1949, 11). For further elaboration on Weber's views on value-neutrality see Ringer (1997) chap. 5. For a generation of IR discipline-defining IR scholars coming out of the experience of value-corrupted knowledge claims of fascist Europe in the 1930s and 1940s, such a commitment is understandable. Values motivate all kinds of negative as well as positive outcomes, an issue with which feminists need to engage further.

relations rather than statist international politics, it is, nevertheless, striking the degree to which many IR feminists have demonstrated similar methodological sensibilities.

I shall now discuss two "second generation" feminist IR texts, exploring their methodological orientations as well as the research methods they use.[23] I have chosen these two as exemplary of the kind of methodological orientation I have outlined because each is concerned with theorizing the state and its security-seeking practices—one from a political/military standpoint, the other from a political economy orientation. Katharine Moon's *Sex Among Allies* deals with national security policy, an issue central to IR, but through the lens of military prostitution, a subject not normally considered part of the discipline. Christine Chin's *In Service and Servitude* deals with issues of development and global political economy but it does so through an examination of the lives of female domestic servants in Malaysia and state policies with respect to regulating their lives. Both these scholars start their research from the lives of some of the most marginalized disempowered women and demonstrate how their lives and work impact on, and are impacted by, national security and the global economy. Both use ethnographic methods and participant observation to conduct in-depth case studies, methods not typical of IR.[24] Both express the hope that their research will help improve the lives of the women they study as well as expose hierarchical exploitative social structures upon which states and their security policies are built.

Sex Among Allies

In her 1997 book, *Sex Among Allies*, which I mentioned briefly in Chapter 2, Katharine Moon takes up a little examined subject and one not normally considered part of the discipline of international relations—prostitution camps around US military bases in the Republic of Korea during the early 1970s. She argues that the cleanup of these camps by the Korean government, which involved imposing health standards on and monitoring of women prostitutes, was directly related to establishing a more hospitable environment for American troops at a time when the United States was in the process of pulling its troops out of Korea as part of the strategy, articulated in the Nixon Doctrine, to place more of the US security burden on regional allies. Through

---

23. "Second generation" is a term that has been used in feminist IR to refer to empirical case studies that have followed from "first generation" feminist critiques of IR theory that challenged the assumptions, concepts, and methodologies of the IR discipline from feminist perspectives.

24. Of course, qualitative case studies are also done in social science IR and are the subject of King, Keohane, and Verba's methodological text. However, such case studies usually employ structured focused comparisons or process tracing methods.

an examination of relevant United States and Republic of Korea government documents and interviews with government officials and military personnel in both states, Moon links efforts to certify the health of prostitutes to policy discussions between the two states about the retention of military bases at the highest level. The challenge for Moon is to show how prostitution, a private issue normally considered outside the boundaries of international politics, is linked to national security and foreign policy. In so doing, she asks questions not normally asked in IR, such as, what factors helped to create and maintain military prostitution and for what ends? She also questions the accepted boundaries that separate private sexual relations from politics among nations and shows how prostitution can be a matter of concern in international politics and a bargaining tool for two alliance partners who are vastly unequal in conventional military power (Moon 1997, 13). Moon demonstrates how private relations among people and foreign relations between governments inform and are informed by each other (Moon 1997, 2).[25]

Moon's analysis led her to rethink the meaning of national security. Claiming that it was the desire of the Korean government to make a better environment for American troops, rather than an effort to improve the conditions under which prostitutes lived and worked, that motivated the government to improve the conditions of the camps, Moon demonstrates how the government's weakness at the international level vis-à-vis the United States caused it to impose authoritarian and sexist control at the domestic level. Moon's evidence supports the broader feminist claim that the security of the state is often built on the insecurity of its most vulnerable populations and their unequal relationships with others, in this case on the lives of its most impoverished and marginalized women. While many of these women felt betrayed by the Korean government and its national security policies, ironically many of them saw the state as their only possible protector against the violence they suffered at the hands of US soldiers. Lack of protection was blamed on the weakness of their own state.[26] Moon concludes that the women

25. In a personal conversation with this author, Moon described her work as being at the intersection of IR and comparative politics. She noted that her research has been more widely recognized in comparative politics and attributed it to the fact that comparative politics asks different questions from IR. Much of IR feminist empirical work is situated at this intersection, although most of these scholars would claim IR as their intellectual training ground.

26. Moon notes that this finding is quite at odds with feminist suspicions of the state, which she dates back to Virginia Woolf's famous indictment of the state's role in war-making. Moon claims that Woolf's indictment is quite middle class and Western. Those who challenge state sovereignty usually live in wealthy countries and are socially, intellectually, and economically empowered enough to talk about opting out of the state (Moon 1997, 158). The high level of awareness of Moon's subjects about the national security policies of the Korean state supports the claim that marginalized people have a deep level of understanding of the privileged world of which they are not a part. See note 19.

saw national sovereignty, or the ability to stand up to the United States, as a means to empower their own lives (Moon 1997, 158). Moon's study challenges the conventional meaning and composition of national (in)security practices; it also challenges us to think about how the relational identities of states are constituted and how often policies deemed necessary for national security can cause insecurity for certain citizens.

Moon's choice of research topic carried considerable personal risk. In reflecting on her role as researcher, Moon speaks of how her frequenting of shantytowns during her research meant that she herself became morally suspect. She was cautioned about publishing her work lest people would question her moral character. Getting women to speak was difficult, and Moon frequently had to use intermediaries because of the feeling of shame that talking about their experiences evoked in many of these women. Many of them had little concept about the structure of a research interview and frequently expressed the view that their opinions were unimportant and not worth recording. Moon states that she did not aim to provide likely-to-be-distorted (by the Korean state) statistical evidence but to show, through narrating the women's lives, how heavily involved they were in US–Korean relations and thus of importance to international politics. While she aims to say something new about state security practices and international politics, one of her principal goals is to give voice to people who were not considered as having anything worthwhile to say, thereby helping to improve their lives. She talks of her work as helping to lift the curtains of invisibility of these women's lives and "offer these pages as a passageway for their own voices," thus allowing them to construct their own identities, rather than having them imposed on them by societal norms and taken-for-granted definitions—definitions that are often imposed when conventional data are used (Moon 1997, 2). Moon concludes that the expansion of the definition of political actor to include individuals without significant resources or control over issues—those not normally defined as actors by IR—can challenge governments' claim to their exclusive definitions of national interest and national security (Moon 1997, 160).

In Service and Servitude

Christine Chin's text examines the importation of Filipina and Indonesian female domestic workers into Malaysia, beginning in the 1970s, and how their labor supported a Malaysian modernization project based on an export-led development model in the context of the neo-liberal global economy. Chin asserts that the global expansion of neo-liberalism has gone hand-in-hand with the free trade in migrant female domestic labor throughout the world. She asks two basic questions of her study, both of which are linked to women's lives: First, why is unlegislated domestic service, an essentially pre-modern social institution with all its attendant hardships, increasingly prevalent in the context of constructing a modern developed society by way of export-led development? And second, why is there an absence of public concern regarding the less-than-human conditions in which some domestic servants work? (Chin 1998, 4) To answer these questions, Chin rejects a "problem-solving" approach, which, she claims, would focus on explaining foreign female domestic labor as a consequence of wage differentials between the labor-sending and labor-receiving countries; instead, she adopts what she terms a critical interdisciplinary approach.[27] According to Chin, problem-solving lacks historicity and divides social life into discrete, mutually exclusive dimensions and levels that have little bearing on one another. Chin's preference for a critically oriented methodology is based on her desire to examine the relationship between domestic service and the developmental state and its involvement with all levels of society from the household to the transnational, the goal of which is to expose power relations with the intention of changing them (Chin 1998, 5).

Chin asks how paid domestic reproductive labor, usually performed by women, supports, shapes, and legitimizes the late-twentieth-century developmental state. As she notes, there has been much work on the Asian "developmental state" and its mechanisms of coercive power but little on how the state has used policies that regulate transnational migrant domestic labor as part of this coercive strategy. Using a Gramscian framework, Chin claims that the developmental state is not neutral but an expression of class, ethnic, racial, and gender-based power, which it exercises through both coercion and co-optation of forces that could challenge it. The state's involvement in regulating domestic service and policing domestic workers in the name of maintaining social order is not just a personal, private issue but one that serves this goal, as the state can thereby provide the good life for certain of its (middle class) citizens through repressing others. Since proof of marriage and children is necessary in order for middle class families to be eligible for foreign domestic workers, domestic service is an institution through which the state has normalized the middle class adoption of the nuclear family (Chin 1998, 198). Winning support of the middle class family by promoting policies that support materialist consumption, including the paid labor of domestic servants, has helped to lessen ethnic divisions in Malaysia and to increase loyalty to the state and hence its security.

Chin questions the assumption, implicit in economic theory, that capitalism is the natural order of life; she claims that critical analysis is designed to

27. Chin is following Robert Cox's famous distinction between problem-solving theory that, according to Cox, accepts the prevailing order as its framework, and critical theory, which stands apart from that order and asks how it came about with the goal of changing it. See Cox (1981, 129–130). I describe this in more detail in Chapter 6.

deconstruct this objective world and to reveal the unequal distribution and exercise of power that inheres in and continues to constitute social relations, institutions, and structures (Chin 1998, 17–18). Thus, many of the questions that Chin asks in her research are constitutive rather than causal. She rejects causal answers that rely solely on economic analysis of supply and demand about why the flow of foreign domestic servants into Malaysia in the 1970s and 1980s increased, in favor of answers that examine the constitution of the developmental state as a coercive structure that gains its legitimacy through seeking support of the middle classes for its export-oriented development at the expense of poor women's lives.

Chin is explicit in positioning herself in the context of her work. She tells us that she came to her study through her own background as an "upper class Malaysian Chinese extended family...whose family members were served twenty-four hours a day by nannies, housemaids and cooks" (Chin 1998, xi). Having been motivated to do this research after witnessing the abuse of a neighbor's Filipina servant, Chin lived in various neighborhoods of Kuala Lumpur, where she could observe working conditions and where she heard many stories of mistreatment and abuse; she spoke with activists who counseled these workers and began to reflect on her own privileged status and the tensions between her class status and being an academic researcher. She had to confront the relationship between domestic service and the political economy of development, a relationship made irrelevant by the dominant discursive practices that characterized a Western, mainstream education on global politics.

Chin's research grew out of her reflection on her own privileged status, her witnessing of the exploitation of those she studied, and her determination to do something about it. She observed how her subjects' everyday lives helped shape decision-making at the national level, as well as how their lives were affected by transnational forces beyond their control (Chin 1998, 22). While many of the employers with whom she spoke did not see how the research could be of intellectual interest, some of the workers asked Chin to publish her work so that the world could know about the harsh conditions under which they worked and lived. Chin acknowledges that coming to know this world forced her to rethink the relationship between theory and practice (Chin 1998, xvii). She also speaks of constructing her own identity as a scholar as the interviewing stage of the project progressed. Questioning "common sense," as well as conventional economics, Chin suggests that the ultimate objective of the study is to help ascertain potentialities for emancipation from the constraints of seemingly natural social relations, institutions and structures (Chin 1998, 27). She defines her project as emancipatory also insofar as it attempts to undo received epistemological boundaries and "social data" collection practices that ignore or silence marginalized voices and fail to present social change in all its complexities (Chin 1998, 29).

Chin describes her research method as "a non-positivist manner of recovering and generating knowledge." She contrasts this with feminist empiricism which, as I claimed earlier, may correct for certain androcentric biases, but risks distilling the complexities of social life into a series of hypotheses that can be labeled as truth (Chin 1998, 20). While acknowledging the usefulness of attitudinal surveys, Chin worries that they may constrain an understanding of the complexities of various forces that shape the performance and consumption of reproductive labor. Chin conducted her research through archival analysis and open-ended interviews, relying on fieldwork notes as evidence. This narrative method allowed Chin's subjects, like Moon's, to recount their lives in their own words and to speak about any issue they pleased, thereby constructing their own identities and challenging identities that had been constructed by others. Chin reflects critically on the interview process as it proceeds; she notes how frequently employers would try to co-opt her by establishing a common relationship. She also reflects on the need to be continually questioning what she had previously taken for granted in everyday life, lending support to the epistemological position, supported by many feminists, that there is no social reality out there independent of the observer.

Like many IR feminists, Chin and Moon rejected conventional social science methodology in favor of qualitative (single) case studies that rely on more empathetic, interpretive methodologies. They use open-ended ethnographic research that relies on narrative accounts of the lives of women at the margins of society, accounts that they prefer over statistical analysis of government-generated data, in which the experiences that Chin and Moon documented are barely reflected. Indeed, no state agency could be convinced to acknowledge the systematic existence of such problems associated with prostitution and the maltreatment of women, let alone collect and publish comparable data on their magnitude.[28] With the goal of making certain women's lives more visible, these studies begin their analysis at the micro level and analyze issues not normally considered part of IR. Looking for meaningful characterizations rather than causes, they seek to understand the foreign policies of states and international politics more generally through the telling of stories of lives rendered insecure by states striving to increase their own security or wealth. Moon documents the Republic of Korea's authoritarian

28. Katharine Moon emphasized this point in a personal conversation with this author. She first envisaged doing a comparative case study of several countries but found that, since data were practically nonexistent, it would have been an impossible task. She emphasized that much of feminist IR is beginning the trench work and compilation of data needed before comparative case studies can be undertaken. These challenges contrast with Steven Van Evera's advice to students selecting a Ph.D. dissertation topic to choose data-rich cases (Van Evera 1997, 79). Van Evera asserts that the more data we have, the more questions we can answer. But feminists are more concerned with the questions that are *not* asked because of the lack of data.

behavior with respect to certain of its citizens as a necessary response to its weak and dependent position vis-à-vis the United States. Looking to promote internal stability and economic growth, Malaysia sought to increase the material welfare of certain of its citizens, including certain middle class women, at the expense of the security of other women's lives. These are nuanced findings that could not be discovered through the use of conventional political or economic indicators.

Both studies attempt to have their research subjects claim their own identities through the telling of their own stories. They see this as a way of rejecting the identities that society has bestowed upon these women, identities that often form the basis of state policies that may render their lives more insecure. Both authors use gender as a category of analysis to help them understand how individuals, families, states, societies, and the international system are constituted through, and in resistance against, hierarchical and often oppressive power relations. While neither of them makes specific reference to the literature on methodology that I outlined in Part One, the degree to which their methodological sensitivities parallel these more general feminist research practices is striking.[29]

QUANTITATIVE RESEARCH: PROBLEMS AND POSSIBILITIES

As these two case studies have demonstrated, fitting women and other marginalized people into methodologically conventional quantitative frameworks has been problematic. Many of the experiences of women's lives have not yet been documented or analyzed, either within social science disciplines or by states. Traditional ways in which data are collected, categorized, and analyzed do not lend themselves to answering many of the questions that feminists such as Moon and Chin raise. The choices that states make about which data to collect is a political act, yet the data that are available to scholars and, more important, the data that are not, shape which research questions are answered and even which questions are asked. Marilyn Waring describes how national accounting systems have been shaped and reshaped to help states frame their national security policies—specifically to understand how to pay for wars.[30] Political decisions about public policy are made on the basis of data that policy elites choose to collect (Waring 1988, 302). In national accounting systems, no value is attached to the environment, to unpaid work, to the reproduction

29. The one exception is that Chin does make reference to Sandra Harding's work on methodology.

30. Waring makes reference to a claim by statistical historians Joseph Duncan and William Shelton that a 1941 paper entitled "Measuring National Income as Affected by War," by Milton Gilbert, was the first clear, published statement of the term gross national product (GNP) (Waring 1988, 55).

of human life, or to its maintenance or care, tasks generally undertaken by women (Waring 1988, 3–4). Under the guise of value-free science, the economics of accounting has constructed a reality which believes that "value" results only when individuals (predominantly men) interact with the marketplace (Waring 1988, 17–18).

Maria Mies also argues that quantitative research methods are instruments for structuring reality in certain ways. Under the guise of "objectivity", statistical procedures can serve to legitimize and universalize certain power relations because they give a "stamp of truth" to the definitions upon which they are based (Mies 1991, 67). As described in Part One, the term "male head of household" came out of a definition of a traditional Western middle class patriarchal family but does not correspond with present reality, given that a majority of women either work in the waged sector to supplement family income or are themselves heads of households. However, it is a term that has been used, either explicitly or implicitly, in national accounting procedures and by international aid agencies and thus has had significant consequences for women's classification as workers, receivers of social benefits, and refugees. Women's work, often unpaid, as farmers, workers in family businesses, and caregivers is frequently overlooked in the compilation of labor statistics. The female domain of production and reproduction that provides the necessary infrastructure for the male world is largely invisible and un-conceptualized (Acker et al. 1991, 134). Redefinitions of labor to include reproductive and caring labor would not only make women's work more visible; it would give us a deeper understanding of the workings of the global economy, which could not function as it does without this substantial body of unremunerated work.[31] Feminist rejection of statistical analysis results both from a realization that the questions they ask can rarely be answered by using standard classifications of available data and from an understanding that such data may actually conceal the relationships they deem important.[32]

These concerns, along with the methodological predispositions described in the first section of this chapter, raise important issues concerning statistical measures of gender (in)equality, measures that are important for answering the research question asked by Keohane as to whether states with highly unequal gendered hierarchies would behave differently internationally from those with less unequal domestic social structures. Since Keohane raised this question in 1998, there have been attempts to answer it using quantitative

31. Spike Peterson begun this task with her reconceptualization of the global economy in terms of the reproductive, productive, and virtual (RPV) economies. See Peterson (2003).

32. For example, even if cross-national aggregate conventional measures of wages and work conditions were available, they would not give an adequate picture of the degree of gender inequality and gender oppression demonstrated in the Chin and Moon case studies.

methods. For example, Mary Caprioli and Mark Boyer have used quantitative social science data and statistical methods—the International Crises Behavior data set and multinomial logistic regression—to investigate whether there is a relationship between domestic gender equality and states' use of violence internationally. Gender equality is measured in terms of percentage of women in parliament and number of years that women had the right to vote at the time of the beginning of the conflict. Their results show that, according to their measures of gender equality, the severity of violence used by states in international crises decreases as domestic gender equality increases.[33]

Caprioli and Boyer admit that social equality is difficult to measure cross-culturally (see also Caprioli 2000, 164). They agree that, as yet, there are no measures to gauge social pressures, associated with gendered role expectations that keep women from certain employment opportunities or out of positions of political power (Caprioli and Boyer 2001, 56).[34] In order to be able to demonstrate empirically that women's leadership would have any effect on foreign policy, certain feminists have argued that there would need to be significant numbers of women in leadership positions—30 percent has sometimes been mentioned. Indeed, Caprioli and Boyer admit that lone female leaders may be pressured to act more aggressively than their male counterparts in order to legitimate their leadership positions (Caprioli and Boyer 2001, 507). They also refer to the difficulty of measuring the impact of female leaders on policy outcomes—leaders who may be constrained by operating in male structures. Indeed, this kind of impact is hard to demonstrate with conventional correlational data. While Caprioli and Boyer feel that these obstacles do not hinder their basic finding—that the severity of violence used by a state in an international crisis decreases as domestic gender equality increases—many feminists would see these problems of measuring gender equality as too serious to allow for such claims to be made, given the social processes lying behind these correlations that remain unexamined.

33. This research builds on Caprioli (2000) and also on Tessler and Warriner (1997), whose study I described in Chapter 2 and who showed a positive correlation between favorable attitudes toward gender equality and favorable attitudes toward peaceful conflict resolution by both women and men in certain states in the Middle East. See also Eichenberg (2003), who investigates to what extent gender differences have the potential to be a significant factor in the political decisions of states to use military force.

34. This caution is supported by Ronald Inglehart and Pippa Norris's empirical study of global attitudes toward gender equality, which stresses the importance of cultural barriers over structural and institutional ones when explaining the lack of women in positions of political power (Inglehart and Norris 2003, 133). They conclude that understanding why women do better in attaining political power in certain societies than others, even those with similar political systems, has proved elusive using existing aggregate data (Inglehart and Norris 2003, 144). The World Values Survey, on which this research is based, is an attempt to document and compare values cross-culturally using attitudinal surveys.

Feminists claim that the lack of gender equality, which they believe exists in all states albeit to widely varying extents, cannot be understood without reference to the historical, gender-laden divisions between public and private spheres that I discussed in Part One. The public/private distinction, upon which the modern Western state was founded, has set up hierarchical gendered structures and role expectations that impede the achievement of true gender equality even today, in states where most legal barriers to women's equality have been removed. Measures such as women's participation in politics and percentage of women in the workforce do not adequately capture the fact that states have been constituted historically as gendered entities with all the attendant problems that this has created for women. Gender inequality, therefore, is not a single variable that can be adequately indexed or measured statistically; rather, it is a historically contingent complex confluence of socio-cultural power relationships, including associated subjective understandings.[35] Such relationships are not easily transferable into numerical data.

It is for these reasons that many feminists have chosen the qualitative case-study methods of the type that I have described—as well as other methods that can be subsumed under methodological post-positivist labels. This does not mean, however, that feminists should be averse to using quantitative measures of gender inequality and gender oppression in appropriate ways as improved partial measures of these phenomena are becoming available.

Due to the efforts of women's international organizing, especially around the United Nations Decade for Women (1975–1985), the UN began to disaggregate data by sex thus helping to bring the plight of women to the world's attention. The United Nations Human Development Report of 1995 focused specifically on women and gender issues for the first time. In that report, the United Nations Human Development Programme first introduced its gender development index (GDI) based on gender differences in life expectancy, earned income, illiteracy, and enrollment in education. It also introduced the gender empowerment measure (GEM) based on the proportion of women in parliament and in economic leadership positions (Benería 2003, 19–20; Seager 2003, 12–13). While still crude indicators, the GDI and the GEM do give us comparative cross-national evidence about the status of women relative to men that can be used for comparative analysis and to suggest directions for improvement.[36] It is data such as these, which go beyond traditional

---

35. These are "social facts" as opposed to "natural kinds." Therefore, they require different types of explanation from those modeled on the natural sciences. Useful for this purpose is John Ruggie's discussion of Polkinghorne's "narrative explanation," a method of interrogative reasoning in which a dialectic process takes place between events which allow them to be grasped as parts of one story which is believable to others looking at the same events (Ruggie 1998, 94).

36. Joni Seager's *Atlas of Women in the World* (Seager 2003) provides a wide range of data on gender inequality in map form, much of it from UN and other international and regional organizations' data. See also UNIFEM (2002).

categorizations of national accounts, that support feminists' claims about gender inequality and help efforts to pressure states and international organizations to design and support public policies that are better for women and other disadvantaged people. They also provide evidence for transnational movements lobbying for the improvement of human rights. Economic data have also provided important evidence for the growing field of feminist economics and the large body of literature on gender in development (see, for example, Benería 2003). Due to efforts by the International Research and Training Institute for the Advancement of Women (INSTRAW) and the Statistical Office of the UN, a consensus has been reached about the need to measure unpaid domestic work through the use of time-use surveys (Benería 2003, 141).

Nevertheless, feminists, who are willing to use indicators of gender inequality and gender oppression descriptively, are often reluctant to take the next step in conventional explanatory social scientific quantitative analysis. Causally oriented explanations of gender inequality that depend on replicable observable regularities are not consistent with feminist understandings of gender as a socially constructed hierarchical relationship of power. Given their skepticism as to the adequacy of causally oriented statistical analyses for understanding or explaining such relationships, it is unlikely that most IR feminists will rely heavily on quantitative data to support and enhance their efforts to understand how states and the global economy are historically constituted as gendered structures and the implications this has for the lives and well-being of their citizens.

CONCLUSION

In this chapter I have offered some reasons that most IR feminists have chosen to conduct their research outside positivist social scientific frameworks. I have suggested that many of the questions they have posed are not yet answerable within such frameworks. While there is no such thing as a feminist method, there are distinct feminist perspectives on methodology that have emerged out of a deep skepticism about traditional knowledge—knowledge that is based largely on certain privileged men's lives and men's experiences. The two case studies that I discussed illustrate the parallels between IR feminists' methodological sensitivities and these methodological perspectives from other disciplines. These IR feminists are asking questions about the linkages between the everyday lived experiences of women and the constitution and exercise of political and economic power at the state and global level. Specifically, they seek to understand how gender and other hierarchies of power affect those at the margins of the system. Their findings reveal states constituted in gendered ways whose security-seeking practices frequently render the lives of their most powerless citizens more insecure. Such redefinitions of security challenge us to think about tensions between state and human security.

IR feminists are asking questions that have rarely or never been asked before in IR; moreover, as I have demonstrated, they are questions that probably *could not* be asked within the epistemological boundaries of positivist social scientific approaches to the discipline. Feminists share with other social constructivists an interest in constitutive questions; however, they are unique in asking questions about socially constructed gender hierarchies and the implications of these gender hierarchies for the behavior of states and the functioning of the global economy. Feminist answers to these questions demonstrate how gender is a pervasive feature of international life and international politics, the implications of which go well beyond its effects on women.

For these reasons, and others that I have discussed, in the foreseeable future at least, IR feminists are likely to favor hermeneutic and interpretive methodologies that expose and help explain these structural relationships. They are also likely to prefer methods that allow subjects to document their own experiences in their own terms. Frequently, these are experiences about which there is little available data since they have been either ignored or categorized in ways that deny their subjects their own identities. As more relevant data become available, it is likely that many feminists will use them to enrich their textured accounts of the lives of those who have not been previously considered as subjects of knowledge. Constructing knowledge from the standpoint of the outsider provides us not only with a wider perspective but also with a unique perspective on knowledge about insiders. Since it offers us a more complex picture of reality, practical knowledge, or knowledge from below, has the potential to extend the boundaries and even transform the discipline in ways that are beneficial for everyone.

While feminists have been skeptical of conventional social science methods for reasons I have illustrated, feminists have been open to combining methods and critically reflecting on which of them are the most useful tools for designing and implementing research that will have the most positive impact on women's (and men's) lives. It is likely that IR feminists will continue to take this pragmatic multimethod approach rather than adhere to the single logic of social scientific inquiry defined by Keohane. But these choices are not easy ones; in the United States they carry considerable professional risk as long as the power inequalities and differential reward structure remain so large between those who adhere to conventional social scientific methodologies and those who employ alternative ones. Should we not ask on whose terms wider agreements about these methodological issues should be based?

CHAPTER 8

Dealing with Difference: Problems and Possibilities for Dialogue in International Relations

2011

The purpose of religious communication among human beings of different commitments is mutual enrichment and enhancement of respect and appreciation rather than hope that the person spoken to will prove to be wrong in what he regards as sacred. Dialogue must not degenerate into a dispute, into an effort on the part of each to get the upper hand.

Heschel, quoted in Jackson 2011, 188

Patrick Jackson uses these words of religious scholar Abraham Heschel to open the concluding chapter of his book, *The Conduct of Inquiry in International Relations*, which he titles "A Pluralist Science of IR." Just as Heschel was seeking interfaith dialogue that respected all religious traditions equally, the purpose of this chapter is to assess the possibilities, as well as the problems, for reaching a mutually respectful dialogue among IR scholars from different methodological persuasions and from different geographic locations. I believe that this would involve envisaging a discipline that is more genuinely international and more pluralist in its methodological commitments than the one we have today.

In the introduction to their book *International Scholarship Around the World*, published in 2009, Ole Waever and Arlene Tickner describe an IR that still speaks from the center about the whole, an IR where there is scant dialogue among competing perspectives; they see a discipline that is neither international nor reflexive about its own practices (Tickner and Waever 2009, 3–4). The various chapters of this important book provide a valuable and unusual look at IR theory from the perspective of scholars in different geographical locations; in the final chapter, Tickner and Waever conclude that, while IR is still dominated by the West, particularly by the United States, Western IR does translate into something different when it travels to the periphery (Tickner and Waever 2009, 338). Nevertheless, as they argue, true dialogue can only begin when there is more than one voice and, I would add, when there is mutual respect across geographical and methodological boundaries and when communication is among equal conversational partners. Tickner and Waever signal that this volume is the first of three; the aim of the third is, in their words, "to seek out more explosive mechanisms for exposing IR's claims of universality. . . . and to explore the role of non-core thinking in creating a post-western discipline (Tickner and Waever 2009, 340).[1] Although I cannot claim to speak from a non-Western perspective, I offer some thoughts on how those of us in the West, who speak from a critical perspective, might contribute to this post-Western vision. I take this up in more detail in Part Three.

Drawing on the observations of scholars who have reflected on the origins and development of what many claim is still a US-dominated field, I begin by briefly revisiting IR's great debates, since they represent the way the discipline has traditionally defined itself. For the most part, these debates have been about challenging the predominance of a US-centered discipline committed to neo-positivist methodologies. Drawing on postcolonial and feminist literatures, I then offer some suggestions as to how we might envisage an IR that is built on more global foundations and on a more pluralist understanding of what we define as scientific knowledge. Since women, and marginalized people more generally, have rarely been the creators or subjects of knowledge, postcolonial and feminist scholars have been on the forefront of critical disciplinary self-reflection. In conclusion, I shall offer some thoughts on possible paths toward placing different scientific traditions on a more equal and mutually respectful footing.

REVISITING THE GREAT DEBATES

As IR theorist Ole Waever claimed in his 1998 article, "The Sociology of a Not So International Discipline," IR scholars have tended to write about the history of the discipline as a series of methodological debates about who is right and who is wrong about how we construct knowledge (Waever 1998, 3). As he pointed out, issues of power and privilege are at stake; the winners, many of them located in the mainstream of what he describes as a US-dominated

---

1. Since this chapter was first written, volumes two and three, both edited by Tickner and David Blaney, have been published. See Tickner and Blaney (2012) and Tickner and Blaney (2013).

social science, have rarely been willing to engage the losers—not a very promising path to dialogue.

The first debate, between realists and idealists, traditionally portrayed as the founding moment of the discipline, was well suited to the emergence of realism as the dominant paradigm, and the United States as the dominant site for IR, in the post–World War II era. The second debate, between traditionalists and social scientists, seemed, in the United States at least, to signal victory for the scientists, where quantification, formal modeling, and rational choice theory have become methodologies of choice (Jackson 2011, 6) Although this shift was less evident in Europe, it did grant American IR a "scientific" legitimacy.

Naming Hans Morgenthau, whose work was discussed in Chapter 1, as the founding father of the discipline, Stanley Hoffmann, in his much-cited 1977 article, asked why it was in the United States that Morgenthau's *Politics Among Nations* received such widespread attention and why henceforward IR became what he, somewhat ironically, termed "an American social science." According to Hoffmann, the realist view of the world was well suited to America's new role as emerging global superpower. Although Morgenthau himself was ambivalent about a "science" of international politics, an issue I will explore more fully in Chapter 10, the postwar United States provided a favorable institutional climate for the receptivity of the scientific tradition, as well as a peculiarly American conviction that all problems are solvable through the scientific method (Hoffmann 1977, 45). As I have claimed in previous chapters, the aura around this very limited and narrow definition of science has placed a burden on other approaches to demonstrate their scientific credibility and has, in my view, been the greatest barrier to constructive dialogue across paradigms.

Hoffmann did note that the popularity of scientific methodologies in the United States did not travel well to other parts of the world. What he saw as the failure of IR to become a truly international discipline has remained a dominant theme among those who have reflected subsequently on the evolution of the field. In 1998, almost ten years after the third, or what some have termed the fourth, debate—variously described as one between positivists and post-positivists, or rationalists and reflectivists—Ole Waever noted a continuation of US hegemony and its continued bias toward rational choice theory (Waever 1998). Four years later, Steve Smith claimed that US IR, which he still regarded as hegemonic, had narrowed rather than broadened in spite of the inability of rational choice theory to explain the events of September 11, 2001. He warned that a discipline dominated by rational choice and positivist methodologies more generally "runs the risk of failing to understand other cultures and identities and thereby becoming more and more a US discipline far removed from the agendas and concerns of other parts of the world" (Smith 2002, 68). For Smith the most irreconcilable divide, and hence the greatest barrier to productive dialogue, was over questions of epistemology, a position with which I strongly agree—at least from my location inside the United States. According to Smith, reflectivists or post-positivists, a category that encompasses a rich array of theoretical approaches, all of which offer a series of alternatives to rationalism, are presented by the mainstream as operating outside the acceptable realm of academic study, not part of the social scientific enterprise (Smith 2002, 72).

While I recognize that there is a much more methodologically pluralist IR scholarship in Europe and elsewhere, it is the case that US theoretical traditions and American foreign policy concerns have shaped, to a disproportionate degree, the agenda of IR as well as its methods of analysis. Following Hoffmann, Thomas Biersteker, in his chapter in the Tickner and Waever volume, points to the interface between the US role of managing and controlling the international system and the preference of IR theorists for causal models and analysis. Biersteker is not making an argument against causal analysis but for the recognition of the legitimacy of interpretive understanding and critical theory also, both of which he finds lacking in US postgraduate education (Biersteker 2009, 322–323). He claims that everyone, including critics, appears to be engaged in US-dominated debates, an engagement that is not reciprocated. Citing his 1984 article coauthored with Hayward Alker, Biersteker claims that it is not the false universalism of an American-dominated discipline but "the oppositions and penetrations (of different theoretical traditions from different parts of the world) [that] make up both the substance and the promise of a truly global 'interdiscipline' of IR" (Biersteker 2009, 322). Building on this vision, evident in the Tickner and Waever volume more generally, I offer some thoughts as to how we might get beyond these unproductive debates that I have outlined here and in previous chapters in Part Two and move toward a more international and pluralist discipline that is built on less West-centric foundations and is more respectful of multiple ways of understanding our complex world, an issue I will take up in greater detail in Part Three.

BUILDING MORE INCLUSIVE FOUNDATIONAL STORIES

As Sandra Halperin has claimed, the historical accounts on which much of mainstream IR theory depends are shaped by a profound mythology about modern European history, one that wrongly places Europe at the center of modernity and transforms Europe's imperial expansion into a story of enlightenment and progress (Halperin 2006, 57). IR dates the beginnings of modern international politics to the Treaty of Westphalia in 1648 and the rise of the modern nation-state in Europe. This Eurocentric account portrays a linear progression toward modernity whereby values of liberty and democracy and economic development were spread around the world through the power, knowledge, and agency of European states. After the collapse of the colonial empires during the twentieth century, the European state system became universalized.

As Halperin reminds us, missing from this story is Europe's brutal expansion that began in 1492 with the so-called "voyages of discovery." Although IR has focused on relations between the great powers in a world of nation-states, it is European colonization and imperialism that have shaped the present and future of more than two-thirds of the world's population. Curiously missing, both from the progressive Eurocentric Westphalian narrative and from the contemporary discipline that describes and analyzes it, are issues of imperialism and race, subjects which were of vital concern to IR scholars at the discipline's founding moments in the early twentieth century. A discipline that claims to be international, of relevance to all peoples and states, traces its modern origins to a time at which imperialism was at its height: yet most recent surveys of IR have little to say about the history of four hundred years of European colonization or of decolonization, one of the most important processes of the twentieth century (Gruffydd Jones 2006, 2).

Any attempt to construct a global IR must recognize this historical legacy of imperialism. In their revisionist account of the early discipline, David Long and Brian Schmidt claim that it was the dynamic interaction between imperialism and internationalism, not the realist/idealist debate, which initially drove IR theory during its founding moments (Long and Schmidt 2005, 1). Many of the IR texts of the early twentieth century evidenced a preoccupation with the administration of the empire. Relatedly, Robert Vitalis claims that white supremacy had a central place in the origins and development of IR (Vitalis 2005, 161). The first IR journal in the United States, founded in 1910, was called the *Journal of Race Development*; later, in 1922, it became *Foreign Affairs,* the official journal of the Council on Foreign Relations. The lead article of the first issue made the case for a research agenda focused on the progress of backward races and states. As the journal's original title makes clear, in 1910, boundaries that were drawn between what is inside and outside the national space were not so much a territorial question as a biological one. An imperialist world order produced administrative problems for the colonizers that begged for scientific study and solutions—an important motivator for the young discipline of international relations (Vitalis 2005, 171). In other words, the importance of scientific study of global issues was recognized well before post–World War II realism. Indeed, postcolonial historians and philosophers of science have long recognized the intimate relationship between Western science and the imperial project (Harding 1998).

Geographer John Willinsky (1998, 27) has linked the way we construct modern knowledge to European imperialism. He claims that five centuries of learning, although generally helpful for humankind, have divided knowledge in certain ways that give certain people agency and authorship while denying them to others. The Cartesian revolution of the seventeenth century shifted knowledge based on resemblances to knowledge based on difference—such as the differences between mind and body, men and women, West and East, and colonizers and colonized. Studying, classifying, and ordering humanity within an imperial context gave rise to peculiar and powerful ideas about race, culture, and nation that were conceptual instruments that the West used to divide up and to educate the world (Willinsky 1998, 3). Willinsky argues that the lessons that were drawn from centuries of European expansion continue to influence, even if subconsciously, how we see and interpret the world today. While Willinsky is not engaging specifically with IR, evidence of these differences can be seen in West-centric modernization stories, clashes of civilizations, and gendered and racial assumptions about who are the creators of knowledge.

Branwen Gruffydd Jones, in the introduction to her edited text *Decolonizing International Relations,* claims that a discipline rooted in European history and classical thought and largely written by and about Americans and Europeans, has forgotten its imperial roots. Echoing Willinsky, she suggests that the way to a more truly "international" understanding of the world is to confront the colonial heritage that modern IR has failed to shed (Gruffydd Jones 2006, 6). Gruffydd Jones does not believe that this can be accomplished by simply applying existing IR knowledge to the rest of the world or by Eurocentric critics: the dispossessed must tell their own history. Authors in the volume consider the question as to how best to puncture the myth of Europe and produce knowledge that is both of and about the international. Too frequently, critical voices are still speaking out of Western knowledge traditions.

Agreeing that one can be Eurocentric at the same time as being critical of the West, John Hobson has observed that many critical IR theorists end up reiterating the conventional Western narrative (Hobson 2007, 93).[2] Focusing on Gramscian IR, Hobson claims that examining the economic and political hegemony of the West by reasoning backward, critical theorists end up imputing inevitability to the rise of the West as endogenously self-generating. He suggests that the way out of this dilemma is to shift toward dialogical thinking that transcends the either/or logic that Willinsky attributes to modern knowledge. Drawing on the work of Jan Nederveen Pieterse, he suggests using the term *hybridity,* a co-constitutive process that recognizes that histories of different civilizations are mutually constitutive of each other. Instead of a clash of civilizations, he suggests a dialogue that demonstrates the multiple non-conflictual ways that each civilization borrows from and emanates others. This happens at what he calls the edges of civilizations, conceptualized

2. For an extensive treatment of the problems of Eurocentrism in world politics, see Hobson (2012).

as *imperial dialectical frontiers,* where a bottom-up logic of emancipation/resistance is intertwined with a top-down logic of imperial domination (Hobson 2007, 107–108). Hobson talks of the pressing need for the creation of political dialogue between West and East, which he defines as all parts of the world outside the West. This would be accomplished by an empathetic approach where all peoples of the world can communicate together as equal partners, where Self and Other are not separate and exclusive but intimately intertwined (Hobson 2007, 115).

Of course, there are major stumbling blocks to Hobson's call for a mutually respectful dialogue among equal partners who respect each other's foundational stories and knowledge traditions. First and foremost is the issue of power—whose knowledge is considered legitimate? Also, there are enormous inequalities in material resources that determine where, and by whom, that knowledge gets produced. As I have emphasized in previous chapters, the problems of creating mutual dialogue in the face of these hierarchies of power, as well as writing history from below, have been central concerns of feminist theory. Drawing on some recent feminist contributions to IR, I shall now suggest some ways that we might envisage a more pluralist discipline that is open to different knowledge traditions.

BUILDING A MORE METHODOLOGICALLY INCLUSIVE IR

As Brooke Ackerly, Maria Stern, and Jacqui True remind us, developing feminist methodologies and conducting feminist research have been major challenges in a state-centric discipline that is notorious for its lack of self-reflection on its own origins (Ackerly, Stern, and True 2006, 1). Yet I believe that the way feminists have gone about meeting these challenges are instructive for thinking about possibilities for constructing a more genuinely pluralist discipline of international relations. As described in previous chapters, IR feminist scholarship has built on a variety of methodologies and methods, both mainstream and critical, and both from inside and outside the discipline. What makes feminist methodologies distinctive is their commitment to constructing knowledge from multiple locations, and from the perspective of both marginalized and non-marginalized subjects. Feminism also alerts us to the importance of studying silences and absences.

In their 2010 book, Brooke Ackerly and Jacqui True conceive of feminist methodologies as involving self-conscious reflection on the purpose of one's research, one's conceptual frameworks, one's ethical responsibilities, one's choices of methods, and one's assumptions about what it means to know rather than just believe something (Ackerly and True 2010, 6). They describe this as a feminist research ethic—"a methodological commitment to any set of practices that reflect on the power of epistemology, boundaries, dimensions of the researcher's own location and to a normative commitment to transforming the social order in order to promote gender justice" (Ackerly and True 2010, 2). A feminist research ethic alerts us to the power of disciplinary boundaries that operate in the way that researchers construct boundaries about what is acceptable and not acceptable in a discipline. IR's frequent dismissal of scholarship deemed unscientific is an example of such disciplining.

Reflexivity, a methodology preferred by many IR feminists, has a long history in the social sciences more generally. The capacity of human beings to reflect on their own situations has served as the foundation for arguments for separating the social from the natural sciences. The knowing subject is located in a variety of hierarchical social structures, such as race, class, and gender, and knowledge of the world begins with the socially situated self, not with a world that can never be independent of the researcher (Jackson 2011, 157–160). Reflexivity is deeper than reflection, or what mainstream scholars mean when they use the term "reflectivist." By way of conclusion, I shall return to Patrick Jackson's book to which I referred at the beginning of this chapter, and its suggestions for constructing a more pluralist science of IR.

POSSIBILITIES FOR A PLURALIST "SCIENCE" OF IR

Patrick Jackson offers one possible way out of these methodological disputes that have inhibited a genuinely international IR and contributed to the dominance of an "American discipline." Like Steve Smith, Jackson (2011, chap. 1) claims that science has been a powerful resource among IR scholars, since accusing work of being "non-scientific" carries very negative connotations. While mainstream IR scholars have lauded the term, there is considerable ambiguity as to what "science" actually means, although, in IR, it has come to be identified with positivism. Jackson argues for a broader Weberian definition that equates science with any empirical inquiry designed to produce systematic and valid knowledge about the world (Jackson 2011, 193). Jackson outlines four scientific approaches, which are all used in IR scholarship: neopositivism, critical realism, analyticism, and reflexivity. He acknowledges the importance of feminism in introducing reflexivity into IR and cites Tickner and Waever's call for a global sociology of IR as an example of reflexive scholarship (Jackson 2011, 185). An important distinction between these four scientific traditions is the relationship between the knower and the known or how their practitioners are hooked up to the world—whether as outsiders or insiders. Positivism and critical realism both accept the Cartesian mind-world dualism while analyticism and reflexivity, typical of some of the literature I have discussed, assume a mind world monism in which the researcher is part of the world that she or he is studying. Whatever approach scholars choose to take is up to them but, importantly, all are granted the status of science, which means that we must all accept that it is not permissible to judge one methodology by standards of evaluation suitable for another, a problem that post-positivist feminists, including myself, encounter frequently.[3]

As I have argued in previous chapters in Part Two, conversations about epistemology will never be productive until methodologies that are labeled "unscientific" by the mainstream are accorded their scientific legitimacy and those who work outside positivist scientific traditions are not asked to redefine their research in positivist terms (Tickner 1997; Keohane 1998). While still speaking from a Western scientific tradition—albeit one that is more broadly defined—Jackson's wider definition of science offers a useful path to more productive dialogues. However, we live in a world in which the majority of the world's population does not live in the West. While we in the West have the responsibility to be reflective about our own knowledge, in Abraham Heschel's words, we must also seek out ways for "mutual enrichment" and dialogue, and show respect for a variety of knowledge traditions, outside our own, each of which can illuminate paths to less conflictual and more just futures.

3. For a feminist critique of Jackson's book see Sylvester (2013). This article is one of several that engage in critical discussion of Jackson's book published in the journal *Millennium: Journal of International Studies* in 2013 (41:1).

PART III

Exploring Some Contemporary Themes and New Directions

In parallel with my methodological engagements over the past ten years, I was inspired to think about what feminist perspectives could tell us about some of the new issues on IR's security agenda, issues that seemed to overwhelm the promise of a new more "cooperative" and "peaceful" world order, - the way the 1990s were portrayed, at least, in the United States.[1]

While I realize that many places in the world were suffering the tragic consequences of conflict through much of the previous decade, the wake-up call for Americans came on September 11, 2001. No longer did the US seem invincible. Looking at this event through gender lenses, it was remarkable the extent to which it stimulated a return to a warrior type of hypermasculinity and even the blaming of feminism and other kinds of critical thinking for the events of 9/11. The sudden popularity of Samuel Huntington's *Clash of Civilizations* that even appeared in airport bookstores, described an over-simplified version of America's new enemies who dwelt on the other side of irreparable civilizational fault-lines. In chapter nine, originally presented at the Council on Foreign Relations in New York in 2002, I offer a feminist analysis of September 11, 2001 and its aftermath. I demonstrate how gendered discourses were used, as they often are in conflict situations, to reinforce mutual hostilities. As discussed in more detail in chapter two, men's association with war-fighting and national security serves to reinforce their legitimacy in world politics while it acts to create barriers for women. I conclude by offering some alternative, less warrior-like models of masculinity and

---

1. I put these terms in quotes because there were many conflicts taking place during the 1990s although they did not engage the great powers directly as had the Cold War. And the fact that the great powers were able to act somewhat cooperatively, at least without a Russian veto, in the First Gulf War and the wars in former Yugoslavia seemed to hold promise for multilateralism.

some cultural representations less dependent on the subordination of women. Often in times of conflict women are seen only as victims. I outline some ways in which the women of Afghanistan were fighting against gender oppression and I conclude with some thoughts on their future prospects.

In its efforts to understand these new conflicts, quite unlike the wars that realist theory was designed to explain, IR began to turn its attention to religion, an area that had being completely neglected by a discipline strongly committed to secular rationalist ways of thinking and the conventional methodologies that I critiqued in Part II. The discipline has shown a strong resurgence of interest in religion in the last ten years but, as is often the case, new work on religion in IR has largely ignored gender. But it is also the case that IR feminists have largely ignored religion –perhaps for the same reason that feminists have been ambivalent about peace and also because all institutionalized religions have diminished women. My research for the 9/11 case stimulated me to explore religion in the context of IR further. Written originally as a contribution to a volume celebrating the work of Robert Keohane (Tickner, 2009), chapter ten takes up IR's inability to fit religion into its conventional explanations of war and begins to explore how methodologies more often used by feminists might help to explain religious motivations. It asks whether western secular theories and knowledge traditions are adequate for understanding the religious motivations and worldviews of those who themselves express a deep hostility to modernity and secular thinking. It suggests that hermeneutic, reflexive and dialogical methodologies, more characteristic of religious thinking and also more typically employed by IR feminists, may be more suitable for understanding these worldviews. It concludes by looking at the work of some Islamic scholars, as well as secular and religious feminist scholarship, looking for possible ways of transcending this religious/secular divide.

Attempts to understand better the views of others, that I discuss in chapters nine and ten, led me to think more deeply about how we might tell more inclusive stories about IR that are less Westcentric. The religious and ethnic conflicts of the post-9/11 world, as well as the recent shocks to a western-led global economy, have raised serious challenges to the liberal modernization story, the dominant narrative in the story we tell about the history of the IR discipline, whereby a secular West would lead the world towards a universalized nation-state system and a capitalist world economy. Chapter eleven goes back to the seventeenth century and the founding of the Westphalian state system where this triumphalist story of the origins of IR is thought to have begun, and critically reexamines some of IR's foundational stories. It draws on feminist and postcolonial approaches to suggest some different foundational stories that start with the lives of those who have rarely been the subjects of International Relations and who inhabit spaces rarely analyzed by the discipline. Originally given as a keynote address at the 2010 meeting of the

Oceanic Conference of International Studies held in Auckland, New Zealand, this chapter reflects the influence of scholars in this region.

It is curious the extent to which IR has written the issues of race and empire out of its conventional history, issues that are fueling contemporary hostility against the West. My engagement with feminist analysis over the past twenty-five years, has convinced me that the way we tell our historical stories about our discipline has an important influence on how we construct contemporary knowledge—whose stories get heard and whose are silenced. This has implications for whose knowledge is seen as legitimate and how that knowledge gets used in both the academic and the policy worlds. And, as I claim in chapter eight, until we accord equal respect to different stories, we cannot hope to build a pluralist discipline that is mutually respectful of a variety of knowledge traditions.

CHAPTER 9

Feminist Perspectives on 9/11

2002

Our brothers who fought in Somalia saw wonders about the weakness, feebleness, and cowardliness of the U.S. soldier.... [W]e believe that we are men, Muslim men who must have the honor of defending [Mecca]. We do not want American women soldiers defending [it].... The rulers in that region have been deprived of their manhood.... By God, Muslim women refuse to be defended by these American and Jewish prostitutes.

Osama bin Laden[1]

As women gain power in these [Western] countries, [they] should become less aggressive, adventurous, competitive, and violent.

Francis Fukuyama (1998, 27)

The operative word is men. Brawny, heroic, manly men.

Patricia Leigh Brown (2001, 5)

I don't want any women to go to my grave...during my funeral or any occasion thereafter.

Mohamed Atta[2]

War gives purpose to life.... Peace brings out the silliness in man; war makes him imitate the tiger.

George S. Patton, Jr.[3]

My nation's wrath has empowered me
My ruined and burnt villages fill me with hatred against the enemy
Oh compatriot, no longer regard me weak and incapable,
My voice has mingled with thousands of arisen women

---

1. December 1998, from an interview with al-Jazeera television, quoted in Judt (2001). I realize that the sufferings associated with these kinds of conflicts had been present for people in many parts of the world before September 11, 2001.

2. Will of Mohamed Atta found in a suitcase at Logan International Airport in Boston. Quoted in the *New York Times*, October 4, 2001, B5.

3. "A World Too Intoxicated by the Wine of War," *Los Angeles Times*, October 8, 2001.

My fists are clenched with fists of thousands of compatriots
To break all these sufferings, all these fetters of slavery.
I'm the woman who has awoken,
I've found my path and will never return.

Meena[4]

GENDERED IMAGES

Following the tragic events of September 11, 2001, in the United States, gendered images were everywhere, many of them threatening. Osama bin Laden taunted the West for becoming feminized; Francis Fukuyama was concerned about it, too. In a 1998 article in *Foreign Affairs*, Fukuyama, although more positive than bin Laden about what they both saw as the feminization of Western culture, pointed to similar dangers. He counseled against putting women in charge of US foreign policy and the military because of their inability to stand up to unspecified dangers (perhaps more specific since 9/11) from "those [non-democratic] parts of the world run by young, ambitious, unconstrained men," (Fukuyama 1998, 36, 38). Five years earlier, Samuel Huntington (1993) warned of a "clash of civilizations," an only slightly veiled reference to a demographically exploding Islam, a "fault line" between Western Christian societies that have progressed in terms of economic development and democratization, and the Muslim world where young men's frustrations are fueled by the failure of these same phenomena.[5]

For others the danger was closer to home; the "real" fault lines were here in the United States. In a 1994 article that lauded Huntington's clash of civilizations thesis, James Kurth focused attention on the "real clash," an internal one. Extolling the rise of Western civilization and the Enlightenment, a secular society based on individualism, liberalism, constitutionalism, human rights, the rule of law, free markets, and the separation of church and state, which came of age at the beginning of the twentieth century, Kurth saw the Enlightenment in decline at the century's end. What he termed "post-industrialism" has moved women into the labor market and out of the home with negative consequences for children, particularly those reared in split family or single-parent households. The United States was, according to Kurth, threatened not only by feminism, which bears the responsibility for the liberation of women, but also by multiculturalism—the presence, and recognition, of large numbers of African Americans, Latino Americans, and Asian

---

4. Meena was the founding leader of RAWA (Revolutionary Association of the Women of Afghanistan). She was assassinated in Quetta, Pakistan, in 1987. Poem from RAWA website, http://www.rawa.org.

5. For a more elaborated version of this argument, see Huntington (1996, 20–32).

Americans who, unlike earlier immigrant populations, remain unassimilated in terms of Western liberal ideas (Kurth 1994, 14).[6]

The fears of these scholars, and Fukuyama's solution—to keep strong men in charge—seemed more real in the aftermath of 9/11 than when they were first articulated. Post–9/11 discourse produced some strange bedfellows. As bin Laden goaded America for its moral decadency and lack of manliness, Jerry Falwell and Pat Robertson blamed 9/11 on the ACLU, homosexuals, and feminists because they "make God mad" (Scheer 2001a). The terrorists were those unconstrained young men, some of whom managed to live among us rather than "out there" beyond the fault line. So, contra bin Laden, masculinity was back in vogue in the United States. Writing in 2002, Peggy Noonan proclaimed that, since 9/11, "the male hero has been a predominant cultural image, presenting a beefy front of strength to a nation seeking steadiness and emotional grounding. They are the new John Waynes... men who charge up the stairs in a hundred pounds of gear, and tell everyone else where to go to be safe."[7] In spite of the Bush administration's appointment of the first female national security adviser, TV screens after 9/11 were full of (mostly white) men in charge, briefing us about "America's New War" both at home and abroad. We felt safer when "our men" were protecting us (against other men) and our way of life.

So where did all the women go? According to an analysis by the British newspaper *The Guardian,* women virtually disappeared from newspaper pages and TV screens after 9/11.[8] Carol Gilligan noted that men's rising star all but eclipsed that of the many heroic women who rose to the occasion, as firefighters or police officers.[9] Women were also among the combat forces deployed in Afghanistan where male warriors waving guns and shouting death to America looked menacing and unrestrained. If we did see women, they were likely to be faceless Afghan women in the now familiar blue *burqa.* Their shadowy and passive presence seemed only to reinforce these gendered images I have drawn.[10]

Yet the picture was more complicated. Bin Laden taunted the West for its feminization, but he also railed against its "crusaders," an image more likely to

---

6. It should be noted that women's equality was not even thought of at the birth of the Enlightenment. For a discussion of women's unequal incorporation into the modern Western state, see Pateman (1988). Males in the workforce have never received much criticism for neglecting their children. For ideas, similar to Kurth's, about the negative effects of cultural diversity, see also Huntington (1996, 304) and Fukuyama (2000). Fukuyama (1999) also emphasizes the negative effects of 1960s women's liberation.

7. Peggy Noonan, quoted in Brown (2001).

8. *The Guardian,* September 20, 2001. Cited from http://www.guardian.co.uk/analysis/story/0,3604,554794,00.html.

9. Quoted in Brown (2001).

10. This gendered image of Afghanistan—men fighting and women invisible—was further reinforced by a comment by US Secretary of Defense Donald Rumsfield on the PBS *Lehrer Newshour* on November 7, 2001, when he claimed that there were no people in Afghanistan who were not armed and fighting.

invoke medieval knights on horseback than the modern-day "feminized" men about whom Fukuyama, as well as bin Laden, was concerned. And the masculinity of bin Laden's own foot soldiers also came under scrutiny. Mohamed Atta, whose last will and testament banned women from his grave lest they pollute it, was "a polite shy boy who came of age in an Egypt torn between growing Western influence and the religious fundamentalism that gathered force in reaction,...[he] had two sisters headed for careers as a professor and a doctor." Grumbling that his wife was raising him as a girl, his father is reputed to have "told him [Atta] I needed to hear the word 'doctor' in front of his name....We told him your sisters are doctors...and you are the man of the family."[11]

And, contra Fukuyama's and Kurth's fears about the feminized weakening of America, American women supported the war effort in overwhelming numbers while Afghan women beneath the *burqa* protested American bombing and exhorted their sisters to fight against gender oppression. The US Catholic bishops gave qualified support to the war on the grounds that it was a just war (Cooperman, 2001), while realist John Mearsheimer (2001) counseled against it. Liberals, such as Laurence Tribe, condoned the use of military tribunals and the detention of more than 1,200 young men, none of whom (as of December 2001) had been charged in connection with the attacks.[12]

So, if the story was not a simple one where gender and other ideological lines were firmly drawn, what can a feminist analysis add to our understanding of 9/11 and its aftermath? The statements with which I begin this chapter offer support for the claim that war both reinforces gender stereotypes and shakes up gender expectations (Goldstein, 2002). The conduct of war is a largely male activity on both sides but Meena, the founder of the Revolutionary Association of the Women of Afghanistan (RAWA), exhorted women to fight, too. Nevertheless, gender is a powerful legitimator of war and national security; our acceptance of a "re-masculinized" society during times of war and uncertainty rises considerably. And the power of gendered expectations and identifications have real consequences for women and for men—consequences that are frequently ignored by conventional accounts of war and civilizational clashes.

Using the gendered framework to analyze war and peace that I developed in Chapter 2, I will show how gendered discourses were used on both sides to reinforce mutual hostilities and their consequences for both women and men. I discuss the much-publicized representation of Afghan women as victims, as well as the less familiar ways—at least to us—in which they were fighting back. Through this case, I suggest how feminist analysis exposes and

11. "A Portrait of the Terrorist: From Shy Child to Single-Minded Killer," *New York Times,* October 10, 2001, p. B9.
12. *The Nation,* December 17, 2001, p. 4.

questions these stereotypical gender representations and demonstrates their negative consequences. I conclude with three generalized lessons that I take from this feminist analysis.

GENDERING 9/11

America under Attack

"This is the warriors' time, the warriors, the martyrs—they're all men."[13] Those we feared after 9/11 were angry young men wielding rifles and shouting "Death to America." Many of them were trained in madrassas—religious schools that teach little except an extreme version of Islam to boys and young men; many of them come from refugee camps where they live in poverty with few prospects in life. Frequently, they are also taught to hate women; in a situation where most of them feel powerless, the wielding of power over women can be a boost to self-esteem. Although Mohamed Atta's middle-class background does not fit this profile, this training must have alleviated his sense of inferiority with respect to the women in his own domestic life.

According to Ian Buruma and Avishai Margalit (2002), this newest form of "Occidentalism," evident in the teaching of madrassas, comes out of a long, warlike tradition of hatred of the West, a hatred that appeals to those who feel impotent, marginalized, and denigrated. Tracing its roots back to nineteenth-century Russia and mid-twentieth-century Japan, they suggest that the objects of hate associated with Occidentalism, all of which played a significant role in the attacks of September 11, are materialism, liberalism, capitalism, rationalism, and feminism. All these phenomena are epitomized in city life with its multiculturalism, wealth, sexual license, and artistic freedom that result in decadence and moral laxity. The twin towers, as powerful symbols of urban secular wealth, were an apt target for vengeance against these evils. Gender symbolism and gender ambivalence borne out of misogyny abound in this discourse; the West is described as individualist, rational, and hard but, at the same time, decadent, effete, and addicted to personal safety at the expense of valuing the heroic self-sacrifice expected of "real men." Today's Occidentalists taunt the West with accusations of moral decadence in this world, yet promise sexual rewards for their men in heaven after their sacrificial death for the cause.

For Occidentalists, it is women's emancipation that leads to decadence. "Westoxification" denotes a plague from the West. Those most vulnerable are women, particularly middle-class women with a Western education; these women must be brought under control and conform to an idealized construct

---

13. Fouad Ajami, quoted in Croisette (2001).

of womanhood (Moghadan 1994, 13). The proper role for women is to be breeders of heroic men. For the Taliban, Occidental sinfulness was present even in Kabul with "girls in school and women with uncovered faces populating and defiling the public domain" (Buruma and Margalit 2002, 5). The ideational and material consequences of this misogynist discourse was brought home to us through the post–9/11 media focus on the plight of women in Afghanistan. But we must remember that it is not only those "out there" who engage in oppositional thinking with its negative gender stereotyping.

America Strikes Back

America may have surprised these warriors with the determination of its response. Belying bin Laden's taunts and Fukuyama's fear that the United States was becoming feminized and thus less able to defend itself, the US military response was swift and strong; it received high approval ratings from men and women alike.[14] From the start, policy-makers framed the attack and the US response as a war between good and evil—the message to the rest of the world was that you are either for us or against us—there could be no middle position. Random attacks on innocent people, identified by their attackers as Muslim, immediately following 9/11, which the Bush administration went to lengths to denounce, manifested an unpleasant form of Orientalism.

Given the massive sense of insecurity generated by the first foreign terrorist attack on American civilians at home, there was something reassuring about "our men" protecting us from "other men." However, even though the war exceeded all expectations in its swift destruction of the Taliban and al Qaeda networks, and despite increased attention to homeland security, the United States remained uncertain about its ability to deter future terrorist attacks.[15]

In light of these continued fears, the US Congress passed the USA Patriot Act, legislation that allowed the attorney general to detain aliens on mere suspicion and without a hearing. Prior to its passage, the United States had already detained more than 1,200 young men without charge; Arab men were subject to ethnic, as well as gender, profiling under the excuse that we were "at war." These measures received strong support across the political spectrum. Criticism was seen as unpatriotic.[16] Equally disturbing was a political climate, typical of countries at war, which fosters intolerance of alternative points of

14. On October 8, 2001, after the beginning of US bombing, support for the war was running at 87 percent of both women and men (Goldstein 2002).

15. Since the original article in was published in 2002, it is clear that these networks have not disappeared and have migrated to many other countries. However, there is evidence to suggest that they have been weakened

16. The naming of the USA Patriot Act was probably to forestall criticism.

view. Illustrations of this intolerance were prevalent in media discussion as well as in political discourse.

In an article in the *New York Times,* Edward Rothstein (2001) articulated his hope that the attacks of September 11 might challenge the intellectual and ethical perspectives of postmodernism and postcolonialism, thus leading to their rejection. Chastising adherents to these modes of thought for their extreme cultural relativism and rejection of objectivity and universalism, Rothstein expressed hope that, as it came to be realized how closely the 9/11 attacks came to undermining the political and military authority of the United States, these ways of thinking would come to be seen as "ethically perverse."

While the author did not mention feminism, feminists are frequently criticized on the same terms; women and feminists often get blamed in times of political, economic, and social uncertainty. Kurth's fear of feminists' destruction of the social fabric of society is one such example, and the association of patriotism with "hegemonic" masculinity challenges women, minorities, and "aliens" to live up to this standard. It is the case that postcolonialists and feminists have questioned objectivity and universalism; but they do so because they claim that these terms are frequently associated with ways of knowing that are not objective but are based only on the lives of (usually privileged) men. Many feminists are sympathetic with postcolonialism, a body of knowledge that attempts to uncover the voices of those who have been colonized and oppressed. It is a form of knowledge seeking that resonates with attempts to recover knowledge about women.

In a rather different piece, which acknowledged the recognition accorded to women of Afghanistan since 9/11, Sarah Wildman (2001) chastised American feminists on the grounds of irrelevance. Claiming that feminists had an unprecedented public platform because of the attention focused on women in Afghanistan, Wildman accused them of squandering their opportunity by refusing to support the war. Equating what she called "feminist dogma" with pacifism, Wildman asserted that there is no logical reason to believe that nonviolent means always promote feminist ends. Wildman fell into the essentialist trap of equating feminism with peace that I discussed in Chapter 2; this allowed her to dismiss feminist voices as irrelevant and unpatriotic. The feminists she selected to quote may have voiced reservations about the war, but feminism encompasses a wide range of opinions, many of which include fighting for justice, particularly gender justice. And feminist voices are not all Western, as is often assumed. In Afghanistan, women have been fighting a war that began well before September 11, a war against women.

Women under Attack

After November 17, 2001, when First Lady Laura Bush used the president's weekly radio address to urge worldwide condemnation of the treatment of women in Afghanistan, a speech that coincided with a State Department report on the Taliban's war against women, their plight was in the headlines in the United States (Stout 2001). Women in Afghanistan had not always been so oppressed. Prior to the Soviet invasion in 1979, women had been gaining rights; they had served in Parliament and in the professions and even as army generals. In 1970, 50 percent of students at Kabul University, 60 percent of teachers, and 40 percent of doctors in Afghanistan were women (Prosser 2001). Frequently, however, steps forward precipitated a backlash from traditional and rural communities (Amiri 2002). In 1989, Arab militants, working with the Afghan resistance to the Soviet Union based in Peshawar, Pakistan, issued a fatwa, or religious ruling, stating that Afghan women would be killed if they worked for humanitarian organizations. Subsequently Afghan women going to work were shot at and several were murdered. Soon after, another edict forbade Afghan women to "walk with pride" or walk in the middle of the street. This was followed by an edict in 1990 that decreed that women should not be educated; if they were, the Islamic movement would be tainted and thus meet with failure.

According to Human Rights Watch (2001), and supported by RAWA, the various parties that made up the United Front or Northern Alliance amassed a deplorable record of attacks on civilians during the civil war that took place in Afghanistan between 1992 and 1996, including the widespread rape of women. The Taliban came to power in 1996, promising to restore law and order and create a pure Islamic state that would guarantee the personal security of women and preserve the dignity of families (Mertus 2000, 56). At first, the restoration of order was seen as beneficial. But soon it was evident that the Taliban sought to erase women from public life and make them invisible in the name of "cleansing" Afghan society. Women were banned from employment, from education, and from going into public places without the accompaniment of a close male relative; they were required to be covered from head to toe in the familiar blue *burqa*. The Ministry for the Promotion of Virtue and the Prevention of Vice ruthlessly enforced these restrictions; in a mockery of female "protection," women were beaten publicly with leather batons containing metal studs for showing their hands or ankles, participating in home-based schooling, or violating any other of these restrictions.[17] For boys who have grown up and been socialized in the madrassas, the sight of a woman is the equivalent of seeing the foreign other, the incarnation of evil itself (Prosser 2001, 2). Given the ban on female employment, many women, particularly those without male relatives or supporters, were forced into begging and

17. It should be noted that men were also policed if their beards were not long enough or their dress not appropriate. However, men retained some control over their lives.

prostitution; restrictions on mobility meant that women and their children did not have access to health care.[18]

After the war, many women and children who were family members of fleeing or killed foreign Taliban fighters were stranded inside Afghanistan with nowhere to go to seek safety. And Afghanistan has always been a large source of refugees; more than 2.5 million Afghans resided in Iran and Pakistan in refugee camps before the war began (Mertus 2000, 53). While all displaced people are vulnerable, displaced women are particularly subject to gender-based violence and abuse (Mertus 2000, 69). Evidence such as this offers a severe challenge to the myth that wars are fought for the protection of women and children.

Women Strike Back

Resistance in Afghanistan faced enormous hurdles as people struggled to meet daily needs and avoid physical harm, but it was ongoing and women were participating. The Revolutionary Association of the Women of Afghanistan (RAWA) was established in Kabul in 1977 as an independent organization of Afghan women fighting for human rights and social justice. RAWA's goal was, and continues to be, to increase the number of women in social and political activities and work for the establishment of a government based on democratic and secular values. After the Soviet occupation in 1979, RAWA became involved in the war of resistance. Its founding leader, Meena, who began RAWA's campaign against Soviet occupation and whose warrior words I quoted at the beginning of this chapter, was assassinated by agents of KHAD (the Afghan branch of the KGB) in 1987.

RAWA continued to work underground in Afghanistan and in the refugee camps of Pakistan to bring education and health care to women, and to mobilize them in defense of their rights.[19] RAWA activities in refugee camps were described as training grounds for a different kind of fighter. Girls received an education and, from these sites, women with hidden cameras were sent on dangerous missions into Afghanistan to document abuse. Even in the camps themselves, operations remained secret since Taliban-style fundamentalism thrives there also (Tempest, 2001). Tahmeena Faryal (an alias she uses for protection), a member of RAWA who visited the United States in November 2001, was described as a "soldier of sorts"; she documented her secret return

---

18. In 2000, life expectancy for Afghan women was 44 years, and one in four children died before the age of five (Mertus, 2000, 59). Of course, these deplorable statistics were as much due to years of warfare as to restrictions on women.

19. Information about RAWA may be found on their website at http://www.rawa.org.

to Afghanistan in 1999 under the *burqa* (Lopez 2001). Faryal, with her goal of giving voice to the women and children of Afghanistan, claimed that no woman she met on her mission complained about the *burqa*; rather, they described the insult of their daily lives and the theft of their identities. In a society where everyday survival became, and has continued to be, an almost insurmountable task, fighting back has been severely constrained.[20] Nevertheless, it is crucial that we see these women as agents as well as victims if we are to get beyond the gender stereotyping that we witnessed after 9/11. I shall now suggest four lessons from this feminist analysis.

WHAT CAN WE LEARN FROM 9/11?

Biology Is Not Destiny Even During Wars

Francis Fukuyama (1998) used his seemingly benign biological assertion that men are warlike and women peaceful to justify the need to channel men's aggression into activities in the political, economic, and military realms, thus diminishing opportunities for women. Yet Joshua Goldstein's study of gender and war, discussed in Chapter 2, suggests that biology is in fact less constraining than culture with respect to the roles that men and women can play in war and peace (Goldstein 2001, 252). But if men are made not born, as Goldstein (2001, 264) claims, could we envisage a new form of "hegemonic" masculinity less validated by a false biological association with war?

Prior to September 11, 2001, we in the United States were becoming accustomed to less militarized models of masculinity. As described in Chapter 5, heroes were men of global business conquering the world with briefcases rather than bullets: Bill Gates, a bourgeois hero who looks distinctly unwarrior-like, amasses dollars not weapons.[21] Robert Connell (2000, 26) depicted this type of "hegemonic masculinity" as embodied in business executives who operate in global markets as well as in the political and military leadership who support them.

Military heroes also were being defined in different ways: they came with a tough and tender image—"a new definition of manliness, forged from the depths of sorrow and loss."[22] Post–9/11 real men cried and tears were no

20. RAWA continues to fight for women's rights against what it sees as a regime, installed by the United States after the war, which still relies on the support of warlords who repress women. RAWA claims that the removal of the Taliban has not meant the end of religious fundamentalism and attacks on women. For a statement about RAWA's continuing struggle, see www.rawa.org.

21. For some IR feminist writings that take up the issue of masculinity, see Zalewski and Parpart (1998 and 2008) and Hooper (2001).

22. Robin Morgan, quoted in Brown (2001).

longer a sign of weakness—"the ideal is that the warrior should be sad and tender, and because of that, the warrior can be very brave as well."[23]

Peace researcher Elise Boulding (2000) has suggested that men in the West are experiencing a great deal of pain due to the questioning of their traditional roles, something that is probably still true today. In this transitional era, so worrying to Kurth and Fukuyama, women's gains are unsettling to many men and women, and men's role expectations have become more complicated. This pain may be one reason for the post–9/11 enthusiasm for old-fashioned masculinity and heroism. Nevertheless, as Boulding claims, men do not necessarily enjoy these assigned macho roles. She suggests that the Men's Movement has provided alternative roles for men; she hypothesizes that, with the diminishing of gender polarities, there are possibilities for a new model of partnership rather than domination.

Sympathetic with these new challenges to gender identities and assuming a strong social constructivist position, Robert Connell (2000, 30) has claimed that the task is not to abolish gender but to reshape it—for example, to disconnect courage from violence and to make boys and men aware of the diversity of masculinities that already exist in the world. Democratic gender relations are those that move toward equality, nonviolence, and mutual respect; Connell claims that this reshaping requires constant engagement with women, rather than the separation that has been characteristic of contemporary men's movements.

While Connell outlined possibilities for shifting forms of masculinity freed from their association with war, Goldstein feared that rearing boys not to become warriors puts them at risk of being shamed by their peers. And Judith Stiehm (2000, 224) has suggested that since women are biologically capable of doing everything men can do, masculinity is fragile and vulnerable; because men's superiority is socially rather than biologically defined, men need to assert and protect it. This makes shifting to new forms of masculinity a difficult task. And, as we know, it is generally harder for men to cross gender lines than it is for women.

Do new forms of masculinity in times of war depend on opening up spaces for new definitions of femininity? Clearly, women's increased visibility in public life, particularly in the military, is shaking up gender expectations. In the US military, women have fought and been killed in the wars in Afghanistan and Iraq with much less attention than in the Gulf War, where the presence of female soldiers in Saudi Arabia was one of the greatest provocations for bin Laden.[24] Yet feminists have been ambivalent about women as

23. Tibetan Buddhist teacher Chogyam Trungpa, quoted in Wax (2001).
24. The *Los Angeles Times* (Perry, 2002) reported the death of seven US Marines on a cargo plane in Pakistan on January 10, 2002, with only passing reference to the fact that one of them was a woman.

war-fighters—whether they should join men's wars in the name of equality or resist them in the name of women's special relationship with peace.

We must also ask what the presence of women in combat ranks does to men's sense of masculinity as a motivator for their war fighting. Judith Stiehm (2000, 224) has argued for ending men's monopoly on the legitimate use of force, thus breaking the link between gender identity and the use of state force. She believes this would reduce the overall use of force; she sees peacekeeping as an activity that challenges the association of masculinity with war. Suspicious of the association of women with peace and of any possibility of "remaking human nature," Jean Elshtain (1987, 352–353) has suggested the notion of a "chastened patriot," a model that could be adopted by both women and men and one that would shed the excesses of nationalism and remain committed to, but detached from and reflective about, patriotic ties and loyalties.

Understanding gender as a social construction and the fluidity of gender identities allows us to see the possibilities of change while acknowledging the power of gendering distinctions to legitimate war as well as other practices that result in the subordination of women. It is not only the gendering of war and peace that constrains women's opportunities; frequently, women are oppressed in the name of culture and religion, a phenomenon that the war in Afghanistan brought to our attention.

Women Bear the Burdens of Religion and Culture

Religious fundamentalists, both Christian and Islamic, used the 9/11 crisis to criticize women's advances: this tendency reflected a much more general phenomenon. As many feminists have pointed out, all fundamentalist religions are, to various degrees, bad for women. Historically, most religions have been as male-dominated as militaries. The connection between religious fanaticism, be it Christian, Judaic, or Islamic, and the suppression of women is almost universal. The patriarchal family, with its control of women, is usually central to fundamentalist movements and is often seen as the panacea for social ills (Yuval-Davis 1997, 63). A paradox of fundamentalist movements is that often women collude with and seek comfort in them; and, in spite of their subservience in religious institutions, women constitute a majority of active members of most religions (Yuval-Davis 1997, 63).

Often, in the name of religion, women bear the brunt of identity politics that is frequently expressed in terms of control over their life choices. At the 1994 United Nations Conference on Population and Development in Cairo and at the UN Women's Conference in Beijing in 1995, the Vatican and other conservative Catholic groups joined with right-wing Muslim forces in their opposition to women's human and reproductive rights. In many Muslim societies, the majority of the population is not literate, so religious knowledge is controlled by the ruling class, who interpret texts for their own benefit and use it to control others. According to Zeiba Shorish-Shamley (2002), the Qur'an gives equal rights to men and women, and women were leaders in early Islam—modest clothing was recommended so that when men and women met in public discussion, intellectuality rather than sexuality would be emphasized.

"When radical Muslim movements are on the rise, women are canaries in the mine" (Goodwin and Neuwirth 2001). In the name of Islamic fundamentalism, the definition of collective identity is increasingly being tied to definitions of gender. According to Women Living Under Muslim Laws (WLUML), an international network of women, construction of the "Muslim woman" is integral to the construction of "Muslimness," explaining, in part, the emphasis on controlling all aspects of women's lives (WLUML 1997, 2–3). Ironically, the weakening of the patriarchal family structure may be a contributing cause of these movements (Moghadan 1994, 15). Azza Karam (2000, 69–70) sees the emergence of "neo-patriarchy," a confluence of patriarchy and dependence that embodies the tension between internal patriarchal power structures and outside pressures of modernization. It is in the reinstatement of cultural values in response to pressures of globalization that women in the Arab world tend to be most affected. Defining "fundamentalism" as the use of religion to gain and mobilize political power, Women Living Under Muslim Laws has argued that, with the ascendancy of identity politics, secular space shrinks, with negative consequences for women (WLUM 1997, 3).[25] And, when women fight for their rights, they are frequently accused of betraying their culture and religion.

Although not reducible to each other, religion bears a close relationship to culture. Gender relations come to be seen as constituting the "essence" of cultures (Yuval-Davis 1997, 43). Women are often required to carry the burden of cultural representation: their "proper" behavior embodies lines that signify a collectivity's boundaries. Women are transmitters of group values and traditions; as agents of socialization of the young, their place is in the home. For some, this is an honor rather than a burden, so all fundamentalist movements have women supporters as well as opponents (Moghadan 1994, 19).

Rina Amiri (2001) has claimed that the Western world has contributed to the perception that the conflict in Afghanistan was a battle between East and West by centering on the place of women in its depiction of Islam as repressive and backward. She has also suggested that a Western approach could damage

---

25. WLUML notes that the use of the term "fundamentalism" is a contested one within the organization. Some, but not all, find it the least objectionable term to name the phenomenon. RAWA also uses the term, at least when speaking to a Western audience.

a long-term vision for an indigenous model of a just society because a Western model can be contextually inappropriate for Afghan women and Islam traditionalists who are sympathetic to women but who will reject what is perceived as Western (Amiri 2002).

Conversely, WLUML (1997, 6) has claimed that well-meaning people, wanting to distance themselves from hatred of Islam as well as the colonial past, epitomized in Orientalist thought, have frequently fallen into the trap of cultural relativism. Consistent with some of Rothstein's more negative assessments of postcolonialism, but in the name of cultural sensitivity, this can lead to endorsement of the right to seclude women.

Issues of culture and religion have been difficult ones for both Western and non-Western feminists. Western feminists have walked a fine line between supporting a "global sisterhood," and thus imposing Western definitions of female emancipation on other cultures, and trying to be culturally sensitive. Third Wave feminism of the 1990s introduced issues of class, race, and cultural variability into its analyses in order to get beyond essentialist generalizations about women that stem from Western middle class women's experiences. As an alternative to the universalism/relativism dichotomy, Nira Yuval-Davis (1997, 1) suggests what she calls "transversal politics," or the politics of mutual support—a form of coalition politics in which differences among women are recognized and given a voice.

In the Muslim world, women's struggles are frequently undermined by the idea of one homogeneous Muslim world, a deliberate myth fostered by both Occidentalism and Orientalism and promoted by interests within and outside (WLUML 1997, 1). In many cases, to be pro-women's rights means to be accused of being Western. Accusing women of being Westernized and, therefore, not representing an "authentic" women's voice allows for the dismissal of women's claims to justice. This has made it difficult for Muslim women to develop a discourse on their rights independent of a cultural debate between the Western and Muslim worlds.

Amiri urges moving beyond the stereotypical premise that Islam as a whole is anti-woman. She suggests that, while it is incumbent on the international community never to tolerate abuses against women in any part of the world, the West should ground its support in the positions of Muslim feminists. WLUML claims that women are frequently hampered by insufficient knowledge about their legal rights, by their inability to distinguish between customs, law, and religion, and by their isolation. To this end, WLUML suggests that women pool information and create strategies across countries; they urge a respect for other voices while condemning bad practices.

All of these attempts to negotiate support for women—attempts that get beyond a false universalism based on Western norms and a type of cultural relativism that condones oppressive practices—depend on seeing women as agents rather than victims. "Moving toward gender equality is a political process—it requires new ways of thinking—in which the stereotyping of women and men gives way to a new philosophy that regards all people, irrespective of gender, as essential agents of change" (UNHDP 1996, 1).[26]

Women's Gains from War May Not Last

Paradoxically, it is sometimes the case that wars are good for women. European and American women first received the vote after World War I, and Japanese women did so after World War II. Frequently, women are mobilized into the paid economy during war, thereby gaining more economic independence. Women have also been mobilized in times of struggle for national liberation, and sometimes they have fought in liberation armies. Quite often, these gains evaporate once the war is over; in the West, the years after both World Wars saw a return to the cult of domesticity and motherhood—a move that had to do with the need for women to step aside and let men resume the jobs they had left to go to war. And women who have fought alongside men in wars of national liberation, and who have been promised a greater role in post-liberation society, often find that these promises evaporate once the struggle is over. Few revolutionary movements directly address women's problems or attempt to solve these problems in post-revolution political and social constitutions and institutions (Tetrault 1992, 92).

When women fight for their rights, they generally get less support than when they are perceived as victims. This is because gender justice demands profound structural changes in almost all societies, changes that would threaten existing elites along with existing political, social, and economic structures. And, frequently, both international governmental and nongovernmental organizations (NGOs) find these types of radical changes too politically risky to support.

A spokesperson for the Feminist Majority suggested in 2002 that never before has the women's movement had such an impact on American foreign policy as it was having at that time (McNamara 2002). The Feminist Majority began its campaign "Stop Gender Apartheid" in 1996, well before the plight of Afghan women was receiving much media attention: it played a key role in the Clinton administration's refusal to recognize the Taliban government. The Feminist Majority's optimism was probably short-lived. Governments are generally reluctant to make women's human rights part of their foreign policies. There is less risk in portraying women as victims than in supporting their empowerment. The image of helpless victims behind the veil is politically less risky than supporting articulate forceful advocates of women's rights. The

26. Although not the most recent, I cite the 1995 Annual Report because it contains the most extensive discussion of gender inequality of any of the Annual Reports.

Bush administration was quoted as having insisted that the campaign to high-light women in Afghanistan must be seen as a "justice issue," not a women's issue (Brant 2001). And even if the Bush administration put the plight of Afghan women on its foreign policy agenda for a short time, it was not par-ticularly progressive on other international women's issues. Twenty-two years after President Jimmy Carter sent the Convention on the Elimination of All Forms of Discrimination Against Women (CEDAW) to the US Senate for rati-fication, the Bush administration reneged on its initial support. As of 2013, the United States is one of a very small minority of countries that still has not ratified CEDAW.

CONCLUSION

American officials described the "war against terrorism" as a new kind of war, a war against a terrorist network, not against another state. In conclusion, one may wonder if there are other, more gendered ways in which this war is unlike the other wars that Americans fought in the twentieth century. The prevalence of gendered images taken to be threatening or used to belittle one's opponents could surely be found in other such wars. But somehow these refer-ences seemed more fundamental in this case.

As quoted above, al Qaeda leaders made a special point of criticizing Western gender relations. Gender relationships are an important aspect of what are taken by many fundamentalists to be key religious or civilizational differences. Even more surprising are the cases of "strange bedfellows" on dif-ferent sides of the war making the same kinds of gendered arguments. Do not these features of the above analysis suggest that the 9/11 crisis reflected a globalization of gender politics, a clash of gendered orders usually hidden by the normalizing practices of unequal societies?

In times of uncertainty, fear of social change rises, as does fear of feminist agendas. However, feminists do not advocate a "feminized society," as some of their critics have suggested, but rather a society where gender differences are less polarized and gender structures are less hierarchical.

CHAPTER 10

On Taking Religious Worldviews Seriously

2009

We need to take alternative worldviews—including religious worldviews—more seriously.

Robert Keohane (2002, 283)

The twenty-first century is dawning...as a century of religion.

Samuel Huntington (2004, 15)

The study of other people's religious beliefs is now no longer merely desirable, but necessary for our very survival.

Karen Armstrong (2004, 304)

Written in the immediate aftermath of the attacks of September 11, 2001, the final chapter of Robert Keohane's *Power and Governance in a Partially Globalized World* challenged scholars of international relations to reflect on whether their theories of world politics are adequate for explaining such acts of what he calls "informal violence."[1] Keohane claimed that incorporating the motivations of those who kill in the name of religion into mainstream IR theory, which he described as relentlessly secular, is difficult. I argue that an important reason for this is that theories built upon the epistemological and ontological foundations of secular rationalism are not particularly useful for understanding religious motivations or worldviews of those who

---

1. Keohane distinguished informal violence, which he described as violence by non-state actors, with the capacity to inflict great harm with small material capabilities, from formal violence that is state-controlled. He preferred this term to "terrorism," because, since terrorism has such negative connotations, it is difficult to define it in an analytically neutral and consistent way (Keohane 2002, 272–274).

express a deep hostility to modernity and secular thinking. Indeed, the social sciences, which have emerged out of Western Enlightenment thought, are themselves part of the secular rationalist thinking that adherents to conservative religious worldviews attack.

Taking up Keohane's challenge to take religious worldviews seriously, I begin this chapter by examining the worldviews of some of those who commit violence in the name of religion. I examine some worldviews of both Christian and Islamic groups that support religious violence. Similarities are striking. The rhetoric of both Christian and Islamic extremist groups demonstrates a sense of rootlessness and loss of identity; all exhibit deep hostility to secular rationalism, modernity, and globalization. While they depend on modern technologies, particularly communication technologies, to spread their message and plan their strategies, all are deeply suspicious of liberal international institutions and the "new world order."[2] I then examine the broader economic and cultural contexts from which contemporary religious violence is emerging. Albeit in an extreme and perverted form, perpetrators of violence and their supporters emerge out of a more prevalent search for identity and cultural values—an attempt to answer the question "Who are we?"—a search that Samuel Huntington has termed the most distinctive feature of the contemporary world (Huntington 2004).

In the second part of the chapter, I suggest that it may not be possible to understand religious violence, and the worldviews that are driving it, within a mainstream IR theoretical framework. To support my position, I first draw on the writings of Hans Morgenthau to demonstrate classical realism's discomfort with secular rationalism for understanding human motivation. I then use constructivist Vendulka Kubálková's work to demonstrate that linguistic constructivism can provide a more useful tool for understanding religious beliefs and quests for meaning and identity that are so important to adherents of the conservative religions that I discuss. I suggest that religious worldviews may be better understood using hermeneutic, reflexive, and dialogical methodologies traditionally associated with religious studies and some forms of linguistic constructivism. These methodologies cannot be fully assimilated within instrumental rationalist conceptions of social science.

In the concluding section, I draw on some feminist secular and religious scholarship that could provide us with some new insights about religious worldviews that seem so pressing in today's world. First, I discuss some Western feminist writings that offer new possibilities for transcending the religious/secular knowledge divide. I then discuss some Islamic scholarship,

---

2. Mark Juergensmeyer states that, in his interviews with supporters of religious violence, he was struck by the intensity of their quest for spiritual values that are deeper than those offered by the superficial values of the modern world. See Juergensmeyer (2000, 222).

critical of conservative religious thought yet sensitive to reactions against Western modernity, that could help us recognize different forms of modernity not so closely linked with Western secularism.

VIOLENCE IN THE NAME OF GOD

Although the overall incidence of terrorism did not increase in the late twentieth century, there was an increase in religious violence.[3] Individuals who support or commit religious violence see themselves as "saints" or "martyrs" striving for a more perfect and more simplified world.[4] They deplore moral ambiguity and uncertainty and see the world in Manichean terms where no compromise is possible. They use militaristic language, frequently from religious texts, to describe a world in a perpetual state of war—a battle between good and evil. If evil means are necessary to achieve good ends, they will be used (Juergensmeyer 2000, 149). In Chapter 9 I described the views of Islamic fundamentalists, but worldviews of religious extremists are surprisingly similar—whether they are Christian, Jewish, or Islamic. All decry secularism, materialism, and modernity, which create confusion and fear amid a general lack of authority and which are manifest through tolerance of "inappropriate" sexual behavior and lack of racial hierarchy.[5] Indeed, identity issues are at the core of a search for certainty in a world where too much choice of identity can seem overwhelming (Stern 2003, 156). Material wealth, engendered by capitalism, leads to moral decadence. Yet motives are material as well as spiritual and emotional; heavenly rewards are promised to perpetrators of religious violence, but so are material incentives.

Extremist religious groups decry international institutions, the building blocks of a liberal world order. They express strong hostility to a world order based on secular morality and on global institutions such as the United Nations (Mead 2006).[6] Kerry Noble, one of the former leaders of an American

---

3. By one measure, the number of terrorist attacks in the 1990s averaged 382 per year, whereas in the 1980s the number averaged 543. However, the number of people killed in each attack increased in the 1990s, as did the number of terrorist organizations classified as "religious." (Cronin 2002, 42–43). Cronin (2006, 13) also reports that groups with spiritual motivations tend to last much longer.

4. My illustrations rely on interviews conducted by Juergensmeyer (2000) and Stern (2003). The goal articulated by both these authors is to study religious violence from the inside—to understand the worldviews of those who commit these acts of violence and the cultural contexts from which they emerge. Both analyze a variety of religions, including Christianity, Islam, and Judaism.

5. Scott Thomas (2005, 10–11) sees the global resurgence of religion, which he claims is a far more wide ranging phenomenon than extremism or fundamentalism, as part of a larger crisis of modernity in the West.

6. Mead asserts that it is no coincidence that the *Left Behind* novels show the Antichrist rising to power as the secretary-general of the UN.

Christian cult, Covenant, the Sword, and the Arm of the Lord (CSA), based in rural Arkansas, stated that the strength of international institutions promoting world government, including the United Nations and international banks, are indications that the Antichrist, whose forces also include the IMF, the Council on Foreign Relations, and the "One-Worlders," is already here (Stern 2003, 11–17). A study of American right-wing rural Christian militias reveals a similar fear of a "new world order" and an "invasion" of the United States by the United Nations (Kimmel and Ferber 2000). Leaders of the Pakistani jihad group Lashkar e Taiba (Army of the Pure), a member of the International Islamic Front, bin Laden's umbrella organization, assert that the West enslaves Muslim countries through debts to the IMF, the World Bank, foreign aid, and loans (Stern 2003, 119). Contrary to CSA's fears of a UN invasion, Army of the Pure claims that the United Nations is a spy for the United States and that international institutions are synonymous with American imperialism (Buruma and Margalit 2004, 8). For many overseas groups, the United States symbolizes the new world order, the greatest enemy of all.

Many of the violent, religiously motivated individuals whom Jessica Stern interviewed indicated a sense of wounded masculinity. Indeed, gender and race are central for understanding the worldviews of perpetrators and supporters of religious violence. Almost all who commit violence in the name of religion are men.[7] Many express ambivalence toward women, homophobia, and fears of being marked "feminine." Followers of right-wing militia movements in the United States consist mainly of lower-middle class white men, and it is through militias that these individuals believe that American manhood can be restored. Militias believe they are engaged in an armed struggle against a state which, they claim, is controlled by feminists, environmentalists, Blacks, and Jews (Kimmel and Ferber 2000, 595). Christian Identity groups see the state as emasculating and blame feminists and their non-white co-conspirators for their humiliation (Stern 2003, 286). Avigdor Eskin, an ultraorthodox Israeli Jew, blames "Afro-Americanism" for the destruction of American culture; surprisingly, he displays a reluctant admiration for Muslims who, unlike Westerners, are willing to die for their ideas (Stern 2003, 99–101). Many members of radical religious movements see themselves as soldiers, and many are military veterans.

While the leaders of extreme religious movements are often middle-aged and affluent, their followers tend to be young urban males experiencing economic hardships, unemployment, and social marginalization. While leaders of

7. Some women have played a prominent role in violent groups; however, groups in which women play a prominent role tend to be motivated by secular political ideologies or ethnic separatism rather than by religion. See Juergensmeyer (2000, 196). This is hardly surprising given that all fundamentalist religions practice severe discrimination against women.

these movements see their role as "purifying" the world, operatives are often influenced by pragmatic incentives such as money that is frequently provided to the families of "martyrs" (Stern 2003, 4–5). In Pakistan many male children are educated at religious schools or madrassas because they receive free books, housing, and board. Often poor families and those in refugee camps cannot afford the cost of textbooks and transportation frequently required at public school (Stern 2003, 296). Racial hierarchies are also prevalent in extremist religious movements. Recruits for Islamic extremism are coming increasingly from Africa, where anti-Americanism is on the rise. But al Qaeda is highly tiered and Africans are, for the most part, not admitted to the upper ranks; they do, however, provide willing foot soldiers for religious violence (Stern 2003, 237–248).

Ian Buruma and Avishai Margalit have claimed that the issue of women lies at the heart of Islamic "Occidentalism," which they define as a dehumanizing picture of the West painted by its enemies (Buruma and Margalit 2004, 7). Most conservative Muslims are not political Islamists but advocates of enforcing public morality, which is largely about regulating female behavior and returning to what they see as a "traditional" way of life (Buruma and Margalit 2004, 128). When he was living in New York, Egyptian Sayyid Qutb, one of the most influential Islamist thinkers of the twentieth century, claimed that what most disturbed him about American society was the immodest behavior of American women (Stern 2003, 32).

Jessica Stern has claimed that the religious violence we face today is not only a response to political and economic grievances, often attributed to neo-liberal economic globalization, but also to what she terms, using the language of Sartre, a "God-shaped hole" where values like tolerance and equal rights for women are irritating to those who feel left behind by modernity (Stern 2003, 282). All extremist religious movements display a deep hostility to modern rationalism, secular thinking, materialism, and economic globalization. They draw selectively on religious texts, often militant or violent, to exhort their followers to "return" to what they define as a "traditional" way of life.[8] They consider themselves to be unconstrained by secular values or laws and display a complete sense of alienation from the existing social system (Cronin 2002, 41). While those who are willing to kill in the name of religion are a small minority, they represent, albeit in an extreme and perverted form, feelings of threat, alienation, and loss of identity that are far more widespread and symptomatic of larger trends—trends that, as I indicated in Chapter 9, are evident in many societies today.

8. The concept of the "traditional," often used by socially conservative groups, consisting of a male breadwinner and a wife who does not work outside the home, is actually an invention of modern capitalism discussed in Chapter 3. It is also a classist definition in that most women, out of economic necessity, have had to work outside the home.

SOME BROADER IMPLICATIONS OF THE RELIGIOUS WAR OF IDEAS

Mark Juergensmeyer has suggested that the moral leadership of the secular state has become increasingly challenged after the end of the Cold War, a struggle, also portrayed in Manichean terms, which provided contesting models of moral politics—communism and democracy (Juergensmeyer 2000, 225–226). Today, communism and democracy have been replaced by the single model of the global market—a model that, according to Juergensmeyer, is devoid of political ideals and lacks clear standards for moral behavior.[9] The political conservatism of the 1980s and the shift in the global economy to the neo-liberal consensus began what has continued to be a widening of income inequality throughout the world. This has reinforced a public sense of insecurity that results in disaffection with political leaders and the growth of right-wing religious movements that feed on the public's perception of the immorality of government.

While disillusionment with the secular state is characteristic of conservative religious groups, their relations with actual states are complex. Many groups, both Christian and Muslim, are using the state to increase their political influence. This is eroding the boundary between religion and politics even in secular societies, a phenomenon that has caught international relations scholars and policy analysts by surprise. Modernization theory, popular in both the academy and the policy world in the 1950s and 1960s, assumed that, as newly independent countries began to follow the path to development previously taken by the West, they would become increasingly secular. Industrialization, urbanization, rationalization, modern science, and secular values would undermine religious beliefs thought to be "left over" from tradition (Lerner 1958). Today, in many parts of the world, when Western values and economic modernization are regarded as culturally alien and a threat to indigenous values, these predictions seem strangely out of place. In the Muslim world there is a positive correlation between supporters of the Islamic faith and educational and occupational prestige, a correlation that challenges the assumption that religious beliefs erode with modernization. Indeed, many leaders of groups that espouse religious violence are members of the professional classes.

Occidentalism epitomizes the resentment against the West's belief in the alleged superiority of secular reason and science as the only way to understand natural phenomena. While modernization theory, which is based on secular rationalist knowledge, has ceased to be of central concern to Western development theory, it has come under increased scrutiny outside the West

---

9. This sense of a lack of morality has only increased since the financial crisis of 2008.

where scholars are searching for definitions of modernity that are more compatible with religion and local cultural values.[10] While Westerners promote the globalizing of Western values as a way to build a democratic international society of states outside the West, the legacy of colonialism and the association of modernity with secularism and Western values play an important role in religion's resurgence.

Fears about loss of identity in the face of secular modernization exist within the West as well as elsewhere. They are intensifying cultural clashes that reinforce exclusionary international (often racialized) boundaries. In the face of what he has famously called a "clash of civilizations," Samuel Huntington suggested that the attacks of 9/11 mobilized America's identity as a Christian nation. Huntington claimed that the religious component of their identity has taken on new meaning for Americans. According to Huntington, this identity is Anglo-Protestant—an identity he clearly favors over a more multiracial, inclusionary one, but one that is unlikely to foster tolerance and cooperation (Huntington 2004, 340). As described in Chapter 9, Huntington's "clash" is mirrored by "jihadists" whose vision of the world is similar. Sayyid Qutb articulated this clash as early as the 1960s, when he claimed that the world was divided into two camps—those who are followers of Islam and those who are not (Esposito and Voll 2003, 240).

I have suggested that the reemergence of conservative religious movements has challenged the predictions of modernization theory and the universal acceptance of a liberal world order based on certain Western values and Western-led international institutions. Their growing influence on the state and politics, even in secular societies, has confounded political analysis that looks to rationalist, materialist explanations for political behavior. To understand these new phenomena requires the IR discipline to pursue some new avenues.

INCORPORATING RELIGION INTO THEORIES OF INTERNATIONAL RELATIONS

Daniel Philpott sees the origins of the secularism of international relations theories in what he calls the "Westphalian synthesis." The Treaty of Westphalia of 1648, often termed a landmark in the origins of the modern state system,[11] signaled the defeat of religion not as a force in politics but as a scheme for

10. Islamic and postcolonial scholars more generally are articulating different conceptions of modernity, or what is often referred to as "multiple modernities." See, for example, Göle (2000).

11. This claim has been the subject of an ongoing dispute. For counter-arguments, see Krasner (1993) and Teschke (2003).

organizing international authority. Denying the right of authorities to enforce religious practices outside their territory, Westphalia established the right of sovereign authorities to govern religion in their territory as they pleased, thus establishing state sovereignty and the norm of nonintervention (Philpott 2002, 73–74). Set in motion by the Protestant Reformation and the subsequent development of religious freedom, the separation of church and state resulted in the gradual secularization of the interstate political realm.

The ontological assumptions of the Westphalian synthesis, together with the commitment to international relations as a social science, so central to the evolution of the International Relations' discipline, particularly in the United States, have reinforced IR's neglect of religion and, more important, its inability to incorporate religion into its theories. The radical revival of Islam has challenged the Westphalian synthesis and its associated modern social scientific commitments. The ultimate goal of radical revivalists is the Islamization of the international political order—replacing the secular state system and Western-led international institutions with an Islamic system under God's rule. Non-state actors claim religious authority and kinship with people outside their state, but they also look to state institutions to promote Islam (Philpott 2002, 89). Support for Islamic movements are statist and transnational at the same time.[12] Given that the fundamental principles around which the Westphalian state system is organized are being questioned, this presents a profound challenge to IR theory. Secular rationalism is ill equipped to understand the mixed motivations, from the transcendental to the materialist, which characterize not only radical Islam, but also the other conservative religious movements that I have described. Therefore, it may be necessary to look beyond conventional social science to other theoretical traditions to help understand these worldviews and to try to design policies and institutions to deal with them. To this end, I now turn to realist Hans Morgenthau's *Scientific Man vs. Power Politics* to help understand deeper problems associated with the reaction against secular modernity and rationalism that I have described.

Morgenthau's Classical Realism

Writing in the aftermath of World War II and deeply affected by European fascism, Hans Morgenthau evoked themes that are strikingly similar to some of those discussed earlier in this chapter. In *Scientific Man vs. Power Politics*, a

12. The Christian Right in the United States tends to look to state institutions to promote Christianity and to see religion and the state as coincidental. Its support for the Iraq war and an imperial foreign policy (God and country) are indications of this. This is quite consistent with the Westphalian principle of *cuius regio, cuius religio* and further complicates the Westphalian synthesis.

book that is strikingly different from his *Politics Among Nations* that I discussed in Chapter 1, Morgenthau pointed to disillusionment with modernity and its association with secular rationalism, a disillusionment which,
as I have indicated, is central to contemporary fundamentalist thinking
in a variety of religions. Morgenthau disputed the liberal claim that, in a
liberal society, reason, revealing itself in the "laws" of economics, would
reign and of necessity bring about harmony, the welfare of all, and world
peace (Morgenthau 1946, 25). Liberals believed that this would come about
through reason that had its own inner force, not dependent on human intervention. In a severe indictment of liberalism and rationalism, Morgenthau
was strikingly pessimistic about the ability of scientific reasoning to solve
social problems. Suggesting that man's [sic] nature has three dimensions—
the biological, the rational, and the spiritual—he concluded that the ratio-
nalistic or instrumentalist conception of man, portrayed by liberal social
science, has completely disregarded the emotional and spiritual aspects of
life (Morgenthau 1946, 122). Disavowing positivism's belief that the social
world is subject to the same kinds of laws as the natural world, Morgenthau
claimed that science may have allowed man to master nature but it has not
answered the reason for man's existence, a search that seems so prevalent
in today's religious resurgence (Morgenthau 1946, 125). While *Scientific
Man vs. Power Politics* is a severe indictment of an attempt to construct a
"scientific" theory of world politics, a "scientific" model is, nevertheless,
the one to which Morgenthau aspired in all his writings. His rigid separation of rationality and emotion, a separation that I described as gendered in
Chapter 1, is itself a product of modern secular reasoning. For Morgenthau,
rationality has the potential to overcome what he sees as dangerous emotions. I shall return to this later in the chapter.

Kubálková's Linguistic Constructivism

Scientific Man vs. Power Politics is grounded in the interpretive or hermeneutic tradition, an intellectual approach that is closer to theology and to contemporary IR post-positivist approaches—approaches that include much
of feminist IR—than to realism's subsequent devolution to a more "scientific" neo-realism. The hermeneutic tradition is also an important foundation for much of contemporary IR constructivism. In an essay whose goal
is to develop what she calls an international political theology, Vendulka
Kubálková claims that it is not possible to study religion adequately in a
positivist framework. Arguing for a rule-oriented constructivist approach,
she asserts that there is a profound difference between positivist and religious understandings of the world. Indeed, positivists' reliance on logic and
the positive evidence of the senses demonstrates a search for non-religious

foundations for secure knowledge. She advocates a shift to an insider's perspective on knowledge building.[13] Such a perspective, characteristic of hermeneutic and post-positivist thought more generally, has religious antecedents in late-eighteenth-century romanticism as a revolt against modern rationalism (Kubálková 2003, 85–89).[14] Kubálková states that, up until two hundred years ago, religions provided the dominant mode of thought, and many schools of thought, such as phenomenology and hermeneutics, have their roots in religious theorizing. The stress on identity, the inside/outside distinction, phenomenology, and hermeneutics, all characteristic of post-positivist thought, has always been central to religious thought and practice. Thus, post-positivist approaches to knowledge cumulation are likely to be better at understanding religious worldviews than positivist ones.

Religious and secular thought start from different ontologies—all religions share a distinction between ordinary and transcendental reality. Religious thinkers see human experience as only one dimension of a multidimensional reality that is ordered by design but is not adequately knowable by sensory perception alone. Creating gods is a necessary feature of the human search for identity and transcendence. A believer must follow the dictates of conscience that are beyond the realm of "rational choice" (Kubálková 2003, 86–90). While constructivism has also been secular, Kubálková claims that approaching human action through linguistic constructivism—as a world created through human action and the meaning that humans give to their actions—is the methodological path by which we can incorporate religion into international relations. I agree that linguistic constructivism is useful for understanding the religious worldviews I have described and for understanding contemporary events, for the way we construct our world is crucial to how we act upon it.[15]

Kubálková and Morgenthau both claim that fundamental questions about human existence cannot be answered in modern secular "scientific" terms. Both are searching for a way to understand human motivations that, as they suggest, are not adequately explainable in instrumental rationalist terms. Both are helpfully suggestive of some ways in which we need to rethink contemporary knowledge production in order to better understand religious

13. For a detailed examination of the contrast between insider and outsider perspectives on knowledge-building and how they are used in IR theory, see Hollis and Smith (1990).

14. Kubálková suggests that romanticism focuses on the irrational and the non-rational and on feeling rather than thought. It does, however, have a much more positive view of human nature than did Morgenthau.

15. Comparison of US responses to the attack on the World Trade Center in 1993, when five people were killed and approximately one thousand injured, and 9/11, where more than three thousand were killed, is illustrative of my argument. Whereas the 1993 attack was considered a crime, 9/11 was declared an act of war. These very different reactions were the result of the comparative levels of destruction rather than the acts themselves, which were motivated by similar goals. See May (2003, 39).

worldviews. Their realist and constructivist analyses take us further into questioning the adequacy of the epistemological foundations of Western modern secular knowledge for understanding religious worldviews. And Kubálková's linguistic constructivism provides some theoretical openings for understanding these worldviews. But I also believe that contributions of secular and religious feminist writings are useful in offering further new and important insights into transcending the divide between secular and religious thinking. Feminists outside the West are also contributing to new thinking about different paths to modernity that are less Western-centered and allow for the inclusion of alternative religious and cultural traditions.

SOME FEMINIST REFORMULATIONS ABOUT MODERN KNOWLEDGE AND MODERNITY

Beyond Gendered Theology

Conservative religions in all the Abrahamic traditions are deeply patriarchal. Reactions from both Western and non-Western critics of modernity are frequently expressed as calls for the (re)activation of restrictive policies on women, which are often justified in the name of religion. Feminist theologians have offered some important critiques of patriarchal religious beliefs and practices and have suggested some reconstructions and revisions of theology which are not only less patriarchal but which can also provide the bases for more benign, more inclusive, and less conflictual religious worldviews. Muslim feminists have claimed that, while Islam is being used as an instrument of oppression against Muslim women, this is because men interpret Islam to suit their purposes. While most *ahadith* (sayings attributed to Mohammad) describe a virtuous woman as one who pleases and obeys her husband, there are no Qur'anic statements that justify the rigid restrictions that have been imposed on women in the name of Islam (Hassan 1999, 260). Marienne Hélie-Lucas, the founder of Women Living Under Muslim Laws, claimed that the laws that Muslim women live under vary widely across societies with differing degrees of oppression. As she claims, these laws are man-made not God given, constructed by political and religious leaders to serve their own purposes. She distinguishes Muslim laws from Islamic doctrine, something that is open and debated by scholars.[16] And when Muslim women fight for their rights, they are frequently accused of betraying their religion and culture and of becoming Western. Indeed, for Islamic feminists, modernity itself is problematic because it is equated with being Western. Rather than reject Islam altogether, Islamic

16. Available at www.wluml.org/sites/wluml.org/files/HeartandSoul.

feminists are attempting to reconstruct an alternative reading of Islam that is less patriarchal and does not endorse the disempowerment of women.

Christian feminist theology has also engaged in both critical analysis of conventional texts and in a constructive re-reading of texts, both of which involve an awareness of the ambivalence that religious texts have created for women. Feminist theologians, following a practice in feminist methodology more generally, question the assumption that there can be a gender-neutral "universal" person who reads a text from an "objective" point of view. A feminist reader of the Scripture assumes a reflexive attitude—that the gender, race, and socioeconomic status of the reader must be taken into consideration when assessing a claim or meaning of a text. Feminist theologians also question the selection of texts that have become part of the canon; a feminist reading of the Scripture is not a reading that focuses only on the content of the Scripture as authoritative, but a hermeneutic one that emphasizes the interactive contextual process of reading, a process that creates meaning for those who participate in the religious community as the people they are (Watson 2003, 7–11).

Feminist theologians in the Christian tradition have drawn inspiration from, but have gone beyond, liberation theology, a radical Christian tradition that emerged in the Black US and Latin American Catholic churches in the 1970s and 1980s. Liberation theology believes that marginalized and oppressed peoples must participate in constructing their own religious thinking out of their lives and experiences (Watson 2003, 1). Rather than invoking the authority of texts selected by religious hierarchies, liberation theology involves a form of knowledge building whereby ordinary people come to understand religion through engagement in a dialogic process. Constructing religious worldviews is reflective, ongoing and emergent. It is consistent with a sense of empathy and compassion—to feel with, which Karen Armstrong suggests is as pivotal in all Abrahamic religious traditions as are the belligerent elements emphasized by fundamentalists (Armstrong 2004, 295). Such non-patriarchal religious interpretations are more inclusive. A non-gendered dialogic reading of religious texts, which suggests that God can be both male and female, is a way to less conflictual religious self-understandings and worldviews.

Beyond Gendered Knowledge

As discussed in more detail in earlier chapters, secular feminists have similar problems with the gendering of secular knowledge. Women have had an ambiguous and complicated relationship with secular rationalism and "objective" reasoning that have been foundations for modern knowledge, including social scientific knowledge. For this reason, secular feminists have constructed useful critiques of the historical development of the kind of secular rationalist thinking of which conservative religions are so critical and about which

Morgenthau was so pessimistic. Modern knowledge, with its claims to universality and objectivity, has generally been constructed by men from knowledge of men's lives in the public sphere. Men's historical roles as political and economic actors have provided the intellectual framework for Western knowledge about politics and economics. The separation of the public spheres, reinforced by the scientific revolution of the seventeenth century, has resulted in the legitimation of what are perceived as the "rational" activities (such as politics and economics) in the former while devaluing the "natural" activities (such as household management, childrearing and caregiving) of the latter (Peterson 1992, 202). Feminists argue that broadening the base from which knowledge is constructed—that is, including the experiences of women—can actually enhance objectivity (Harding 1991, 123).[17]

Modern knowledge depends on the Cartesian separation of the intellect (valued in public sphere behavior) and the emotions (more acceptable in the private sphere).[18] These are hierarchically ordered and gendered, where the mind is associated with men and emotions with women and where, as Morgenthau claims, it is the task of (masculine) reason to tame dangerous (female) emotions. Feminists believe that emotion and intellect are mutually constitutive and sustaining, and that emotions can be a positive as well as a negative force. Armstrong claims that, since the scientific revolution of the seventeenth century, even Western theology has been characterized by inappropriate reliance on reason. This has reinforced the tendency to impose dogmatic religious beliefs that are causing many of today's problems (Armstrong 2004, 294).

As discussed in Part Two, for feminists, rationality is contextual and emergent out of social relations in which the individual is embedded. Contextualized rationality, whereby the producer of knowledge is reflexive of her or his role in the production of knowledge, is a more robust ideational foundation from which to build less conflictual worldviews. Like feminist theologians, many secular feminists also advocate a dialogic contextual model of knowledge-building whereby knowledge emerges through conversations with texts and subjects. For example, Brooke Ackerly has built on, but goes beyond, democratic political theory in designing a deliberative democratic model of social criticism that she defines as an ongoing process to bring about incremental un-coerced models of social change (Ackerly 2000, 14). Working with rural women and social activists in Bangladesh, Ackerly constructed a framework that combines scholarship with action. She argues that effecting social change in social, political, and economic institutions must come, not just from

17. Harding uses the term "strong objectivity" to describe this inclusive form of knowledge building. Strong objectivity was described in more detail in Chapter 6.
18. Recent work in neuroscience has called into question the scientific evidence for this claim. See Damasio (2005).

theorists, but also from the experiences of those whose lives are impacted by injustices that they seek to remedy. Participants in such a dialogue are not theorists or elites but ordinary individuals who must have mutual respect and equal ability to influence outcomes. Analogous to processes used by liberation theologians, Ackerly recounted meetings among rural women and social activists who used stories, analogies, and emotions in non-institutionalized settings to construct better understandings of their situations in order to change them. Building knowledge through an interactive dialogic process that includes multiple voices, rather than constructing knowledge aimed at discovering some objective universal truth, could provide a useful foundation for the construction of less conflictual worldviews.[19] Although not specifically religious, such an approach could also contribute to bridging religious and secular divides.

Beyond Traditional/Modern Divides

As political theorist Chris Brown has suggested, there are a number of different ways of being modern; the modernity associated with the liberal, largely post-Christian, humanist West is not a universal model (Brown 2002, 299). Feminists outside the West are contributing to a reconceptualization of modernity that could allow for the incorporation of local religious and cultural traditions. Islamic feminists have made important contributions to a growing literature on "multiple modernities" that is offering a critique of the adequacy of Western modernization theory. This literature is attempting to get beyond the traditional/modern divide and the exclusive association of modernity with the spread of Western secular norms, institutions, and economic arrangements that are a source of such hostility to conservative religious groups both inside and outside the West (Eisenstadt and Schluchter 2001).[20] The conceptualization of non-Western modernities is a theoretical effort to create new ways of reading and seeing some aspects of social life that have been judged and dismissed as regressive and backward (Göle 2000, 41–45).

Turkish feminist Nilufer Göle criticizes modernization theory for its portrayal of non-Western countries as being temporally behind the West in terms of their development. In the second half of the twentieth century, when modernization theory was popular in the West, modernization and Westernization were believed to be synonymous. Göle claims that, today, she sees evidence

19. This is a methodology that is quite compatible with feminist methodologies more generally. For a comprehensive introduction to feminist methodologies for political and social sciences, see Ackerly and True (2010).

20. For an historical account of non-Western contributions to Western modernity, see Hobson (2004).

of a decoupling of these two concepts. She points to concomitant processes of the globalization of capitalism and the indigenization of modernity. She hypothesizes alternative forms of "hybrid" modernity—the blending of global capitalism with the recognition of different sets of values and cultures. Göle's analysis suggests that modernization can take different forms in different contexts. She is attempting to build alternative visions of modernity that would allow for mutual respect for, and understanding of, different worldviews.

CONCLUSION

In this chapter, I have attempted to offer some insights to help us better understand the worldviews of those who commit violence in the name of religion. I believe that these views are an extreme version of more general frustrations with secular modernity and liberal capitalism and the policies, institutions, and knowledge supporting them, which date back to the Westphalian era when a system of secular states began to replace religiously based polities. An adequate understanding of the religious worldviews that are fueling many of today's conflicts requires building knowledge that is itself critically reflective of secular rationalism—a form of knowledge that is limited in its ability to explain religious motivations and practices. I have outlined some ways in which insights from classical realism and linguistic constructivism are useful for such an endeavor. Going beyond these IR theoretical traditions, I have discussed some feminist writings that offer insights into a radical rewriting of religion and more synthetic forms of knowledge building. In part, humans create their world through the meaning they give to their actions. Less patriarchal religious interpretations can help us get beyond the constitutive gendered hierarchies of conservative religious worldviews—worldviews that are generating conflict and violence. Less gendered, more reflexive understandings of modern knowledge-building can help us get beyond religious/secular divides and the exclusive association of modernity with a secular Western model. Dialogic, reflexive forms of knowledge can produce greater understanding of the "other's" religious beliefs—an understanding that, as Karen Armstrong's epigraph at the beginning of this chapter suggests, may no longer be merely desirable but necessary for our very survival.

CHAPTER 11

Retelling IR's Foundational Stories: Some Feminist and Postcolonial Perspectives

2011

For the most part, conventional IR, particularly in the United States, has been remarkably unreflective about its disciplinary history.[1] As Ole Waever and Arlene Tickner have claimed, the IR scholarly community has very little knowledge about how it itself is shaped by global relationships of power, knowledge, and resources (Tickner and Waever 2009, 1). Certain critical theorists broadly defined, who identify with more sociologically and historically grounded research traditions, many of whom work outside the United States, have been more open to examining the foundations of the discipline. In this chapter, I begin to retell some of the foundational stories of the IR discipline from the perspective of those whose voices and lives have rarely been included in what we define as international relations. I have done this with no pretense to being a historian—rather to demonstrate that the way any discipline frames its foundational myths has important consequences for the questions it asks and the knowledge it deems necessary for answering them.

IR's conventional disciplinary history credits the Peace of Westphalia of 1648 as the symbolic starting point in the history of modern interstate relations. Spatial relations began to be defined by territorial boundaries within which states claimed exclusive sovereignty and the right to prohibit other states from interfering in their internal affairs. As I described in Chapter 10,

---

1. According to Jason Sharman and Jacqui True (Sharman and True 2011), this may be less true in the Oceanic region, where the influence of British IR is greater and the commitment to positivist social science is weaker.

Westphalia ended wars fought over religion; henceforward, European wars would be fought over (secular) sovereign spaces and securing territorial boundaries against external threats.

More or less coincidental with the birth of the modern state—in the sixteenth and seventeenth centuries—the early beginnings of the modern global economy can be seen—a less definable space, which spawned the birth of industrialization in eighteenth- and nineteenth-century Europe and the gradual movement of work from home to factory. The Eurocentric liberal version of "World History" portrays a linear progression toward modernity whereby universal values of liberty and democracy, as well as technology and economic development, were spread around the world through the power and knowledge of European nations. In this story, colonized peoples usually appear as objects of action, those upon whom the power and influence of the West is exerted (Young 2007, 16–17). During the twentieth century, as decolonization proceeded, former empires joined this international society of states and were expected to conduct their international politics according to its norms and laws. The collapse of Soviet style communism at the end of the 1980s, famously termed the "end of history," appeared to be an important final marker on this triumphalist journey.

Philosopher Stephen Toulmin also locates the traditional view of the rise of modern knowledge in seventeenth-century Europe. Political and economic crises and the collapse of tolerance, manifest in that century's wars of religion, motivated a quest for rationality, accompanied by a distrust of the emotions. In the search for certainty in an uncertain world, modern Cartesian science, based on the separation of the rational mind from the bodily emotions, replaced Renaissance humanism. A belief in the possibility of a timeless, objective, and universal understanding of the world, independent of context—what has been described as "the view from nowhere"—formed the basis for modern scientific knowledge (Toulmin 1990, 175).

As we stand today in what is variously described as late modernity or post-modernity—a time when the triumphalist vision of the 1990s has receded even in the West—what are we to make of these foundational stories about modern states and modern knowledge that have been so important in framing our understandings of international politics? The political and economic supremacy of Europe, around which these stories were constructed, has ended; many are predicting an erosion of US power and a shift to Asia as the next global economic center. As I described in more detail in Chapters 9 and 10, non-state actors, supported by global networks, are declaring war on states; secularism, the foundation of the modern state system, is under attack, confounding boundaries between public and private, and reason and emotion. Global communications and economic transactions are speeding up time and shrinking space but are often leading to clashes of civilizations rather than to increased intercultural understandings. Economic collapses in one location are felt throughout the global economy. In other words, IR's foundational stories and teleological accounts of progressive journeys toward a secular liberal modernity appear less and less relevant for understanding contemporary problems. Firmly rooted in the European historical experience and in European knowledge traditions, it is doubtful whether they were ever relevant for much of the world's population.

As Maori scholar Makere Stewart-Harawira tells us, indigenous people tell markedly different stories about the development of the world order—about the impact of imperialism, genocide, and dispossession (Stewart-Harawira 2005, 16). The rise of the modern state in Europe and the initial stages of European expansion abroad occurred simultaneously. Imperialism was essential in shaping the character of *both* Europe *and* the non-European world; as Tarak Barkawi and Mark Laffey suggest, it is their common history (Barkawi and Laffey 2002, 113). Given that IR dates its disciplinary origins at the beginning of the twentieth century, the height of European imperialism, it is quite remarkable how little attention the discipline has paid to imperialism and colonialism, the major defining historical experience for much of the world's population (Gruffydd Jones 2006, 4).

This purpose of this chapter is to suggest some alternative readings of IR's foundational stories. I am aware that challenges to the accuracy of the Westphalian story are being mounted by both conventional and critical scholars within the discipline; however, it is not my purpose to engage these debates about the historical accuracy of these foundational stories but, rather, to suggest that the way we frame our historical myths have important influences on how we construct contemporary knowledge and how that knowledge gets used in both the academic and the policy worlds.

Drawing on feminist and postcolonial approaches, both of which write from positions of marginality, I offer some different historical stories about those who have rarely been the subjects of international relations and who inhabit spaces rarely analyzed by our discipline. Although it is only recently that they have engaged each other, feminism and postcolonialism share a commitment to producing histories and sociologies of knowledge that counter the familiar Western narratives. They also share a skepticism about claims to universalism and objectivity of modern knowledge. I suggest how these stories might be helpful in understanding persistent structures of gender and racial inequalities that are a constitutive feature of global politics and economics. I also suggest how these different stories might help us build a more truly global IR that could help us better understand our contemporary problems.

FEMINIST FOUNDATIONAL STORIES

History is usually written by the winners and rarely includes the voices of those whose lives have been hidden, either by virtue of conquest or by the fact that they were not in a position to write their own history—at least not in a form that seems intelligible to the winners. Since, historically, most women could not read or write (or at least were not permitted to write for a public audience), women have rarely been chroniclers of their own past. Consequently, until recently, the average woman in history has remained almost invisible.

Historians have marked certain historical times as moments of great change. Conventionally, the year 1500 has been taken as such a moment in European history—a breaking point between the medieval era and the rise of modernity—a marker for modern international politics. As I suggested in earlier chapters, feminists often claim that historical moments, marked as progressive, have rarely been so for women. A feminist reexamination of the early modern era reveals that it was not a good time for women. During the early stages of state formation and the beginnings of capitalism in Europe, women as a group experienced a contraction of social and personal options (Kelly-Gadol 1977, 139). While traditional modes of thought were challenged, gender relations were not. In fact, in spite of women's varied circumstances throughout European history, gender discrimination, albeit in a variety of forms, remained remarkably consistent.

Sixteenth- and seventeenth-century Europe also experienced political disorder, natural disasters, epidemics, and economic hard times. As is often the case, desire for order resulted in greater policing of women and a revival of misogynist attitudes, since the maintenance of rigid gender difference is often taken as a mark of a well-ordered society. (As was suggested in the previous two chapters, such attitudes are prevalent in times of uncertainty.) Religion was deeply embedded in the worldviews of sixteenth- and seventeenth-century Europeans, and women's subordinate position in religious ordering was accepted as God's punishment for Eve's disobedience in the Garden of Eden by men and women alike (Karant-Nunn 1998, 168). In both Protestant and Catholic Europe, there was a growing concern for moral rectitude and orderliness that had serious consequences for women.

The end of the fifteenth century saw the beginning of a massive persecution of witches in Europe; the fear of witches lasted until the eighteenth century. What has been termed by historians as the first phase of the Age of Reason was also a time when many thousands of women were burned alive or hung. Although historians have paid little attention to witchcraft, William Monter claims that this misogynist heritage was inscribed in European laws and religion (Monter 1977, 134).

As discussed in Part One, feminists have also drawn our attention to an emerging gendered division of labor that can be seen in seventeenth-century Europe, when definitions of male and female were becoming polarized in ways that were suited to the growing division of labor between work and home required by early capitalism. Evolving notions of citizenship were based on male, property-owning heads of households: since the status of men defined that of their wives and children, gender discrimination became a constitutive feature of the modern state (Toulmin 1990, 133). Not only did the growth of capitalism in Europe have an effect on the gendered division of labor and the meaning of work; gender structures also shaped economic change (Wiesner 1998, 203). With the development of capitalism, work was increasingly defined as an activity for which one was paid; reproductive and caring tasks, the majority of which were performed by women, were not considered work. Even work for which women were paid, such as sewing, began to be thought of as domestic, whereas men's work, even in the same field, was considered productive (Wiesner 1998, 207). According to historian James Belich, in nineteenth-century settler societies, such as New Zealand and Australia, women worked staggeringly hard at both reproductive and subsistence (non-paid) tasks, often without the help of a resident male partner. While their work was primarily on family farms, when they did do paid work, settler women's wages were typically half those of men's (Belich 2009, 649).

The assignment of space within a socio-spatial structure denotes distinctive roles, capacities for action, and access to power within any social order (Harvey, quoted in Rose 1993, 18). Democratic theory and practice have been built on the male-as-norm engaged in narrowly defined political and economic activities associated with the public sphere (Pateman 1988, chap. 1). The spatial separation of the public and private spheres, typical of both capitalist and, later, socialist models of development, has had important ramifications for the construction and historical evolution of political and economic institutions at all levels, ramifications that are still in evidence today.

COLONIAL STORIES

As women were losing status in early modern Europe, "voyages of discovery" allowed Europe to identify itself against the otherness of a multitude of races, religions, languages, and cultures (Guha 2002, 8). The origins of European colonization date back to the late fifteenth century to what Europeans at that time referred to as the "discovery" of the fourth and final continent, the "New World" of the Americas. This "discovery" of a world inhabited by strange and savage peoples, as they were described by early European explorers, unsettled Europeans' view of the world and challenged their linear story about creation and the progressive evolution of Christian humankind. Europeans typically treated non-Europeans as representing a lower stage of political, social, and economic development that Europeans had left behind (Kiel 2003, 56). In other words, past and present could exist at the same time in different places (McGrane 1989, 93). Paul Kiel claims that this cultural incommensurability was a crucial element in the development of relations between Europeans and non-Europeans.

The year that Christopher Columbus set sail for the Americas, 1492, is often marked as the early beginning of European colonization. According to Tzvan Todorov, Columbus's first observations about the Indians noted that they were naked and lacked culture, law, or religion; those with lighter skin were looked on more favorably. In subsequent observations, Columbus appeared to express two contrasting attitudes toward the Indians that persisted in the way colonizers saw the colonized, traces of which still exist today, albeit in a more muted form. First, by projecting his own values onto the Indians, Columbus saw them as potential equals who, therefore, were open to conversion to Christianity. The subsequent contrasting view saw them as different, which translated into inferiority. In Todorov's opinion, these contrasting views leave no room for a true other—someone capable of being not merely an imperfect state of one's self (Todorov 1984, 42).

The name of Columbus is associated with a complete transformation of the European geographical imagination. Europe became a continent, and the notion of Christian man was seen in relation to others who were different (McGrane 1989, 27). Difference was signified by gender as well as race. In the borders of Janszoon Visscher's world map, published in Amsterdam in 1639, ten years before the Treaty of Westphalia, Europe and Asia are represented by well-dressed "ladies," while Africa and America, the latter described on seventeenth-century maps as the strangest of all known continents, are represented by semi-naked women sitting on animals (Mignolo 1995, 273). Walter Mignolo (1995, 309) claims that the goal of these Eurocentric maps was not necessarily accuracy but was related to controlling territories and diminishing non-European conceptualizations of space.

These gendered and racial representations of newly discovered peoples lasted well into the eighteenth century. Anthropologist Margaret Jolly describes how *Observations Made During a Voyage Around the World*, written by J. R. Forster, a naturalist on James Cook's second voyage to the South Pacific, established a gradation of Pacific peoples. To the lighter skinned island populations Forster ascribed more benevolent behavior than to those who were darker and described as somewhat mistrustful (Jolly 2007, 517). People of the Pacific Islands were also ranked by temporal stages associated with infancy and adolescence; adulthood was a stage that only Europeans had reached, giving them the right to oversee the growth of other races. Representations of women were crucial to Forster's racial typologies. Women from the lighter skinned islands to the east were described as beautiful and alluring, while darker skinned women from the west were depicted as ugly and sexually unappealing (Jolly 2007, 520).

Geographer John Agnew claims that the idea of race has been vital to the substantive distinctions drawn between different regions of the world and their different stages of economic and moral development (Agnew 1998, 23). He notes that nineteenth-century Europeans' encounters with Australian

Aborigines attributed their actions to the context of the European past rather than to those of a different culture coexisting in time and space. Agnew asserts that converting time into space is a fundamental characteristic of modern geopolitical thought (Agnew 1998, 36).

As anthropologist Johannes Fabian has argued, the ascription of temporality is political. The relationship between the West and non-West has been formed through a spatialization of time, evidence of which still exists today (Fabian quoted in Oke 2009, 311). Similarly, Bernard Cohn claims that, from the eighteenth century on, European states made their power visible by defining and classifying space. Creating and codifying vast amounts of information formed the basis of their capacity to govern. In the case of Britain, this process of state-building was closely linked to its emergence as an imperial power. Cohn claims that many aspects of the state's documentation projects were first developed in India, where they were seen as necessary if India were to be controlled (Cohn 1996, 1–4). The British believed that they could conquer India by making the unknown and the strange knowable; for many British officials from the seventeenth century on, India was a vast collection of numbers, and a number was a form of certainty to be held onto in a strange world (Cohn 1996, 8). The term "statistics" implied the collection and dissemination of information thought necessary and useful to the state (Cohn 1996, 81). Cohn suggests that the British were most comfortable surveying India numerically and categorically from a distance—from a horse, an elephant, or a train—rather than in streets and bazaars, where they were surrounded by their Indian subjects (Cohn 1996, 10).

For many Europeans, India was a vast museum, a source of collectibles that could be brought back for display in European museums and gardens. India was not only exotic and bizarre but also symbolic of Europe's past; however, Europe had progressed, whereas India was static and mired in the past. Like other colonized peoples, Indians were seen as people without a history for whom a history must be constructed in order to rule them. Nineteenth-century colonial discourse saw in India a double lack of history; first, India did not have documents, records, or chronicles of the type with which the West had constructed its own history; second, since India had no history, it had not progressed (Cohn 1996, 93).

Creating new stories and new histories for colonized peoples, as well as cataloging, analyzing, and putting the world on display scientifically from an objective distance, were acts of power. Modern science, history, and geography played a large role in legitimizing stories about colonized people and in dividing the world in ways that objectified those who were not white and who resided outside the West. Contemporary scholars from these same disciplines, as well as those from other social sciences and humanities, have contributed important critical reflections on how our knowledge structures may still serve to perpetuate, even if unconsciously, some of the imperial legacies that contribute to the hierarchical gendered, racial, and geographic structures of inequalities that still exist today. Divisions between civilized and uncivilized, evident in the effort to impose Western knowledge on colonial people, were reinforced by this dualistic knowledge structure that emphasized difference. This has had important implications for modern, and even contemporary, conceptions of autonomy and agency, with men, generally Western privileged men, more often being seen as both the knowers and the subjects of knowledge.

Feminists have also argued that knowledge that claims to be universal and objective is actually knowledge based largely on the lives of privileged men. Analyzing the foundations of modern scientific knowledge construction, feminist philosopher Sandra Harding (1987, 6) claims that traditional social science has typically asked questions about nature and social life that certain (usually privileged) men want answered. She traces the relationship between the development of modern Western science and the history of European expansion. Challenging the claim to value-neutrality that modern science makes with respect to the questions it asks, she argues that European voyages of discovery went hand in hand with the development of modern science and technology—Europeans who were colonizing the world needed to know about winds, tides, maps, and navigation, as well as botany, the construction of ships, firearms, and survival in harsh environments. Such questions became intellectually interesting in order to solve colonialism's everyday problems (Harding 1998, 39–54). It was men who went to the colonies to collect and name specimens from the animal, plant, and even the human world and who brought them back to the West to display in museums or study in laboratories.[2] Cataloging, analyzing, and putting the world on display were acts of power. This collecting and renaming, which resulted in forgetting how much knowledge actually originated outside the West, was, for the most part, done by men.[3] Few women went to the colonies, and women were excluded from the design and management of the three major corporate sponsors of imperial knowledge: the Jesuits, the trading companies, and the imperial governments themselves. Like science and history, geography, particularly mapmaking, was also an important aspect of imperial knowledge.

2. A particularly egregious example of human display was Saartjie Baartman, a sixteen year old Xhosa girl from South Africa, who was brought to London in 1810 and put on display as the "Hottentot Venus." Thought to identify a primitive level of sexuality, she fed into the nineteenth century European fascination with African female sexuality (Willinsky 1998, 59).

3. Mary Kingsley was one of the few female travelers of the late nineteenth century to go to what were deemed the wild parts of the earth not considered fit for Western women. She wrote that the last words a distinguished scientist said to her before embarking on her travels in West Africa were "always take measurements, Miss Kingsley, and always take them from the adult male" (quoted in Willinsky 1998, 35).

The association of women with danger and disorder, evident in the seventeenth century's persecution of witches, was extended outward to the dangers of unknown places; indeed, the intersection of race and gender was a significant marker for unknown others, seen either as dangerous or as at a less advanced stage of development. As I discussed in Chapter 9, the dangers that we face today are frequently framed in similarly gendered and racial terms. But even when the intentions of those who construct these frames are benign, the sense of the other being at an earlier stage of development remains with us. In an analysis of attitudes toward the Pacific Islands by Australian policy-makers and academic economists during the 1990s, Greg Fry presents a set of images associated with what these policy-makers saw as development failures—a region "falling off the map," an image that is strikingly similar to that depicted in seventeenth-century maps to which I alluded earlier. For the Islands, the only hope for salvation from these "developmental failures" is to give up inappropriate traditions and open their economies to the global market (Fry 1997, 305–306). As John Agnew suggests, the language of modern thought is filled with the fusion of time and space into binary distinctions between those areas that are "ahead" or "advanced" and those that are "backward" or "behind"—distinctions that are also reflected in our intellectual division of labor between those who study Third World development and those who study advanced capitalist states, the latter being accorded a higher status in the IR intellectual hierarchy (Agnew 1998, 33).

RECONSTRUCTING OUR DISCIPLINARY STORIES

Drawing on these insights from feminist and postcolonial scholars, how might we construct a less Eurocentric, more multicultural story about our disciplinary foundations—one that is critically sensitive to the androcentric and Eurocentric biases that are built into our teaching and research? Postcolonial scholar Homi Bhabha suggests a reinterpretation of modern history as *hybrid* whereby the subjectivity of previously colonized people is recognized. He challenges the linear Eurocentric story of the progressive universal World History, described earlier. Such histories ignore the fact that all societies and institutions are the products, not of a one-way imposition of knowledge, but of multidimensional cultural interactions between European peoples and others. Rather than a one-way process, history becomes an encounter with, and learning from, cultural difference. John Hobson has proposed a similar model in his work on the Eastern origins of Western civilization (Hobson 2004). This recognition of a two-way process challenges the negative implications of dualities such as self versus other, inside versus outside, and modern versus primitive (Bhabba, cited in Young 2007, 16–17).

Tarak Barkawi and Mark Laffey suggest that a less Eurocentric IR could be achieved by a thicker conception of the international that is directly attentive to imperial relations. Such a framework involves constructing knowledge from the diversity of people's everyday lives; this opens up space for a richer account of the international which reveals the connections between concrete struggles of people the world over (Barkawi and Laffey 2002, 119–120). Much of feminist IR over the last twenty years has been grounded in stories of the everyday lives of those who have not been the subjects of history and their connectivity through various structures of gendered and racial hierarchies.

Many of these scholars whose work I have discussed claim that Western knowledge cannot be separated from its implication in the history of imperialism. Stephen Toulmin advocates an alternative knowledge structure that might help us to a more empathetic understanding of the other, more suited to the kind of reinterpretation of history that these scholars suggest. Instead of the High Science model, associated with the detached observer—a model that feminists have critiqued for its androcentric and elite biases—Toulmin (1990) suggests a return to practical reasoning, based on experiential knowledge about the concrete and particular, that comes out of participant observation and thick description. Rather than surveying other cultures from a distance, as the British did in India, this kind of knowledge-building requires an empathetic understanding of the Other constructed through dialogic encounters. As I have described throughout this book, many feminists also advocate a dialogic contextual model of knowledge-building whereby knowledge emerges through conversations with texts and subjects (Ackerly 2000). And Linda Tuhiwai Smith draws on *kaupapa* Maori theory, a theory that is premised on the centrality of being and identifying as Maori and as a Maori researcher—what she calls doing research as an "outside-insider" (Tuhiwai Smith 1999). *Contextualized* rationality, whereby the producer of knowledge is critically reflexive about her or his role in the production of knowledge and the power structures in which that knowledge is embedded, is a more robust ideational foundation on which to build less ethnocentric and conflictual worldviews.

Modern Western knowledge has been built on dichotomous oppositional frameworks that are not helpful for understanding many of our contemporary global problems. And, as Spike Peterson tells us, our fear of contaminating objective reason and research by acknowledging the role of emotion has left us tragically ill informed in the face of violent forms of nationalism and fundamentalism (Peterson 2000, 19). As I described in more detail in Chapters 9 and 10, conflictual spatial and temporal divisions between the West and the Rest, and the civilized and the non-civilized, embodied in Cartesian knowledge structures, as well as the appropriation of colonial history by Western imperial powers, are fueling contemporary tensions. Non-Western peoples are demanding respect, dignity, and the right to tell their own histories. The rise of religious fundamentalisms and ethnically driven conflicts are fueled in part by colonial legacies. Confronting the negative implications of these legacies depends in part on reconstructing the history of modernity, democracy, and state-building from the point of view of previously colonized peoples (Young 2007, 16).

In the words of Makere Stewart-Harawira, "the reclaiming, retelling and rewriting of our histories is critical to reaffirming identities and to healing the deeply embedded scars of the past" (Stewart-Harawira 2005, 23). I conclude with these words because they remind us all that, rather than searching for one universal history, we need to uncover stories about forgotten spaces that respect difference, show tolerance and compassion, and are skeptical about absolute truths. Such stories can help us to build a more inclusionary, more open minded, and more reflexive international relations that transcends the structures of domination that all of us still carry within ourselves from the past. More inclusive stories about our discipline's foundations, which respect multiple ways of being and knowing, are needed if we are to conceptualize a more just, less hierarchical global politics.

PART FOUR

Conclusions

CHAPTER 12
Looking Back: Looking Forward

As I look back over twenty-five years of feminist scholarship in international relations, I see a remarkable body of wide-ranging, provocative scholarship that crosses disciplines and international boundaries.[1] It challenges IR to think about new issues that have never been part of the discipline and to see more familiar issues in new ways. As I have tried to show through a presentation of some of my own contributions, I see how the exciting scholarship being produced by an intellectually alive, engaged, and supportive feminist community has challenged my own thinking and moved it in new directions.

IR feminism has moved far beyond its initial goals of demonstrating how IR's concepts and theoretical assumptions are gendered, and it is now embarking on new journeys—some into uncharted territories. I will reflect on this later in this chapter. I believe that many of the misunderstandings about methodologies that I discussed in Part Two still exist, and I will revisit some issues that other IR feminists have thoughtfully raised in response to my call for conversations in my 1997 article in *International Studies Quarterly* (Chapter 6 in this volume). I do so because so much of my own work has addressed these methodological questions and also because they signal some broader issues with which feminists continue to be concerned as we move forward into the next twenty-five years.

Although my calls for conversation did not generate much discussion from the IR mainstream, they did generate responses from other IR feminists, most of them in British journals.[2] Some took issue with my arguments, but most focused on the problems and possibilities for conversations with other IR scholars and, more fundamentally, whether we should still be trying to engage

---

1. Portions of this chapter are based on Tickner (2010).
2. The exception being, as I mentioned in Chapter 7, a symposium that *International Studies Quarterly* published in the subsequent issue (*ISQ* 42:1).

the field in such conversations at all.[3] One of the most contentious issues has been that of engaging with feminist scholars (as well as non-feminists who use gender as a variable), who use positivist, usually quantitative, methods. I will take up this controversy, which I too have addressed in some of my work, later in this chapter. It is important to stress that, while this scholarship is providing important and valuable data about women's lives and raising interesting research questions (not all of which are feminist questions, as I discussed in Chapter 7), it is the work that receives the most recognition in US IR mainstream journals.[4] This relates to the issue of the power of knowledge and whose knowledge gets taken seriously. As I have emphasized throughout my own work, this is a critical question for feminists.

First, I will elaborate on some of the feminist scholarship that has taken up the issue of conversation with the broader discipline (or lack of it). In an article entitled "Engaging from the Margins: Feminist Encounters with the "Mainstream" of International Relations," Jill Steans observed in 2003 that, in spite of the post–Cold War opening of IR to some critical theoretical approaches, feminism continued to suffer from marginalization (Steans 2003). According to Steans, IR scholars have engaged selectively with IR feminists, ignoring those who work with unsettled notions of gender while engaging with those who work with stable and unproblematic gender categories. The latter group to which Steans is referring are scholars, not all of whom self-identify as feminists, who work within a positivist/rationalist approach to social science. They often use quantitative methods, and they see gender as one among many variables that might inform theories of causality (Steans 2003, 430).

Three years later, in an article entitled "You Still Don't Understand," this time aimed at critical IR scholars rather than at the mainstream, Georgina Waylen castigated critical international political economy (IPE) for barely mentioning gender, despite feminist attempts to engage in conversation (Waylen 2006). Waylen claimed that critical IPE and feminism have much in common, an ontology that gives primacy to social relations and is not state centric, and a normative belief that the purpose of social theorizing is to understand and challenge global structures of domination (Waylen 2006, 147). However, in spite of these similar ontological and normative commitments, Waylen claimed in 2006 that critical IPE continued to focus on class while ignoring

3. I am not talking about conversations among feminist scholars and with their research subjects. Creating knowledge reflexively through conversation is an important aspect of feminist methodology (Ackerly and True 2010). See also Tickner and Sjoberg (2011).

4. Feminist questions are those that are asking questions that have relevance for women's lives (see Chapter 7). I am defining feminist theory as theory that uses gender as an analytical category.

race and gender. Her examination of influential edited volumes on globalization revealed only a few references to women and only one to any feminist critiques of globalization (Waylen 2006, 151). Waylen attributed this silence, in part, to the power differentials between critical IPE scholars and feminists, which allow IPE scholars to ignore gender; more fundamentally, however, she still saw a lack of understanding about the most fundamental goal of feminist theory—what it means to use gender as an analytical category that is fundamentally constitutive of important processes in the global economy, an issue that I discussed in some detail in Chapters 3 and 4 (Waylen 2006, 164). More recent interventions into this debate indicate that we may have moved into a period of fatigue—questioning whether attempts at engagement are even worthwhile. I cite three examples from a British, a US, and an Australian perspective, respectively.

The misunderstanding theme continued with Marysia Zalewski's contribution to a 2007 special issue of *The British Journal of Politics and International Relations* that assessed British contributions to gender and international relations. Echoing Steans, Zalewski devoted quite a bit of her article to criticizing what she called "neo-feminist" scholarship that uses social scientific quantitative methods. She claimed that the power, which is so deeply embedded in incompatible ontological and epistemological sensibilities, is too deep to overcome. If we assume, as does Zalewski, that understanding across epistemological divides is an impossible task, she asks us to consider whether feminism has undone itself rather than succeeding in undoing IR. She suggests that holding feminism to the demands of an established discipline invites critical atrophy; while acknowledging a need for feminist-informed critical analyses of international politics, Zalewski suggests that such analyses must play an important role in unsettling the established norms that reproduce the discipline and that continued misunderstandings may be productive in this task (Zalewski 2007, 303).

Writing ten years after "You Just Don't Understand," Laura Sjoberg claimed that there is a sense among feminists that the mainstream will never understand and, therefore, it may no longer be a worthwhile project to try to "mainstream" feminist IR (I should add that many, including Zalewski, have never felt it to be a worthwhile project). Sjoberg claimed that feminist IR and mainstream IR are different worlds—besides its commitment to gender-based analysis as crucial to its disciplinary inquiry, feminism, to quote Sjoberg, "is a world of contingency, subjectivity, emancipation and empathy" (Sjoberg 2008, 2). She cites Sarah Brown's claim in 1988, before the field was established, that only with feminist IR can the mainstream have a complete understanding of global politics. Nevertheless, like Zalewski, Brown worried that feminist IR might lose something were it to try to fit into the discipline (Brown 1988). With these concerns in mind, Sjoberg asked where we would go if we left IR, a point to which I will return.

Painting a more optimistic picture of feminist IR's acceptance in Australia, Katrina Lee-Koo also suggested that feminist IR scholarship's goal to make gender visible "is not well served by rehashing decades-long debates in the top-tier journals about the relevance of gender to IR" (Lee-Koo 2009, 430). In spite of being someone who has attempted this, I am inclined to agree with her argument at this point. Nevertheless, these reflective conversations (if only among IR feminists) raise some important issues that are still worth considering as we move forward into the next twenty-five years. The first is the issue of marginality: Where do, or where should, feminists locate themselves in the IR discipline (if at all)? If feminist conversations are not being heard by non-feminists, mainstream or critical, should they be abandoned? And second, what about the social scientific quantitative work, dismissed by most of the IR feminists who have participated in these conversations?[5] With the increasing prominence of this type of work in mainstream journals, this is an important issue that post-positivist feminists need to address further. While I realize that this issue has more resonance for those located inside the United States, it does speak to a third issue, namely the wider concern about knowledge and power—that is, whose knowledge is recognized and validated as legitimate.[6] I now take up each of these three questions.

MARGINALITY?

Also writing in the special issue of the *British Journal of Politics and International Relations* to which I referred earlier, Judith Squires and Jutta Weldes, who see gender as having achieved considerable success in international relations scholarship, challenged feminists to abandon what they term "unhelpful preoccupation with their marginal status," (Squires and Weldes 2007, 196). Squires and Weldes claimed that what they called auditing practices, a category in which they would place the articles that I have discussed, run the risk of reproducing the mainstream, even while they attempt to criticize it (Squires and Weldes, 2007, 194). Claiming that there has been a tendency to critique rather than to demonstrate the ways in which gendered analyses of the international fundamentally shift our understanding of the international, they encouraged feminists to build on the remarkable legacy of empirically rich and theoretically and conceptually sophisticated gendered analysis that they argue fundamentally transforms the horizons of international relations.

5. It is important to note that there have been responses to feminist critiques of positivist methodologies from feminist quantitative scholars. See, for example, Caprioli (2004).

6. Feminist philosopher of science, Sandra Harding has written extensively on this issue. See, for example, Harding (2008).

While I agree with Squires and Weldes that feminists should, and indeed are, building on this rich legacy, the issue of abandoning marginality is more contentious among feminist scholars. As Zalewski and Brown both suggested at different times, it is important to maintain feminism's critical edge. And as Bina D'Costa and Katrina Lee-Koo observed in their introduction to *Gender Politics in the Asia-Pacific*, there is also merit in recognizing, as their volume does, that feminist IR might *want* to sit on the margins (D'Costa and Lee-Koo 2009, 11). As they claim, the margins of IR have produced exciting, innovative, and challenging work. Their book, which is a celebration of the scholarship of Jindy Pettman, one of the founding figures of feminist IR, is evidence of this. The editors situate the contributions in what they term the field of critical feminist IR. Although primarily focused on the Asia Pacific region, this volume is broad in its scope and subject matter; it emphasizes another link that has always been important to feminists, that between social activism and scholarship

Neither this volume, nor other recent texts in feminist IR, feel compelled to situate themselves in previous debates with IR.[7] Feminists have become more self-confident in articulating the multiple, but uniquely feminist, methodologies that inform their work. While not bound to any one way of doing research, feminist research is committed to a reflective sensibility that engages with the relationship between the researcher and her subjects. The 2006 volume *Feminist Methodologies for International Relations*, edited by Brooke Ackerly, Maria Stern, and Jacqui True, as well as the more recent Ackerly and True volume (2010) on feminist methodologies for political and social science that I cited earlier, provide an honest and self-reflective account of how feminists conduct their work in international relations. Both are a refreshing change from mainstream positive accounts; importantly, they offer guides for ethical engagements and begin to offer a distinctive array of feminist methodologies for IR (Lee-Koo 2009, 422).

This new work is but one snapshot of the exciting work that has been done by feminist IR scholars in the first decade of the twenty-first century. Feminist research is providing us with vibrant research programs and supports my claim that feminism is breaking disciplinary and geographical boundaries and expanding what, and who, are included in the subject matter of global politics, as well as how to go about studying it. All of this research challenges Squires and Weldes's claim that there has been too much focus on critique and engaging with the mainstream; it indicates feminism's rapidly maturing and expanding research programs. I shall now turn to the more contentious issue about quantitative methodology.

---

7. See, for example, Shepherd (2009). This is a textbook for use in the classroom that covers a broad range of global issues, using a feminist perspective and gendered analysis. It also includes a section on feminist theories and feminist methodologies.

SHOULD IR FEMINISTS USE QUANTITATIVE METHODOLOGIES?

While feminist IR has drawn on multiple methodologies, much of it has tended to stay away from positivist and quantitative ones, for reasons I elaborated in Part Two. And, as I said earlier, the most contentious debates in feminist IR have taken place on this terrain. It is interesting to note that feminist researchers in other social science disciplines have been more willing to adopt mainstream methodological frameworks. Certainly this has been true in feminist economics and much of feminist scholarship in American politics, as well as some branches of sociology.

A series of articles, edited by Brooke Ackerly, in *Politics and Gender*, the journal of the Women and Politics Section of the American Political Science Association, take up this issue. Claiming that there is a role for feminist theory in informing positivist-oriented research, Ackerly calls for a more productive conversation with IR feminists who use quantitative methods (Ackerly 2009, 432).[8] Ackerly suggested that post-positivist IR feminists should not reject such methodologies outright but, rather, should adopt what she calls a "feminist rigor" that reflects on all stages of their methodological choices, from choices about the questions that are asked, to the method of data collection, to the method of analysis; these choices can include empirical inquiry. Indeed, Ackerly contends that we need empirical work to help us better understand injustices in the world and how we might go about mitigating them (Ackerly 2009, 431).

The *Politics and Gender* edited collection included contributions from three scholars who self-identify as IR feminists and who use quantitative positivist research methods. Laura Parisi, one such scholar, asked how we might reconcile feminist theorizing with quantitative methods. Situated in an interdisciplinary women's studies department and influenced by work in feminist economics and development studies, Parisi reflects on her own journey, which has taken her beyond asking whether we should engage in positive research methods to an attempt to understand their limitations as well as their promise. Parisi claimed that IR feminists should not reject all positivist models because they are positivist, but rather, they should reject those models that do not draw on theoretical insights from feminist scholars about gender relations (Parisi 2009, 411). For Parisi, the question becomes how "we might effectively utilize quantitative methodologies in our goal of transforming hierarchical gender, racial, ethnic, class, and sexual relations that feminize and marginalize

8. Ackerly describes my exchange with Robert Keohane in *International Studies Quarterly* (Tickner 1998) as closing off rather than opening up conversation. She claims that a normative theorist asking a positivist theorist to reconceptualize the building blocks of IR and a positivist theorist asking a normative theorist for a positivist research agenda is untenable.

many, including men." For Parisi, the biggest challenge is to overcome the tension between sex-disaggregated data that places too much emphasis on the material dimensions of power to the exclusion of social and ideological power relations. She concludes that we can use feminist theorizing to explain why this is so and to frame our interpretations of statistical findings (Parisi 2009, 416). Parisi also concludes that quantitative tools can provide an entry point for deeper qualitative analysis.

Clair Apodaca, another author in this volume, identifies herself as a positivist, quantitatively trained feminist researcher whose normative goal is to empower women and create social change (Apodaca 2009, 420). She affirmed that feminists like her do believe that feminist research questions can be answered using social scientific explanatory frameworks. She claims that, if one is working for incremental change within the existing system, there are benefits in using the dominant language of the patriarchal system and that using data and statistical analysis is no less feminist than other forms of research. The major obstacle she sees for this type of research is the politically motivated and biased acts of data collection by states and international institutions that decide which segments of the population are considered worthy of being counted and which are ignored—with women, particularly marginalized women, usually in the latter category, an issue I also raised in Chapter 7. Apodaca concedes that most quantitative feminists would agree that knowledge is not neutral but is situated in structures of social, economic, and political power. While the researcher's interpretations must take this into account, Apodaca concludes that we need more, not less, data. She quotes the Convention to Eliminate All Forms of Discrimination Against Women's (CEDAW) plea "that statistical information is absolutely necessary in order to understand the real situation of women in each of the states that are parties to the Convention" (Apodaca 2009, 422).

One response to this call for more and better data has been the creation of WomanStats—a multidisciplinary central repository for cross-national data on women,[9] which allows researchers to find information they need for their research. Mary Caprioli, one of the creators of this data set and the third author in the *Politics and Gender* issue, admits to its limitations. Being mostly at the state level, it does not permit disaggregation across racial, class, and socioeconomic lines (Caprioli 2009, 431). Nevertheless, WomenStats is a very valuable resource that is constantly being updated, enlarged, and improved.

Given the strong link between feminist activism and feminist scholarship, any effort to compile more and better data, which can help us understand the multiple realities of women's lives, should be welcomed. As Apodaca says, using statistics can and should be one of the tools that feminists employ

9. Available at http://www.womanstats.org.

where appropriate. Not to do so risks stereotyping women as not up to dealing with numbers. Statistics on discrimination, poverty, human rights violations, and sexual harassment can be used to formulate public policy and initiate legal redress for these problems (Apodaca 2009, 420). International women's movements over the past forty years have demanded better data from international organizations in order to support their claims of a variety of gender oppressions. Activists want scholars to provide them with analyses that depend on empirical investigations that they do not have the time or resources to conduct.[10] Nevertheless, we must remember that doing empirical research is not the same as an unquestioning commitment to empiricism, which carries with it the deep imprint of positivist science and its universalist and masculinist assumptions that I discussed in Part Two.

The authors just discussed give us some ideas about how we might conduct empirical analysis using feminist sensibilities. Parisi, Apodaca, and Caprioli reflectively assess the political implications of their findings, the politics of data collection, the way data are interpreted, and the relative merits of variables that might best demonstrate gender inequality. This leads Ackerly to conclude that these authors show that feminist theory has the potential for bridging philosophical and social science methods (Ackerly 2009, 435). While agreeing that quantitative analysis with a feminist sensibility can yield important empirical research that is valuable for feminist goals, I remain skeptical about the promise of bridging deeper epistemological divides.

For example, in a 2008 article in *International Security*, a mainstream US journal in which most feminists, who do not use social scientific methodologies, would have a hard time getting their work published, Caprioli and her five coauthors, all of whom are associated with the WomenStats program, addressed the issue of the marginalization of contributions to feminist security studies; the contributions to which they refer consist of research that does not use conventional methodologies. The authors attribute this marginality to the use of what they called "unconventional methodologies"; their implied solution seemed to be that feminists should adopt social scientific methodologies if they want to be accepted and taken seriously (Hudson et al. 2008/2009, 29). As I claimed in Part Two, the gulf between positivist and post-positivist research traditions, feminist or otherwise, is far greater than such comments would indicate. What this piece described as "unconventional methodologies" encompass a wide array of rich historical, hermeneutic, humanistic, and philosophical traditions of knowledge-building that can also provide us with equally valid understandings of insecurity and oppression. Whether these

10. The relationship between activism and critical scholarship is a complicated one. See Australian feminist legal scholar Diane Otto (2009) for a thoughtful engagement with this issue.

traditions can be bridged, as Ackerly suggested, or whether their differences are too fundamental is a matter of much scholarly debate.[11] Comments such as these suggest that it is hard for the mainstream, even if it self-identifies as feminist, to understand or accept that there are many valuable and legitimate ways of conducting "scientific" research outside positivist social sciences practices. While, as I have suggested, many post-positivist feminists have moved beyond a concern with bridging these divides, the issue of knowledge and power remains a central one and one that I believe that feminists should continue to raise.

KNOWLEDGE AND POWER

Observations on their own writings, such as those presented by the authors in *Politics and Gender*, go quite some way in introducing a feminist sensibility into quantitative research and recognizing these epistemological issues; they are an important contribution to this debate. However, Parisi and Apodaca's observation that knowledge is not neutral but situated in unequal structures of power is a deep problem that is hard to solve. As I have emphasized throughout this book, feminists in all disciplines have been acutely aware of the relationship between knowledge and power and the ways that conventional knowledge has been constructed in the interests of the powerful. Feminist scholarship emerged from a deep skepticism about knowledge that, while it claims to be universal and objective, is, in reality, partial and subjective.

Feminists have made unique contributions in drawing attention to unequal power structures, gendered, racial, or otherwise, that impact negatively on so many people's lives—both women and men. Importantly, they have also alerted us to ways in which knowledge itself is complicit in legitimating these hierarchical structures—the unequal terrain on which feminists attempt to engage with social scientific research, and the lack of engagement, even with other critical approaches noted by Georgina Waylen, are examples of this. And, as Marysia Zalewski claims, power differentials in the discipline of international relations allow both mainstream and critical approaches to ignore gender. The fact that the mainstream in any discipline rarely reflects on these epistemological issues, or feels itself obliged to respond to calls for conversations across these divides, is an indication of the power of hegemonic knowledge structures. By studying issues not normally considered part of IR, feminists have alerted us to the ways that certain subjects and issues have been silenced through the drawing of these epistemological and disciplinary boundaries.

---

11. For the classic statement that supports their incompatibility, see Hollis and Smith (1990). It is a position with which I tend to agree.

While it is up to each of us to choose our own methodological pathways, we should all be tolerant of non-conventional methodologies that may be more suited to analyzing some of the research questions that IR feminists have raised. New questions, concepts, and definitions, and new modes of analysis are essential tools for seeing beyond the ideological and epistemological boundaries that drive global politics and inhibit our quest to understand them. Nevertheless, it may be time to put aside these debates and pursue the many fruitful ways that IR feminists, however they define themselves, are investigating oppressive power structures, both material and ideational, and seeking ways to change them. The location from which we do our research, whether it is inside or outside what has been defined as the discipline of IR, is for each of us to decide.

In 2002, Anne Runyan, a feminist scholar who has moved from political science/IR to women's studies, posed the question as to whether feminists should seek to be at home in IR—that is, to have their perspectives legitimated within the discipline—or whether they should forget IR in order to build more hospitable local/global homes for giving voice to the world's inhabitants, especially those marginalized by world politics as usual (Runyan 2002, 361). Given my belief that knowledge and power cannot be separated, this is a question that feminists must continue to ask themselves, particularly in the United States, where the hold of social scientific methodologies is strong and where the implications of whose knowledge gets heard and validated is so problematic. With these questions always in mind, I conclude with some thoughts on possible future directions.

FUTURE DIRECTIONS?

In 2010, the Center for International Studies at the University of Southern California (USC) hosted a conference to celebrate twenty years of feminist IR scholarship.[12] The intention of this third gender conference at USC was to highlight some of the innovative work being done by younger IR feminist scholars. The volume that came out of the conference, *Feminism and International Relations: Conversations about the Past, Present and Future*, (Tickner and Sjoberg 2011) showcased feminist IR scholars who had been at USC as graduate students, postdoctoral fellows, or participants in past USC conferences. Coedited with Laura Sjoberg, one of my former students, this is a book of which I am particularly proud. Indeed, one of the most rewarding aspects of my own journey has been the students with whom I have had the privilege to work. Some, whose work is contained in this volume, have chosen feminist paths, while

---

12. Organized by Jane Jaquette, one of the organizers of the first USC conference in 1990, Laura Sjoberg of the University of Florida, a USC Ph.D., and myself.

others have not. But all have showed courage in pursuing their passion and their interests rather than what is currently fashionable in what remains, in the United States at least, a rather narrow discipline.

Demonstrating the range of interests that is characteristic of feminist IR scholarship more generally, the edited volume included chapters exploring topics such as the Women's International League for Peace and Freedom (WILPF), human rights discourse at the United Nations, gender mainstreaming in global governance, an emancipatory perspective on security, the Chechen wars, US drone warfare, targeting civilians in wars, and the global political economy of beauty. Some authors brought a gender perspective to existing IR approaches such as realism, constructivism, and critical security studies; some drew more directly on feminist methodological approaches, such as Third World social criticism (Ackerly 2000) and feminist science studies (Harding 1986, 1991), or on concepts such as militarized masculinity (Enloe 2000) and Peterson's reproductive, productive, and virtual (RPV) framework for studying the global economy (Peterson 2003). A unique feature of the book is the conversations between the authors and senior scholars, some of whose theoretical frameworks the authors drew upon.

While this book is but one snapshot of some of the topics that IR feminists are addressing, its commitment to conversation and reflexivity is a particularly feminist way of building knowledge that, I am sure, will continue to be a hallmark of feminist IR scholarship in the future. Participants at the conference emphasized that the goal of feminist IR is, and should continue to be, an ongoing conversation rather than a destination. As IR feminism has become more confident and less constrained by disciplinary boundaries, participants saw feminist IR as expanding into new theoretical domains, such as queer theory and intersectional analysis, as well as addressing more complex and nuanced definitions of sex and gender that problematize the boundaries between the two. However, all agreed that, in addition to expanding its theoretical and methodological boundaries, feminist IR must also produce research that is useful and accessible to those who work in policy communities and who must convince policy-makers that gender and women matter in all aspects of global policy-making. Mindful of its roots in social activism, feminism must stay committed to effecting social change that can benefit those marginalized by global politics, both women and men.

Conversations such as those at the 2010 conference demonstrate that, from whatever locations they choose to position themselves, it is certain that IR feminists will continue to expand the definition of what we mean by global politics and how, and from what location, we choose to study them. While some have chosen homes outside what we conventionally define as IR, I have chosen to stay at home in IR, even though my continuing journey is now taking me to some remote places. The goal of my intellectual journey has been to speak to a broader IR audience, an audience that includes students who will go on to work in the policy world, and for whom I hope I may have succeeded in some small way in making gender visible.

It is now twenty-five years since Sarah Brown asserted that only with feminist analysis could the field of IR come to a complete understanding of global politics (Brown 1988). Twenty-five years later, most IR feminists of various methodological persuasions would agree with this assertion; however, it is doubtful that the discipline as a whole is ready to accept such a claim. The first twenty-five years of feminist scholarship has demonstrated that feminist IR has traveled far and has much to celebrate, but there are still challenges ahead if IR feminism is to achieve this transformative goal.

ORIGINAL SOURCES

CHAPTER 1
"Hans Morgenthau's Principles of Political Realism: A Feminist Reformulation,"
   Millennium: Journal of International Studies 17, no. 3: 429–440, 1988.

CHAPTER 2
"Feminist Perspectives on Peace and World Security in a Post-Cold War Era." In *Peace*
   and World Security Studies: A Curriculum Guide, 6th ed., ed. Michael Klare.
   Boulder, CO: Lynne Rienner Publishers: 43–54, 1994. Reprinted by permission
   of the publisher. and
"Feminist Responses to Security Studies." *Peace Review: A Journal of Social Justice*
   16, no. 1: 43–48, 2004. Reprinted by permission of the publisher (Taylor &
   Francis Ltd, http://www.tandf.co.uk/journals).

CHAPTER 3
"On the Fringes of the World Economy: A Feminist Perspective." In *The New*
   International Political Economy, eds. Craig N. Murphy and Roger Tooze, Boulder,
   CO: Lynne Rienner Publishers: 191–206, 1999. Reprinted by permission of the
   publisher.

CHAPTER 4
"States and Markets: An Ecofeminist Perspective on International Political Economy,"
   International Political Science Review 14, no. 1, 1993.

CHAPTER 5
"The Gendered Frontiers of Globalization," *Globalizations* 1, no. 1: 15–23, 2004.
   Reprinted by permission of the publisher (Taylor & Francis Ltd, http://
   www.tandf.co.uk/journals).

CHAPTER 6
"You Just Don't Understand: Troubled Engagements Between Feminists and IR
   Theorists." *International Studies Quarterly* 41: 611–632, 1997.

CHAPTER 7
"What Is Your Research Program? Some Feminist Answers to IR's Methodological
   Questions," *International Studies Quarterly* 49: 1–21, 2005.

CHAPTER 8

"Dealing with Difference: Problems and Possibilities for Dialogue in International Relations," *Millennium: Journal of International Studies,*" 39, no. 3: 607–618, 2011.

CHAPTER 9

"Feminist Perspectives on 9/11." *International Studies Perspectives* 3, no. 4: 333–350, 2002.

CHAPTER 10

"On Taking Religious Worldviews Seriously," Chap. 12 in *Power, Interdependence and Nonstate Actors in World Politics*, eds. H. Milner and A. Moravcsik. Princeton: Princeton University Press: 223–239, 2009. Reprinted by permission of the publisher.

CHAPTER 11

"Retelling IR's Foundational Stories: Some Feminist and Postcolonial Perspectives," *Global Change, Peace and Security* 23, no. 1: 5–13, 2011. Reprinted by permission of the publisher (Taylor & Francis Ltd, http://www.tandf.co.uk/journals).

CHAPTER 12

"You May Never Understand: Prospects for Feminist Futures in International Relations," *The Australian Feminist Law Journal* 32, June: 9–20, 2010. Reprinted by permission of the publisher.

BIBLIOGRAPHY

Acker, Joan, Kate Barry and Johanna Esseveld. 1991. "Objectivity and Truth: Problems in Doing Feminist Research," In *Beyond Methodology: Feminist Scholarship as Lived Research*, eds. Mary Margaret Fonow and Judith Cook. Bloomington: Indiana University Press: 133–153.

Ackerly, Brooke. 2009. "Why a Feminist Theorist Studies Methods." *Politics and Gender* 5, no. 2: 431–436.

Ackerly, Brooke. 2000. *Political Theory and Feminist Social Criticism*. Cambridge: Cambridge University Press.

Ackerly, Brooke, and Jacqui True. 2010. *Doing Feminist Research in Political and Social Science*. New York: Palgrave Macmillan.

Ackerly, Brooke, Maria Stern, and Jacqui True, eds. 2006. *Feminist Methodologies for International Relations*. Cambridge: Cambridge University Press.

Addams, Jane, Emily G. Balch, and Alice Hamilton. 1916. *Women at The Hague: The International Congress of Women and Its Results*. New York: Macmillan.

Agnew, John. 1998. *Geopolitics: Re-visioning World Politics*. London: Routledge.

Amiri, Rina. 2002. "Afghanistan: Women in Government and Society." Panel discussion, U.S. Institute of Peace, Jan. 29. http://www.usip.org/oc/newsroom/es20020129.html.

Amiri, Rina. 2001. "Muslim Women as Symbols—and Pawns." *New York Times Magazine,* Nov. 27, A21.

Apodaca, Clair. 2009. "Overcoming Obstacles in Quantitative Feminist Research." *Politics and Gender* 5, no. 3: 419–426.

Arendt, Hannah. 1969. *On Violence*. New York: Harcourt, Brace and World.

Armstrong, Karen. 2004. *The Spiral Staircase: My Climb out of Darkness*. New York: Alfred A. Knopf.

Axelrod, Robert. 1984. *The Evolution of Cooperation*. New York, NY: Basic Books

Azar, Edward E., and John W. Burton. 1986. *International Conflict Resolution: Theory and Practice*. Brighton, Sussex: Wheatsheaf Books.

Azar, Edward, and Chung-in Moon. 1984. "Third World National Security: Toward a New Conceptual Framework." *International Interactions* 11, no. 2: 103–135.

Barkawi, Tarak, and Mark Laffey. 2002. "Retrieving the Imperial: Empire and International Relations." *Millennium: Journal of International Studies* 31, no. 1: 109–127.

Basu, Soumita. 2011. "Security as Emancipation: A Feminist Perspective." In *Feminism and International Relations: Conversations about Past, Present and Future*, eds. J. Ann Tickner and Laura Sjoberg. New York: Routledge, 98–114.

Beitz, Charles. 1979. *Political Theory and International Relations*. Princeton, NJ: Princeton University Press.

Belich, James. 2009. *Replenishing the Earth: The Settler Revolution and the Rise of the Anglo-World, 1783–1939*. Oxford: Oxford University Press.

Benería, Lourdes. 2003. *Gender, Development and Globalization: Economics as if All People Mattered*. New York: Routledge.

Benería, Lourdes, and Rebecca Blank. 1989. "Women and the Economics of Military Spending." In *Rocking the Ship of State*, eds. Adrienne Harris and Ynestra King. Boulder, CO: Westview Press.

Benhabib, Seyla. 1987. "The Generalized and the Concrete Other." In *Feminism as Critique: Essays on the Politics of Gender in Late-Capitalist Societies*, eds. Seyla Benhabib and Drucilla Cornell. Cambridge: Polity Press, 77–95.

Biersteker, Thomas J. 2009. "The Parochialism of Hegemony: Challenges for 'American' International Relations." In *International Relations Scholarship Around the World*, eds. Arlene Tickner and Ole Waever. New York: Routledge: 308–327.

Bloom, Leslie Rebecca. 1998. *Under the Sign of Hope: Feminist Methodology and Narrative Interpretation*. Albany: State University of New York Press.

Bookchin, Murray. 1980. *Toward An Ecological Society*. Montreal: Black Rose Books.

Booth, Ken. 2007. *Theory of World Security*. Cambridge: Cambridge University Press.

Booth, Ken. 1991. "Security and Emancipation." *Review of International Studies* 17, no. 4: 313–326.

Boulding, Elise. 2000. *Cultures of Peace: The Hidden Side of History*. Syracuse, NY: Syracuse University Press.

Boyle, Francis Anthony. 1985. *World Politics and International Law*. Durham, NC: Duke University Press.

Brandes, Lisa. 1994. "Public Opinion, International Security Policy, and Gender: The United States and Great Britain since 1945." PhD dissertation, Yale University.

Brant, Martha. 2001. "The Bushes Unveil the Women's Issue." *Newsweek*, Nov. 26, p. 7.

Broverman, Inge K., Susan R. Vogel, Donald M. Broverman, Frank E. Clarkson, and Paul S. Rosenkranz. 1972. "Sex-Role Stereotypes: A Current Appraisal." *Journal of Social Issues* 28, no. 2: 59–78.

Brown, Chris. 2002. "Narratives of Religions, Civilization and Modernity." In *Worlds in Collision: Terror and the Future of Global Order*, eds. Ken Booth and Tim Dunne. New York: Palgrave-Macmillan: 293–302.

Brown, Patricia Leigh. 2001. "Heavy Lifting Required: The Return of Manly Men." *New York Times Magazine*, Oct. 28, Sec. 4, p. 5.

Brown, Sarah. 1988. "Feminism, International Theory and International Relations of Gender Inequality." *Millennium: Journal of International Studies* 17, no. 3: 461–475.

Bunch, Charlotte, and Roxanna Carrillo. 1994. "Global Violence Against Women." In *World Security: Challenges for a New Century*, eds. Michael Klare and Daniel Thomas. New York: St. Martin's Press: 256–273.

Burguières, Mary K. 1990. "Feminist Approaches to Peace: Another Step for Peace Studies." *Millennium: Journal of International Studies* 19, no. 1: 1–18.

Buruma, Ian, and Avishai Margalit. 2004. *Occidentalism: The West in the Eyes of Its Enemies*. New York: Penguin Press.

Buruma, Ian, and Avishai Margalit. 2002. "Occidentalism." *New York Review of Books*, vol. 49, no. 1, Jan. 17, 4–7.

Caprioli, Mary. 2009. "Making Choices." *Politics and Gender* 5, no. 3: 426–431.
Caprioli, Mary. 2004. "Feminist IR Theory and Quantitative Methodology: A Critical Analysis." *International Studies Review* 6, no. 2: 253–269.
Caprioli, Mary. 2000. "Gendered Conflict." *Journal of Peace Research* 37, no. 1: 51–68.
Caprioli, Mary, and Mark Boyer. 2001. "Gender, Violence and International Crisis." *Journal of Conflict Resolution* 45, no. 4: 503–518.
Carpenter, Charli R. 2006. "Women and Children First: Gender Norms and Humanitarian Evacuation in the Balkans." *International Organization* 57, no. 4: 428–477.
Carr, E. H. 1964. *The Twenty Years Crisis, 1919–1939*. New York: Harper and Row.
Castells, Manuel. 1997. *The Information Age: Economy, Society and Culture*, vol. 2. Oxford: Blackwell Publishers.
Charlesworth, Hilary. 1994. "Women's Rights and Traditional Law: A Conflict." *Third World Legal Studies*.
Charlesworth, Hilary, Christine Chinkin, and Shelley Wright. 1991. "Feminist Approaches to International Law." *The American Journal of International Law* 85, no. 4: 613–645.
Chase-Dunn, Christopher K. 1982. "International Economic Policy in a Declining Core State." In *America in a Changing World Political Economy*, eds. William P. Avery and David P. Rapkin. New York: Longman Publishing Group.
Chin, Christine B. N. 1998. *In Service and Servitude: Foreign Female Domestic Workers and the Malaysian "Modernity" Project*. New York: Columbia University Press.
Choucri, Nazli, and Robert C. North. 1975. *Nations in Conflict*. San Francisco, CA: W. H. Freeman.
Claude, Inis L., Jr. 1962. *Power and International Relations*. New York: Random House.
Code, Lorraine. 1991. *What Can She Know? Feminist Theory and the Construction of Knowledge*. Ithaca, NY: Cornell University Press.
Cohn, Bernard S. 1996. *Colonialism and Its Forms of Knowledge*. Princeton, NJ: Princeton University Press.
Cohn, Carol. 1993. "Wars, Wimps, and Women: Talking Gender and Thinking War." In *Gendering War Talk*, eds. Miriam Cooke and Angela Wollacott. Princeton, NJ: Princeton University Press, 227–246.
Cohn, Carol. 1990. "'Clean Bombs' and Clean Language." In *Women, Militarism, and War: Essays in History, Politics, and Social Theory*, eds. Jean Bethke Elshtain and Sheila Tobias. Savage, MD: Rowman & Littlefield, 33–57.
Cohn, Carol. 1987. "Sex and Death in the Rational World of Defense Intellectuals." *Signs: Journal of Women in Culture and Society* 12, no. 4: 687–718.
Cohn, Carol, ed. 2013. *Women and Wars*, Cambridge, UK: Polity Press.
Collins, Patricia Hill. 1991. "Learning from the Outsider Within: The Sociological Significance of Black Feminist Thought." In *Beyond Methodology: Feminist Scholarship As Lived Research*, eds. Mary Margaret Fonow and Judith Cook. Bloomington: Indiana University Press, 35–59.
Collins, Patricia Hill. 1989. "The Social Construction of Black Feminist Thought." *Signs: Journal of Women in Culture and Society* 14, no. 4: 745–773.
Confortini, Catia C. 2012. *Intelligent Compassion: Feminist Critical Methodology in the Women's International League for Peace and Freedom*. New York: Oxford University Press.
Confortini, Catia C. 2006. "Galtung, Violence and Gender: The Case for a Peace Studies/Feminism Alliance" *Peace and Change* 31, no. 3: 333–367.

Connell, R. W. 2000. "Arms and the Man: Using the New Research on Masculinity to Understand Violence and Promote Peace in the Contemporary World." In *Male Roles, Masculinities and Violence: A Culture of Peace Perspective*, eds. Ingeborg Breines and R. W. Connell, Paris: UNESCO, 21–33.

Cook, Judith A., and Mary Margaret Fonow. 1990. "Knowledge and Women's Interests: Issues of Epistemology and Methodology in Feminist Sociological Research." In *Feminist Research Methods*, ed. Joyce McCarl Nielsen. Boulder, CO: Westview Press, 69–93.

Cooperman, Alan. 2001. "Roman Catholic Bishops Declare U.S. War Is Moral." *Washington Post*, Nov. 16, A37.

Cox, Robert. 1981. "Social Forces, States and World Orders: Beyond International Theory." *Millennium: Journal of International Studies* 10, no. 2: 126–155.

Crapol, Edward P., ed. 1987. *Women and American Foreign Policy*. Westport, CT: Greenwood Press.

Cronin, Audrey Kurth. 2006. "How al-Qaida Ends: the Decline and Demise of Terrorist Groups." *International Security* 31, no. 1: 7–48.

Cronin, Audrey Kurth. 2002. "Behind the Curve: Globalization and International Terrorism." *International Security* 27, no. 3: 30–58.

Damasio, Antonio R. 2005. *Descartes' Error: Emotion, Reason and the Human Brain*. London: Penguin Books Publishers.

Dankelman, Irene, and Joan Davidson. 1988. *Women and Environment in the Third World: Alliance for the Future*. London: Earthscan Publications.

D'Costa, Bina, and Katrina Lee-Koo. 2009. *Gender and Global Politics in the Asia-Pacific*. New York: Palgrave Macmillan.

Der Derian, James. 1995. *International Theory: Critical Investigations*. New York: New York University Press.

Deutsch, Karl W. 1957. *Political Community and the North Atlantic Area*. Princeton, NJ: Princeton University Press.

Diamond, Irene, and Gloria F. Orenstein. 1990. *Reweaving the World: The Emergence of Ecofeminism*. San Francisco, CA: Sierra Club Books.

Doyle, Michael W. 1983. "Kant, Liberal Legacies and Foreign Affairs." *Philosophy and Public Affairs* 12, no. 3: 205–235.

Eichenberg, Richard. 2003. "Gender Differences in Public Attitudes Toward the Use of Force by the United States, 1990-2003." *International Security* 28, no. 1.

Eisenstadt, Shmuel, and Wolfgang Schluchter. 2001. "Paths to Early Modernities—A Comparative View." In *Public Spheres and Collective Identities*, eds. Shmuel Eisenstadt, Wolfgang Schluchter, and Bjorn Wittrock. Piscataway, NJ: Transaction Publishers 2001, chap. 1.

Eisenstein, Zillah. 2004. *Against Empire: Feminisms, Racism, and the West*. London/New York: Zed Books.

Elshtain, Jean Bethke. 1988. "The Problem with Peace." *Millennium: Journal of International Studies* 17, no. 3: 441–449.

Elshtain, Jean Bethke. 1987. *Women and War*. New York: Basic Books.

Elshtain, Jean Bethke. 1985. "Reflections on War and Political Discourse: Realism, Just War, and Feminism in a Nuclear Age." *Political Theory* 13, no. 1: 39–57.

Elshtain, Jean Bethke, and Sheila Tobias. 1990. *Women, Militarism, and War: Essays in History, Politics, and Social Theory*. Savage, MD: Rowman & Littlefield.

Enloe, Cynthia. 2000. *Maneuvers: The International Politics of Militarizing Women's Lives*. Berkeley: University of California Press.

Enloe, Cynthia. 1990. *Bananas, Beaches and Bases: Making Feminist Sense of International Politics*. Berkeley: University of California Press.

Enloe, Cynthia. 1983. *Does Khaki Become You? The Militarisation of Women's Lives.* London: Pluto Press.

Ferber, Marianne, and Julie A. Nelson, eds. 1993. *Beyond Economic Man: Feminist Theory and Economics.* Chicago: University of Chicago Press.

Fisher, Anne. 2013. "Why Are There Still So Few Women in Top Leadership Jobs?" January 17. http://management.fortune.cnn.com/tag/senior- executive-women/.

Flax, Jane. 1987. "Postmodernism and Gender Relations in Feminist Theory." *Signs: Journal of Women in Culture and Society* 12, no. 4: 621–643.

Fonow, Mary Margaret, and Judith A. Cook. 1991. "Back to the Future: A Look at the Second Wave of Feminist Epistemology and Methodology." In *Beyond Methodology: Feminist Scholarship as Lived Research,* eds. Mary Margaret Fonow and Judith A. Cook. Bloomington: Indiana University Press: 1–15.

Fry, Greg. 1997. "Framing the Islands: Knowledge and Power in Changing Australian Images of 'the South Pacific.'" *The Contemporary Pacific* 9, no. 2: 305–344.

Fukuyama, Francis. 2000. "What Divides America." *Wall Street Journal*, Nov. 15, A26.

Fukuyama, Francis. 1999. *The Great Disruption: Human Nature and the Reconstitution of Social Order.* New York: Free Press.

Fukuyama, Francis. 1998. "Women and the Evolution of World Politics." *Foreign Affairs* 77, no. 5: 24–40.

Gallagher, Nancy. 1993. "The Gender Gap in Popular Attitudes Toward the Use of Force." In *Women and the Use of Military Force*, eds. Ruth Howes and Michael Stevenson. Boulder, CO: Lynne Rienner.

Galtung, Johan. 1971. "A Structural Theory of Imperialism." *Journal of Peace Research* 8, no. 2: 81–117.

Galtung, Johan. 1969. "Violence, Peace and Peace Research." *Journal of Peace Research* 6, no. 3: 167–191.

Giddens, Anthony. 1994. *Beyond Left and Right: The Future of Radical Politics.* Stanford, CA: Stanford University Press.

Gill, Stephen, and David Law. 1989. "Global Hegemony and the Structural Power of Capital." *International Studies Quarterly* 33, no. 4: 475–499.

Gill, Stephen, and David Law. 1988. *The Global Political Economy: Perspectives, Problems and Policies.* Baltimore, MD: The Johns Hopkins University Press.

Gilligan, Carol. 1982. *In a Different Voice: Psychological Theory and Women's Development.* Cambridge, MA: Harvard University Press.

Gilpin, Robert. 1987. *The Political Economy of International Relations.* Princeton, NJ: Princeton University Press.

Goldstein, Joshua. 2012. *International Relations*, 10th ed. New York: Harper Collins.

Goldstein, Joshua. 2002. "John Wayne and G.I. Jane." In *The Christian Science Monitor*, Jan. 10.

Goldstein, Joshua. 2001. *War and Gender: How Gender Shapes the War System and Vice Versa.* Cambridge: Cambridge University Press.

Göle, Nilufer. 2000. "Global Expectations, Local Experiences: Non-Western Modernities." In *Through a Glass Darkly: Blurred Images of Cultural Tradition and Modernity over Distance and Time*, ed. Wil Arts. Leiden. Boston, MA: Brill Academic Publisher, 40–55.

Goodwin, Jan, and Jessica Neuwirth. 2001. "The Rifle and the Veil." *The New York Times Magazine*, Oct. 1. Cited from http://www.rawa.org.

Grant, Rebecca. 1991. "The Sources of Gender Bias in International Relations Theory." In *Gender and International Relations,* eds. Rebecca Grant and Kathleen Newland. Indianapolis: Indiana University Press, 8–26.

Gruffydd Jones, Branwen, ed. 2006. *Decolonizing International Relations*. Lanham, MD: Rowman and Littlefield.

Guha, Ranajit. 2002. *History at the Limits of History*. New York: Columbia University Press.

Habermas, Jürgen. 1971. *Knowledge and the Human Interests*. Boston, MA: Beacon Press.

Halliday, Fred. 1988. "Hidden From International Relations: Women and the International Arena." *Millennium* 17: 3.

Halperin, Sandra. 2006 "International Relations Theory and the Hegemony of Western Conceptions of Modernity."In *Decolonizing International Relations*, ed. Branwen Gruffydd Jones. Lanham, MD: Rowman and Littlefield, 43–63.

Hansen, Lene. 2000. "The Little Mermaid's Silent Security Dilemma and the Absence of Gender in the Copenhagen School." *Millennium: Journal of International Studies* 29, no. 2: 285–306.

Haraway, Donna. 1988. "Situated Knowledges: The Science Question in Feminism and the Privilege of Partial Perspective." *Feminist Studies* 14, no. 3: 575–599.

Harding, Sandra. 2008. *Science from Below: Feminisms, Postcolonialities and Modernities*. Durham, NC, and London: Duke University Press.

Harding, Sandra. 1998. *Is Science Multicultural? Postcolonialism, Feminisms, and Epistemologies*. Bloomington: Indiana University Press.

Harding, Sandra. 1991. *Whose Science? Whose Knowledge? Thinking from Women's Lives*. Ithaca, NY: Cornell University Press.

Harding, Sandra. 1987. "Introduction: Is There a Feminist Method?" In *Feminism and Methodology*, ed. Sandra Harding. Bloomington: Indiana University Press, 1–14.

Harding, Sandra. 1986. *The Science Question in Feminism*. Ithaca, NY: Cornell University Press.

Harris, Adrienne, and Ynestra King, eds. 1989. *Rocking the Ship of State: Toward a Feminist Peace Politics*. Boulder, CO: Westview Press.

Hartsock, Nancy C. M. 1983. *Money, Sex and Power: Toward a Feminist Historical Materialism*. Boston, MA: Northeastern University Press.

Hassan, Riffat. 1999. "Feminism in Islam." In *Feminism and World Religion*, eds. Arvind Sharma and Katherine K. Young. Albany: State University of New York Press, 248–278.

Hekman, Susan. 1990. *Gender and Knowledge: Elements of a Postmodern Feminism*. Boston, MA: Northeastern University Press.

Hobden, Stephen, and J. Hobson. 2003. *Historical Sociology of International Relations*. Cambridge: Cambridge University Press.

Hobson, John M. 2012. *The Eurocentric Conception of World Politics: Western International Theory, 1760–2010*. Cambridge: Cambridge University Press.

Hobson, John M. 2007. "Is Critical Theory Always *for* the White West and *for* Western Imperialism? Beyond Westphilian to a Post-Racist Critical IR." *Review of International Studies* 33: 91–116.

Hobson, John M. 2004. *The Eastern Origins of Western Civilisation*, Cambridge: Cambridge University Press.

Hoffman, Stanley. 1981. *Duties Beyond Borders: On the Limits and Possibilities of Ethical International Politics*. Syracuse, NY: Syracuse University Press.

Hoffman, Stanley. 1977. "An American Social Science: International Relations." *Daedalus* 106, no. 3: 41–60.

Hollis, Martin, and Steve Smith. 1990. *Explaining and Understanding International Relations*. Oxford: Oxford University Press.

hooks, bell. 1984. *Feminist Theory: From Margin to Center*. Boston, MA: South End Press.

Hooper, Charlotte. 2001. *Manly States: Masculinities, International Relations, and Gender Politics*. New York: Columbia University Press.

Hooper, Charlotte. 1998. "Masculinist Practices and Gender Politics: The Operation of Multiple Masculinities in International Relations." In *The Man Question in International Relations*, eds. Marysia Zalewski and Jane Parpart. Boulder, CO: Westview Press.

Hudson, Valerie, Mary Caprioli, Bonnie Ballif-Spanvill, Rose McDermott, and Chad E. Emmett. 2008/2009. "The Heart of the Matter: The Security of Women and the Security of States." *International Security* 33, no. 3: 7–45.

Human Rights Watch. 2001. "Poor Rights Record of Opposition Commanders." Oct. 6. Cited from RAWA website, http://www.rawa.org.

Huntington, Samuel P. 2004. *Who Are We? The Challenges to America's National Identity*. New York: Simon and Schuster.

Huntington, Samuel P. 1996. *The Clash of Civilizations and the Remaking of World Order*. New York: Simon and Schuster.

Huntington, Samuel P. 1993. "The Clash of Civilizations?" *Foreign Affairs* 72, no. 3: 22–49.

Independent Commission on Disarmament and Security Issues. 1982. *Common Security: A Blueprint for Survival*. New York: Simon & Schuster.

Inglehart, Ronald, and Pippa Norris. 2003. *Rising Tide: Gender Equality and Cultural Change around the World*. Cambridge: Cambridge University Press.

International Labour Organization. 2011. *Global Wage Report 2010/11: Wage Policies in Times of Crises*. Geneva: ILO.

International Labour Organization. 2004. *Global Employment Trends for Women*. Geneva: ILO. Accessible at www.ilo.org.

Jackson, Patrick Thaddeus. 2011. *The Conduct of Inquiry in International Relations: Philosophy of Science and its Implications for the Study of World Politics*. New York: Routledge.

Jagger, Alison M. 1983. *Feminist Politics and Human Nature*. Totowa, NJ: Rowman and Allanheld.

Jaquette, Jane. 2003. "Feminism and the Challenges of the 'Post-Cold War' World." *International Feminist Journal of Politics* 5, no. 3: 331–354.

Jaquette, Jane S. 1984. "Power as Ideology: A Feminist Analysis." In *Women's Views of the Political World of Men*, ed. Judith H. Stiehm. Dobbs Ferry, NY: Transnational Publishers.

Jayaratne, Toby Epstein, and Abigail Stewart. 1991. "Quantitative and Qualitative Methods in the Social Sciences: Current Feminist Issues and Practical Strategies." In *Beyond Methodology: Feminist Scholarship as Lived Research*, eds. Mary Margaret Fonow and Judith A. Cook. Bloomington: Indiana University Press, 85–106.

Jolly, Margaret. 2007. "Imagining Oceania: Indigenous and Foreign Representations of a Sea of Islands." *The Contemporary Pacific* 19, no. 2: 508–545.

Judt, Tony. 2001. "America and the War." *New York Review of Books* 48, no. 10. Nov. 15.

Juergensmeyer, Mark. 2000. *Terror in the Mind of God: The Global Rise of Religious Violence*. Berkeley: University of California Press.

Kaldor, Mary. 1986. "The Global Political Economy." *Alternatives* 11, no. 4: 431–460.

Karam, Azza. 2000. "Democrats Without Democracy: Challenges to Women in Politics in the Arab World." In *International Perspectives on Gender and Democratization*, ed. Shirin Rai. New York: St. Martin's Press, 64–83.

Karant-Nunn, Susan C. 1998. "The Reformation of Women." In *Becoming Visible: Women in European History*, 3rd ed., eds. Renate Bridenthal, Susan Mosher Stuard, and Merry E. Wiesner. Boston, MA: Houghton Mifflin, 175–202.

Keck, Margaret, and Kathryn Sikkink. 1998. *Activists Beyond Borders: Advocacy Networks in International Politics*. Ithaca, NY: Cornell University Press.

Kegan, Robert. 1982. *The Evolving Self: Problem and Process in Human Development*. Cambridge, MA: Harvard University Press.

Keller, Evelyn Fox. 1985. *Reflections on Gender and Science*. New Haven, CT: Yale University Press.

Keller, Evelyn Fox. 1983. *A Feeling for the Organism: The Life and Work of Barbara McClintock*. New York: Freeman.

Kelly-Gadol, Joan. 1977. "Did Women Have a Renaissance?" In *Becoming Visible: Women in European History*, eds. Renate Bridenthal and Claudia Koonz, Boston: Houghton Mifflin Company, 137–164.

Kelman, Herbert C. 1986. "Interactive Problem Solving: A Social-Psychological Approach to Conflict Resolution." In *Dialogue Toward Inter-Faith Understanding*, ed. W. Klassen. Tantur/Jerusalem: Ecumenical Institute for Theoretical Research, 293–314.

Keohane, Robert O. 2002. *Power and Governance in a Partially Globalized World*. New York: Routledge.

Keohane, Robert O. 1998. "Beyond Dichotomy: Conversations Between International Relations and Feminist Theory." *International Studies Quarterly* 42, no. 1: 193–198.

Keohane, Robert O. 1989. "International Relations Theory: Contributions of a Feminist Standpoint". *Millennium: Journal of International Studies* 18, no. 2: 245–253.

Keohane, Robert O. 1984. *After Hegemony: Cooperation and Discord in the World Political Economy*. Princeton, NJ: Princeton University Press.

Ketchum, Sara Ann. 1980. "Female Culture, Womanculture and Conceptual Change: Toward a Philosophy of Women's Studies." *Social Theory and Practice* 6, no. 2: 151–162.

Kiel, Paul. 2003. *European Conquest and the Rights of Indigenous Peoples: The Moral Backwardness of International Society*. Cambridge: Cambridge University Press.

Killborn, Peter. 1996. "Cause for Sibling Rivalry at Teamsters." *New York Times Magazine*, July 17, A16.

Kimmel, Michael, and Abby L. Ferber 2000. "'White Men Are This Nation': Right-Wing Militias and the Restoration of Rural American Masculinity." *Rural Sociology* 65, no. 4: 582–604.

King, Gary, Robert Keohane, and Sidney Verba. 1994. *Designing Social Inquiry: Scientific Inference in Qualitative Research*. Princeton, NJ: Princeton University Press.

Kramerae, Cheris, and Dale Spender, eds. 1991. *The Knowledge Explosion*. Elmsford, NY: Pergamon Press.

Krasner, Stephen D. 1982. "American Policy and Global Economic Stability." In *America in a Changing World Political Economy*, eds. William P. Avery and David P. Rapkin. New York: Longman Publishing Group.

Krasner, Stephen. 1993. "Westphalia and All That." In *Ideas and Foreign Policy: Beliefs, Institutions and Political Change*, eds. Judith Goldstein and Robert O. Keohane. Ithaca, NY: Cornell University Press, 235–264.

Kubálková, Vendulka. 2003. "Toward an International Political Theology." In *Religion in International Relations: The Return from Exile*, eds. Fabio Petito and Pavlos Hatzopoulos. New York: Palgrave Macmillan, 79–105.

Kurth, James. 1994. "The Real Clash." *The National Interest*, no. 37 (Fall): 3–15.

Lakatos, Imré, and Alan Musgrave. 1970. *Criticism and the Growth of Knowledge*. Cambridge: Cambridge University Press.

Lapid, Yosef. 1989. "The Third Debate: On the Prospects of International Theory in a Post-Positivist Era." *International Studies Quarterly* 33, no. 3: 235–254.

Lee-Koo, Katrina. 2009. "Feminist International Relations in Australia." *Australian Journal of Politics and History* 55, no. 3: 415–432.

Leiss, William. 1972. *The Domination of Nature*. New York: George Braziller.

Lerner, Daniel. 1958. *The Passing of Traditional Society: Modernizing the Middle East*. Glencoe, IL: Free Press.

Light, Margot. 1988. *The Soviet Theory of International Relations*. New York: St. Martin's Press.

Linklater, Andrew. 1982. *Men and Citizens in the Theory of International Relations*. London: Macmillan.

Long, David, and Brian C. Schmidt, eds. 2005. *Imperialism and Internationalism in the Discipline of International Relations*. Albany: State University of New York Press.

Lopez, Steve. 2001. "Afghan Woman's Tale Rises From Bottomless Well of Sadness." *Los Angeles Times*, Nov. 14, B1.

Martin, Jane Roland. 1994. "Methodological Essentialism, False Difference, and Other Dangerous Traps." *Signs: Journal of Women in Culture and Society* 19, no. 3: 630–657.

May, Elaine Tyler. 2003. "Echoes of the Cold War: The Aftermath of September 11 at Home." In *September 11 in History: A Watershed Moment?*, ed. Mary L. Dudziak. Durham, NC: Duke University Press, 35–54.

McClelland, David. 1975. "Power and the Feminine Role." In *Power, The Inner Experience*, ed. David McClelland. New York: Wiley.

McGrane, Bernard. 1989. *Beyond Anthropology: Society and the Other*. New York: Columbia University Press.

McNamara, Mary. 2002. "With Shift to L.A., Feminist Majority Builds on Momentum." *Los Angeles Times*, Jan. 16, E 1.

Mead, Walter Russell. 2006. "God's Country?" *Foreign Affairs*. September/October: 24–43.

Mearsheimer, John J. 2001. "Guns Won't Win the Afghan War." *New York Times Magazine*, Nov. 4, Sec. 4, 13.

Merchant, Carolyn. 1989. *Ecological Revolutions: Nature, Gender and Science in New England*. Chapel Hill: University of North Carolina Press.

Merchant, Carolyn. 1980. *The Death of Nature: Women, Ecology and the Scientific Revolution*. San Francisco, CA: Harper & Row.

Mertus, Julie A. 2000. *War's Offensive on Women: The Humanitarian Challenge in Bosnia, Kosovo, and Afghanistan*. Bloomfield, CT: Kumarian Press.

Mies, Maria. 1991. "Women's Research or Feminist Research? The Debate Surrounding Feminist Science and Methodology." In *Beyond Methodology: Feminist Scholarship as Lived Research*, eds. Mary Margaret Fonow and Judith A. Cook. Bloomington: Indiana University Press: 60–84.

Mies, Maria. 1986. *Patriarchy and Accumulation on a World Scale: Women in the International Division of Labour.* London: Zed Books.

Mignolo, Walter D. 1995. *The Darker Side of the Renaissance: Literacy, Territoriality, and Colonization.* Ann Arbor: University of Michigan Press.

Mitchell, Juliet. 1987. "Women and Equality." In *Feminism and Equality,* ed. Anne Phillips. Oxford: Basil Blackwell.

Moghadan, Valentine M. 1994. "Women and Identity Politics in Theoretical and Comparative Perspective." In *Identity Politics and Women: Cultural Reassertions and Feminisms in International Perspective,* ed. Valentine M. Moghadan. Boulder, CO: Westview Press, 3–26.

Mohanty, Chandra Talpade. 2003. *Feminism Without Borders: Decolonizing Theory, Practicing Solidarity.* Durham, NC: Duke University Press.

Monter, E. William. 1977. "The Pedestal and the Stake: Courtly Love and Witchcraft." In *Becoming Visible: Women in European History,* eds. Renate Bridenthal and Claudia Koonz, Boston, MA: Houghton Mifflin Company, 119–136.

Moon, Katherine. 1997. *Sex Among Allies: Military Prostitution in U.S.–Korea Relations.* New York: Columbia University Press.

Moore, Henrietta L. 1988. *Feminism and Anthropology.* Minneapolis: University of Minnesota Press.

Morgenthau, Hans. 1995. "The Intellectual and Political Functions of Theory." In *International Theory: Critical Investigations,* ed. James Der Derian. New York: New York University Press, 36–52.

Morgenthau, Hans. 1973. *Politics Among Nations: The Struggle for Power and Peace,* 5th ed. New York: Alfred Knopf.

Morgenthau, Hans. 1946. *Scientific Man vs. Power Politics.* Chicago: University of Chicago Press.

Murray, Sally, and Andrew Mack. 1985. "Women, Feminism, and Peace Research." In *Peace Research in the 1980s,* ed. Andrew Mack. Canberra: Australian National University, 91–102.

Nayak Meghana V. 2009. "The Influence of *International Feminist Journal of Politics:* Possibilities of Mentorship and Community for Junior Feminist Faculty." *International Feminist Journal of Politics* 11, no. 1: 21–29.

Nielsen, Joyce McCarl, ed. 1990. *Feminist Research Methods: Exemplary Readings in the Social Sciences.* Boulder, CO: Westview Press.

North, Robert C. 1990. *War, Peace, Survival: Global Politics and Conceptual Synthesis.* Boulder, CO: Westview Press.

Nussbaum, Martha, and Jonathan Glover, eds. 1995. *Women, Culture and Development: A Study of Human Capabilities.* Oxford: Oxford University Press.

Ohmae, Kenichi. 1991. *The Borderless World: Power and Strategy in the Interlinked Economy.* New York: Harper Collins.

Oke, Nicole. 2009. "Globalizing Time and Space: Temporal and Spatial Considerations in Discourses of Globalization." *International Political Sociology* 3, no. 3: 310–326.

Okin, Susan Moller. 1989. *Justice, Gender and the Family.* New York: Basic Books.

Okin, Susan Moller. 1980. *Women in Western Political Thought.* Princeton, NJ: Princeton University Press.

Olsson, Louise, and Torunn Tryggestad, eds. 2001. *Women and International Peacekeeping.* London: Frank Cass.

Orr, David W., and Marvin S. Soroos, eds. 1979. *The Global Predicament: Ecological Perspectives on World Order.* Chapel Hill: University of North Carolina Press.

Otto, Diane. 2009. "The Exile of Inclusion: Reflections on Gender Issues in International Law Over the Last Decade." *Melbourne Journal of International Law* 10, no. 1: 11–26.

Parisi, Laura. 2009. "The Numbers Do(n't) Always Add Up: Dilemmas in Using Quantitative Research Methods in Feminist IR Scholarship." *Politics and Gender* 5, no. 3: 410–419.

Parker, Geoffrey. 1985. *Western Geopolitical Thought in the Twentieth Century.* New York: St. Martin's Press.

Pateman, Carole. 1994. "The Rights of Man and Early Feminism." *Schweizerisches Jahrbuch für Politische Wissenschaft* 34: 19–31.

Pateman, Carole. 1988. *The Sexual Contract.* Stanford, CA: Stanford University Press.

Peterson, V. Spike. 2004. "Feminist Theories Within, Invisible To, and Beyond IR." *Brown Journal of World Affairs* 35: 37–41.

Peterson, V. Spike. 2003. *A Critical Rewriting of Global Political Economy: Integrating Reproductive, Productive and Virtual Economics,* New York: Routledge.

Peterson, V. Spike. 2000. "Rereading Public and Private: The Dichotomy That Is Not One." *SAIS Review: A Journal of International Affairs* 20, no. 2: 11–29.

Peterson, V. Spike. 1992a. "Security and Sovereign States: What Is at Stake in Taking Feminism Seriously?" In *Gendered States: Feminist (Re) Visions of International Relations Theory,* ed. V. Spike Peterson. Boulder, CO: Lynne Rienner, 31–64.

Peterson, V. Spike. 1992b. "Transgressing Boundaries: Theories of Knowledge, Gender and International Relations." *Millennium: Journal of International Studies* 21, no. 2: 183–206.

Pettman, Jan Jindy. 2009. "IFjP Tenth Anniversary Reflections: In the Beginning…" *International Feminist Journal of Politics* 11, no. 1: 2–9.

Pettman, Jan Jindy. 1996. *Worlding Women: A Feminist International Politics.* London: Routledge.

Pettman, Jan Jindy. 1993. "Gendering International Relations," *Australian Journal of International Affairs* 47: 47–60.

Philpott, Daniel. 2002. "The Challenge of September 11 to Secularism in International Relations." *World Politics* 55, no. 1: 66–95.

Pietilä, Hilkka, and Jeanne Vickers. 1990. *Making Women Matter: The Role of the United Nations.* London: Zed Books.

Pirages, Dennis. 1989. *Global Technopolitics: The International Politics of Technology and Resources.* Belmont, CA: Wadsworth.

Pitkin, Hanna Fenichel. 1984. *Fortune Is a Woman: Gender and Politics in the Thought of Nicollo Machiavelli: With a New Afterword.* Chicago: University of Chicago Press.

Prosser, S. E. 2001. "Taliban and Women—Oil and Water." Women in International Law (WILIG), Washington Steering Committee. *Newsletter* 14, no. 2: 2–3.

Prügl, Elisabeth. 1999. *The Global Construction of Gender: Home-Based Work in the Political Economy of the 20th Century.* New York: Columbia University Press.

Reardon, Betty A. 1985. *Sexism and the War System.* New York: Teachers College.

Reinharz, Shulamit. 1992. *Feminist Methods in Social Research.* New York: Oxford University Press.

Ringer, Fritz. 1997. *Max Weber's Methodology: The Unification of the Cultural and Social Sciences.* Cambridge, MA: Harvard University Press.

Rothstein, Edward. 2001. "Attacks on U.S. Challenge the Perspectives of Postmodern True Believers." *New York Times Magazine,* Sept. 11, A17.

Rose, Gillian. 1993. *Feminism and Geography: The Limits of Geographical Knowledge.* Minneapolis: University of Minnesota Press.

Rosenberg, Emily S. 1990. "Gender." *Journal of American History* 77, no. 1: 116–124.

Ruddick, Sara. 1984. "Preservative Love and Military Destruction: Some Reflections on Mothering and Peace." In *Mothering: Essays in Feminist Theory*, ed. Joyce Treblicot. Totowa, NJ: Rowman and Allanheld.

Ruggie, John Gerard. 1998. *Constructing the World Polity: Essays on International Institutionalization*. New York: Routledge.

Runyan Anne Sisson. 2002. "Still Not 'At Home' in IR: Feminist World Politics Ten Years Later." *International Politics* 39: 361–368.

Runyan, Anne Sisson. 1988. "Feminism, Peace, and International Politics: An Examination of Women Organizing Internationally for Peace and Security." Ph.D. diss., American University.

Russett, Bruce. 1993. *Grasping the Democratic Peace: Principles for a Post-Cold War World*. Princeton, NJ: Princeton University Press.

Sassen, Saskia. 1998. *Globalization and Its Discontents*. New York: W. W. Norton.

Scheer, Robert. 2001. "Falwell Should Have Listened to the Feminists." *Los Angeles Times*, Sept. 25, p. 20.

Scott, Joan W. 1986. "Gender: A Useful Category of Historical Analysis." *The American Historical Review* 91, no. 5: 1053–1075.

Seager, Joni. 2008 *The Penguin Atlas of Women in the World*, 4th ed. Harmondsworth, UK: Penguin Books.

Seager, Joni. 2003. *The Penguin Atlas of Women in the World*. Revised and updated. Harmondsworth, UK: Penguin Books.

Sen, Gita, and Caren Grown. 1987. *Development, Crises and Alternative Visions: Third World Women's Perspectives*. New York: Monthly Review Press.

Sharman, Jason, and Jacqui True. 2011. "Anglo-American Followers or Antipodean Iconoclasts? International Relations in Australia and New Zealand." *Australian Journal of International Affairs* 65, no. 2:148–166.

Shepherd Laura. 2009. *Gender Matters in Global Politics*. London: Routledge.

Shiva, Vandana. 1995. "Gender Justice and Global Apartheid." *Third World Resurgence*, no. 61, Sept/Oct.

Shiva, Vandana. 1989. *Staying Alive: Women, Ecology and Development*. London: Zed Books.

Shorish-Shamley, Zeiba. 2002. "Afghanistan: Women in Government and Society." Panel discussion, U.S. Institute of Peace. Cited from http://www.usip.org/oc/newsroom/es20020129.html, Jan. 29.

Sjoberg, Laura. 2013. *Gendering Global Conflict: Toward a Feminist Theory of War*. New York: Columbia University Press.

Sjoberg, Laura ed. 2009. *Gender and International Security: Feminist Perspectives*. New York: Routledge.

Sjoberg, Laura. 2008. "Will They Ever Understand? The Impossible Relationship Between Feminism and International Relations," unpublished paper presented at the 2008 annual meeting of the International Studies Association.

Smith, Steve. 1997. "New Approaches to International Theory." In *The Globalization of World Politics*, eds. John Baylis, Patricia Owens, and Steve Smith. Oxford: Oxford University Press, 165–190.

Smith, Steve. 2002. "The United States and the Discipline of International Relations: 'Hegemonic Country, Hegemonic Discipline.'" *International Studies Review* 4, no. 2: 67–85.

Sprout, Harold and Margaret Sprout. 1971. *Toward a Politics of the Planet Earth*. New York: Van Norstrand Reinhold.

Squires, Judith, and Jutta Weldes. 2007. "Beyond Being Marginal: Gender and International Relations in Britain." *British Journal of Politics and International Relations* 9, no. 2: 185–203.

Steans, Jill. 2003. "Engaging from the Margins: Feminist Encounters with the 'Mainstream' of International Relations." *British Journal of Politics and International Relations* 5, no. 3: 428–454.

Stern, Jessica. 2003. *Terror in the Name of God: Why Religious Militants Kill.* New York: Harper Collins.

Stern-Petterson, Maria. 1998. "Reading Mayan Women's In/Security." *International Journal of Peace Studies* 3, no. 2.

Stewart-Harawira, Makere. 2005. *The New Imperial Order: Indigenous Responses to Globalization.* London: Zed Books.

Stiehm, Judith Hicks. 2000. "Neither Male nor Female: Neither Victim nor Executioner." In *Male Roles, Masculinities and Violence: A Culture of Peace Perspective,* eds. Ingeborg Breines, Robert W. Connell, and Ingrid Eide. Paris: UNESCO: 223–230.

Stiehm, Judith Hicks. 1996. "The Civilian Mind." In *It's Our Military Too,* ed. Judith Hicks Stiehm. Philadelphia, PA: Temple University Press.: 270–294.

Stiehm, Judith Hicks. 1983. *Women and Men's Wars.* Oxford: Pergamon Press.

Stienstra, Deborah. 2000. "Dancing Resistance from Rio to Beijing." In *Gender and Global Restructuring: Sightings, Sites and Resistances,* eds. Marianne Marchand and Anne Sisson Runyan. New York: Routledge: 209–224.

Stout, David. 2001. "Mrs. Bush Cites Women's Plight under Taliban." *New York Times Magazine,* Nov. 18, B4.

Sylvester, Christine, 2013. "The Elusive Arts of Reflexivity in the 'Sciences' of International Relations." *Millennium: Journal of International Studies* 41: 309–325.

Sylvester, Christine. 2002. *Feminist International Relations: An Unfinished Journey.* Cambridge: Cambridge University Press.

Sylvester, Christine. 1994a. "Empathetic Cooperation: A Feminist Method for IR." *Millennium: Journal of International Studies* 23, no. 2: 315–334.

Sylvester, Christine. 1994b. *Feminist Theory and International Relations in a Postmodern Era.* Cambridge: Cambridge University Press.

Sylvester, Christine. 1990. "The Emperor's Theories and Transformations: Looking at the Field Through Feminist Lenses." In *Transformations in the Global Political Economy,* eds. Dennis Pirages and Christine Sylvester. New York: Macmillan.

Sylvester, Christine. 1987. "Some Dangers in Merging Feminist and Peace Projects." *Alternatives* 12, no. 4: 493–509.

Tannen, Deborah. 1990. *You Just Don't Understand: Women and Men in Conversation.* New York: William Morrow.

Tempest, Rone. 2001. "Training Camp of Another Kind." *Los Angeles Times,* Oct. 15, A1.

Teschke, Benno. 2003. *The Myth of 1648: Class, Geopolitics and the Making of Modern International Relations.* London: Verso Press.

Tessler, Mark, and Ina Warriner. 1997. "Gender, Feminism, and Attitudes Toward International Conflict: Exploring Relationships with Survey Data from the Middle East." *World Politics* 49, no. 2: 250–281.

Tetrault, Mary Ann. 1992. "Women and Revolution: A Framework for Analysis." In *Gendered States: Feminist (Re)Visions of International Relations Theory,* ed. V. Spike Peterson. Boulder, CO: Lynne Rienner, 99–121.

Thomas, Scott M. 2005. *The Global Resurgence of Religion and the Transformation of International Relations: The Struggle for the Soul of the Twenty-First Century.* New York: Palgrave Macmillan.

Tickner, Arlene B., and David Blaney, eds. 2013. *Claiming the International (Worlding Beyond the West).* New York: Routledge.

Tickner, Arlene B., and David Blaney, eds. 2011. *Thinking the International Differently (Worlding Beyond the West).* New York: Routledge.

Tickner, Arlene B., and Ole Waever, eds. 2009. *International Relations Scholarship Around the World,* New York: Routledge.

Tickner, J. Ann. 2011. "Retelling IR's Foundational Stories: Some Feminist and Postcolonialist Perspectives." *Global Change, Peace and Security* 23, no.1: 5–13.

Tickner, J. Ann. 2010 "You May Never Understand: Prospects for Feminist Futures in International Relations." *The Australian Feminist Law Journal* 32: June: 9–20.

Tickner, J. Ann. 2009. "On Taking Religious Worldviews Seriously." In *Power, Interdependence and Nonstate Actors in World Politics,* eds. Helen V. Milner and Andrew Moravcsik. Princeton: Princeton University Press, 223–240.

Tickner, J. Ann. 2004. "Feminist Responses to Security Studies." *Peace Review* 16, no. 1: 43–48.

Tickner, J. Ann. 2002. "Feminist Perspectives on 9/11." *International Studies Perspectives* 3, no. 4: 333–350.

Tickner, J. Ann. 2001. *Gendering World Politics: Issues and Approaches in the Post-Cold War Era.* New York: Columbia University Press.

Tickner, J. Ann. 1998. "Continuing the Conversation..." *International Studies Quarterly* 42: 1.

Tickner, J. Ann. 1997. "You Just Don't Understand: Troubled Engagements Between Feminists and IR Theorists." *International Studies Quarterly* 41, no. 4: 611–632.

Tickner, J. Ann. 1994. "Feminist Responses to Peace and Security in the Post-Cold War Era." In *Peace and World Security Studies: A Curriculum Guide,* ed. Michael Klare, 6th ed. Boulder, CO: Lynne Rienner, 43–54.

Tickner, J. Ann 1987. *Self-Reliance versus Power Politics: American and Indian Experiences in Building Nation-States.* New York: Columbia University Press.

Tickner, J. Ann, and Laura Sjoberg, eds. 2011 *Feminism and International Relations: Conversations about the Past, Present and Future.* New York: Routledge.

Tobias, Sheila. 1990. "Shifting Heroisms: The Uses of Military Service in Politics." In *Women, Militarism, and War: Essays in History, Politics, and Social Theory,* eds. Jean Bethke Elshtain and Sheila Tobias. Savage, MD: Rowman & Littlefield, 163–187.

Todorov, Tzvetan. 1984. *The Conquest of America: The Question of the Other.* Translated from the French by Richard Howard. New York: Harper and Row.

Tong, Rosemarie Putnam. 1998. *Feminist Thought: A More Comprehensive Introduction.* 2nd ed. Boulder, CO: Westview Press.

Toulmin, Stephen Edelston. 1996. "Concluding Methodological Reflections: Elitism and Democracy among the Sciences." In *Beyond Theory: Changing Organizations Through Participation,* eds. Stephen Edelston Toulmin and Björn Gustavsen. Amsterdam: John Benjamins Publishing, 203–225.

Toulmin, Stephen Edelston. 1990. *Cosmopolis: The Hidden Agenda of Modernity.* Chicago: University of Chicago Press.

Tronto, Joan. 1993. *Moral Boundaries: A Political Argument for an Ethic of Care.* New York: Routledge.

True, Jacqui. 2003. "Mainstreaming Gender in Global Public Policy." *International Feminist Journal of Politics* 5, no. 3: 368–396.

Tuana, Nancy. 1992. "Reading Philosophy as a Woman." In *Against Patriarchal Thinking*, ed. Maja E. Pellikaan-Engel. Amsterdam: VU University Press, 47–54.

Tuhiwai Smith, Linda. 1999. *Decolonizing Methodologies: Research and Indigenous Peoples.* London: Zed Books.

United Nations. 1996. *United Nations Human Development Report 1995.* New York: Oxford University Press.

United Nations Development Fund for Women (UNIFEM). 2002. *Progress of the World's Women 2002*, vol. 2. New York: UNIFEM.

United Nations Development Programme. 2010. *United Nations Human Development Report 2010.* New York: Palgrave Macmillan.

United Nations Educational, Scientific, and Cultural Organization (UNESCO), Institute for Statistics. 2004. *Educational Statistical Tables.* New York: United Nations. Accessible at www.unesco.uis.org.

UN Women. 2011. "Women, Poverty & Economics." http://www.unifem. org/gender_issues/women_poverty_economics/.

Van Evera, Stephen. 1997. *Guide to Methods for Students of Political Science.* Ithaca, NY: Cornell University Press.

Vasquez, John A. 1979. "Colouring it Morgenthau: New Evidence for an Old Thesis on Quantitative International Studies." *British Journal of International Studies* 5, no. 3: 210–228.

Ver Beek, Kurt Alan. 2001. "The Maquiladoras: Emancipation or Exploitation?" *World Development* 29, no. 9: 1553–1567.

Vitalis, Robert. 2005. "Birth of a Discipline." In *Imperialism and Internationalism in the Discipline of International Relations,* eds. David Long and Brian C. Schmidt. Albany: State University of New York Press, 159–181.

Waever, Ole. 1998. "The Sociology of a Not So International Discipline: American and European Developments in International Relations." *International Organization* 52, no. 4: 687–727.

Walker, R. B. J. 1992. "Gender and Critique in the Theory of International Relations." In *Gendered States,* ed. V. Spike Peterson. Boulder, CO: Lynne Rienner, 179–202.

Walker, R. B. J. 1989. "History and Structure in the Theory of International Relations." *Millennium: Journal of International Studies* 18, no. 2: 163–183.

Wallensteen, Peter. 1988. "The Origins of Peace Research." In *Peace Research: Achievements and Challenges,* ed. Peter Wallensteen. Boulder, CO: Westview Press, 7–29.

Walt, Stephen M. 1991. "The Renaissance of Security Studies." *International Studies Quarterly* 35, no. 2: 211–239.

Waltz, Kenneth N. 1979. *Theory of International Relations.* Reading, MA: Addison-Wesley.

Waltz, Kenneth N. 1959. *Man, the State and War.* New York: Columbia University Press.

Waring, Marilyn. 1988. *If Women Counted: A New Feminist Economics.* San Francisco, CA: Harper & Row.

Watson, Natalie K. 2003. *Feminist Theology.* Grand Rapids, MI: Wm. B. Eerdmans Publishing.

Wax, Naomi. 2001. "Not To Worry. Real Men Can Cry." *New York Times Magazine,* Oct. 28, Sec. 4, 5.

Waylen, Georgina. 2006. "You Still Don't Understand: Why Troubled Engagements Continue Between Feminists and (Critical) IPE." *Review of International Studies* 32, no. 1: 145–164.

Weber, Cynthia. 1994. "Good Girls, Little Girls and Bad Girls." *Millennium: Journal of International Studies* 23, no. 2: 337–348.

Weber, Max. 1949. *The Methodology of the Social Sciences*. Trans. and ed. Edward A. Shils and Henry A. Finch. Glencoe, IL: Free Press.

Wendt, Alexander. 1998. "On Constitution and Causation in International Relations." *Review of International Studies* 24, no. 5: 101–117.

West, Lois. 1999. "UN Women's Conferences and Feminist Politics." In *Gender Politics in Global Governance*, eds. Mary K. Meyer and Elisabeth Prügl. Lanham, MD: Rowman and Littlefield, 177–193.

Whitworth, Sandra. 1989. "Gender in the Inter-Paradigm Debate." *Millennium: Journal of International Studies* 18, no. 2: 265–272.

Wiesner, Merry E. 1998. "Spinning out Capital: Women's Work in Preindustrial Europe, 1350–1750." In *Becoming Visible: Women in European History*, 3rd ed., eds. Renate Bridenthal, Susan Mosher Stuard, and Merry E. Wiesner, Boston, MA: Houghton Mifflin, 203–232.

Wight, Martin. 1995. "Why Is There No International Theory?" In *International Theory: Critical Investigations*, ed. James Der Derian. New York: New York University Press, 15–35.

Wildman, Sarah. 2001. "Arms Length: Why Don't Feminists Support the War?" *The New Republic*, Nov. 5, p. 23.

Willinsky, John. 1998. *Learning to Divide the World: Education at Empire's End*. Minneapolis: University of Minnesota Press.

Women Living Under Muslim Laws. 1997. "Plan of Action Dhaka 1997." Cited from http://www.wluml.org/english/publications/engpofa.htm.

Yost, David S. 1994. "Political Philosophy and the Theory of International Relations." *International Affairs* 70, no. 2: 263–290.

Young, Iris Marion. 2007. *Global Challenges*. Cambridge: Polity Press.

Youngs, Gillian. 2000. "Breaking Patriarchial Bonds: Demythologizing the Public/Private." In *Gender and Global Restructuring: Sightings, Sites, and Resistances*, eds. Marianne H. Marchand and Anne Sisson Runyan. New York: Routledge: 44–58.

Yuval-Davis, Nira. 1997. *Gender and Nation*. London: Sage.

Zalewski, Marysia. 2007. "Do We Understand Each Other Yet? Troubling Feminist Encounters with(in) International Relations." *The British Journal of Politics and International Relations* 9, no. 2: 300–312.

Zalewski, Marysia. 1995. "Well, What Is the Feminist Perspective on Bosnia?" *International Affairs* 71, no. 2: 339–356.

Zalewski, Marysia, and Jane Parpart, eds. 2008. *Rethinking the Man Question: Sex, Gender and Violence in International Relations*, London: Zed Books.

Zalewski, Marysia, and Jane Parpart, eds. 1998. *The "Man" Question in International Relations*. Boulder, CO: Westview Press.

INDEX

Hooper, Charlotte, 25, 61–62, 140
Hottentot Venus, 169n2
Huntington, Samuel, 127, 132,
    147–148, 153
Huysmans, Jef, 90n25
hybridity, 122, 170

idealist school of international relations,
    79–80, 119
imperial dialectical frontiers
    (Hobson), 123
imperialism. *See* colonialism
India, 68, 104, 168, 171
informal violence (Keohane), 147
Inglehart, Ronald, 113n34
In Service and Servitude (Chin), 105
International Brotherhood of
    Teamsters, 76
International Congress of Women, 27
International Crises Behavior data
    set, 113
International Islamic Front, 150
International Labor Organization
    (ILO), 68
International Monetary Fund (IMF), 40,
    66, 69, 150
international political economy (IPE).
    See also economic globalization
    basic needs approach to, 48–49
    comprehensive security and, 2–3
    counterhegemonic perspective on, 49
    critical IPE scholarship and, 176–177
    ecofeminist perspective on,
        50–51, 59–60
    ecological perspectives on, 3, 58–59
    environmental issues and perspectives
        on, 3, 45, 49–51, 58
    feminist approaches to, 36–37, 45–49,
        60, 176–177
    gendered categories in, 3,
        36–37, 43, 45
    liberal school of, 3, 36–41, 45–46
    Marxist school of, 3, 36, 38–39, 43–45
    nationalist school of, 36, 40–43,
        45–46, 57
    the state and, 3, 97
international relations academic
    discipline
    analyticism and, 124
    colonialism and, 121–122, 129, 164

constructivism and, 148, 155–157,
    161, 185
critical realism and, 124
critical theory and, 83, 120, 122
dialogue in, 117–119, 122–123, 125
environmental perspectives and,
    38, 56–57
epistemology in, 2, 14–15, 24,
    71–72, 74, 76, 81–84, 88–90, 116,
    119–120, 125, 177, 184
Eurocentric aspects of, 120–122
feminist perspectives and approaches
    in, 1–2, 7–8, 11, 16–18, 22–23,
    71–80, 83–85, 88–96, 98–99, 101,
    105–116, 118, 123–124, 127–129,
    164, 170–171, 175–184
foundational myths of, 162–164
gendered notions and concepts in,
    7–8, 21, 71, 74, 76, 79–80, 85, 88,
    116, 175–176, 178
Grotian tradition and, 79, 89
"inside tradition" *versus* "outside
    tradition" and, 82n15, 88
Kantian tradition and, 79–80, 89
methodology and, 71–72, 74–77, 84,
    90, 92–95, 97–98, 105, 107–115,
    117–118, 123–125, 162, 176–177,
    179–185
misunderstandings with feminism
    and, 73–77, 80–85, 89, 97, 177
neopositivism and, 93–94, 124
ontology of, 22, 71, 75–76, 80, 89,
    99–100, 154, 177
positivism in, 93, 119, 124, 176,
    180–183
postcolonial perspectives in, 118, 122,
    128, 162, 164, 170–171
post-positivism in, 1, 83–84, 120, 155,
    182–183
quantitative methods in, 95, 176–177,
    180–183
rational choice theory and, 21,
    82, 119
religious worldviews and, 128,
    147–148, 153–154
scientific theory notions in, 1, 9–11,
    81–83, 85, 99, 103, 119, 124,
    155, 184
state-oriented focus of, 3, 11–12,
    97–99, 128, 153–154, 162–163

international relations academic
   discipline (*Cont.*)
   theory building in, 21, 24, 78–79,
      81–82, 92–95
   traditionalists and social scientists
      debate in, 119
   unitary state actor assumption in, 22
   United States and, 72–73, 77–78,
      81–82, 90, 116, 118–120, 124, 154,
      162, 184–185
   white supremacy in, 121
   women's underrepresentation in,
      6–7, 21
International Research and Training
      Institute for the Advancement of
      Women (INSTRAW), 115
International Scholarship Around the World
      (Waever and Tickner), 117–118,
      124, 162
International Security, 182
International Studies Quarterly (ISQ), 71,
      92, 175
Iraq, 30, 154n12
Islam. *See also* Islamic fundamentalism
   The Qur'an and, 143, 157
   women in, 143–144, 151, 157–158
Islamic fundamentalism. *See also*
      religious fundamentalism
   anti-secular emphasis in, 148–152,
      154, 158–159
   "clash of civilization" thesis and, 153
   economic globalization and, 151–152
   political mobilization and, 152
   views of women and, 142–143,
      150–151

Jackson, Patrick, 92n1, 117, 124–125
Jaggar, Alison, 39
Jaquette, Jane, 12–13, 69, 184
Jesuits, 169
Jolly, Margaret, 167
Journal of Race Development, 121
Juergensmeyer, Mark, 148n2, 152

Kant, Immanuel, 79–80, 86
Karam, Azza, 143
kaupapa theory (Maoris), 171
Keller, Evelyn Fox
   on demarcation between public and
      private, 10

dynamic objectivity and, 15–16
   feminist critiques of natural science
      and, 9, 16
   on McClintock, 15–16, 95n8
Keohane, Robert
   on feminism and international
      relations methodology, 71, 92–98,
      100, 112, 180n8
   informal violence and, 147
   on religious worldviews, 147–148
   on social science inquiry, 93n3, 95n7,
      102n20, 104, 105n24, 116
Kiel, Paul, 166
King, Gary, 93n3, 95n7, 102n20, 105n25
King, Ynestra, 27
Kingsley, Mary, 169n3
Kirkpatrick, Jeane, 6
knowledge
   Cartesian notions of, 103, 122–124,
      159, 163, 171
   colonialism and, 121–122,
      168–169, 171
   as emancipation, 103–104
   feminist approach to construction of,
      9, 43, 86–87, 96, 100–101, 110,
      116, 159, 169, 183, 185
   gendered assumptions behind, 100,
      158–159
   High Science model of, 103, 171
   postcolonial approaches to, 170
   social construction of, 9, 43, 86–87,
      93, 96, 100
   thick description and, 171
Kohlberg, Lawrence, 10–11
Korea, Republic of. *See* South Korea
Kuala Lumpur (Malaysia), 109
Kubálková, Vendulka, 148, 155–157
Kurth, James, 132–134, 137, 141

Laffey, Mark, 164, 171
Lapid, Yosef, 1, 83
Lashkar e Taiba (Army of the Pure,
      Pakistan), 150
Law, David, 49
Lee-Koo, Katrina, 178–179
Leiss, William, 58–59
Leviathan (Hobbes), 55–56
liberalism school of international
      political economy
   environmental issues and, 38

export-led development strategies
and, 40
feminist critique of, 37–40
gendered aspects of, 36, 38
the individual and, 36–39, 45–46
Marxist critiques of, 38–39
nationalist critique of, 41
rational economic man assumption in,
37–39, 45–46
self-interest and, 37–38
valuation of capital over labor in, 39
Western liberal political theory
and, 38
liberation theology, 158
linguistic constructivism. *See*
constructivism
Linklater, Andrew, 79
Long, David, 121

Machiavelli, Niccolo, 56n3
Malaysia, 105, 107–111
Maoris, 171
maquiladoras, 65
Margalit, Avishai, 135–136, 151
Marxist school of international political
economy
class and, 36, 43, 45
core and periphery notions in, 43
critiques of liberalism and, 38–39
feminist critique of, 3, 43–45
gendered aspects of, 36, 44
women's reproductive roles and, 44
masculinity. *See also* gender
business leadership and, 140
hegemonic masculinity, 25, 137, 140
military service and, 29–30, 140–141
models of, 127–128, 140–141
religious violence and, 150
September 11, 2001 terrorist attacks
and, 133, 136, 141
terrorism and, 134
war and, 20–22
maternal thinking (Ruddick), 14–15
McClintock, Barbara, 15–16, 95n8
Mearsheimer, John, 134
Meena (RAWA founding member),
131–132, 134, 139
Meier, Golda, 75, 85
Men's Movement, 141
mercantilism, 40, 42, 50

Merchant, Carolyn, 14, 16, 52–56, 59
Mexico, 65, 68
Mies, Maria, 31–32, 49, 104, 112
Mignolo, Walter, 167
militia movement (United States), 150
Mitchell, Juliet, 41
modernity
different models of, 160–161, 163
economic globalization and, 161
feminism and, 160, 165
Westernization and, 160–161
modernization theory, 152–153,
160–161
Monter, William, 165
Moon, Katharine, 23, 105–107,
110–112
moral development
gendered conceptions of, 11, 14
Kohlberg's stages of, 10–11
Morgan, Robin, 140
Morgenthau, Hans
Hoffman on, 119
political man concept and, 10, 16, 81
political realism principles of, 1,
7–10, 15–18
on power, 12–13
realist school of international
relations and, 1, 7–11, 15, 78n8,
119, 148, 154–155
secular rationalism and, 155, 156,
158–159
self-criticism of, 11n10
World War II and, 11, 154

Nalgonda (India), 104
national accounting systems,
111–112
nationalism school of international
political economics
Enlightenment and, 42
environmental issues and, 57
feminist critique of, 40–43
gendered aspects of, 36
international division of labor
and, 41
mercantilism and, 40, 42
national security and, 41, 46
Prisoners Dilemma games and, 42
the state and, 41, 45–46, 57
National Organization of Women, 21

Scott, Joan, 77
Seager, Joni, 114n36
security. *See also* national security;
   security studies
   basic material needs and, 13–14
   binary Western metaphysical notions
      and, 25
   community building and, 13
   comprehensive notions of, 2–3,
      23–25, 27–28, 33–34, 46, 99, 101
   conflict resolution and, 14
   environmental issues and, 32–33, 49
   gendered perspectives on, 29,
      45–46, 127
   of individuals, 2, 25, 101,
      106–107, 116
   interdependence and, 14
   structural violence and, 13, 28
security studies
   bottom-up approach to, 22
   critical security studies and, 24–25
   discourse analysis and, 23–24
   feminist approach to, 2, 19–20, 22–24,
      27–29, 33–35, 182
   gender and, 2, 19–20
   masculine discourse in, 23–24, 30
   rational actor assumptions in, 24
Self Employed Women's Association
   (SEWA), 68
September 11, 2001 terrorist attacks
   compared to World Trade Center
      attack (1993), 156n15
   feminist perspectives on, 127,
      131–137, 140–144, 146
   gendered responses to, 135–136, 142
   Huntington on, 153
   impact on U.S. security policy from,
      127, 133, 135–136
   international relations discipline and,
      119, 128, 147
   rational choice theory and, 119
   religious fundamentalists' response
      to, 142
   renewed emphasis on masculinity and,
      133, 136, 141
Sex Among Allies (Moon), 105–106
shipbuilding, 53
Shorish-Shamley, Zeiba, 143
Sjoberg, Laura, 177, 184
Smith, Linda Tuhiwai, 171

Smith, Steve, 88, 119–120, 124
"The Sociology of a Not So International
   Discipline" (Weaver), 118–119
Southern African Development
   Co-ordination Conference
   (SADCC), 13
South Korea
   government of, 105–106, 110–111
   military prostitution in, 23, 105–107
   Nixon Doctrine and, 105
   United States and, 23, 105–107, 111
Soviet Union, 13n12, 163
Squires, Judith, 178–179
states
   colonialism and, 164
   developmental state and, 108–109
   The Enlightenment and, 51–52
   environmental issues and, 51, 57
   feminist perspective on, 48–49, 69,
      106, 115–116
   as focus of international relations,
      3, 11–12, 97–99, 128, 153–154,
      162–163
   gendered conception of, 19, 36,
      41–43, 98, 115–116, 166
   natural resource exploitation and,
      55–56, 58, 60
   war and, 20–21, 23
   Westphalian system and, 128,
      153–154
Steans, Jill, 176
Stern, Jessica, 150–151
Stern-Petterson, Maria, 102, 123, 179
Stewart-Harawira, Makere, 164, 172
Stiehm, Judith, 22, 30–31, 34, 141–142
Stop Gender Apartheid campaign, 145
strong objectivity, 87, 103
structural adjustment programs
   (SAPs), 66, 68
structural violence, 13, 31, 33–35
Sun Tzu, 61
Sylvester, Christine, 80

Taliban, 136, 138, 145
Tannen, Deborah, 73–74, 76–77, 83,
   88n23, 91
Tessler, Mark, 25–26, 113n33
Thatcher, Margaret, 75, 85
"The Third Debate" (Lapid), 1
third-wave feminism, 96n9, 144

Third World. *See also* Global South
  development in, 39–40, 43, 48
  global economy and, 43
  Marxist analysis of, 43–45
  terminology of, 37n1
  women in, 39–40, 44–45, 48
Tickner, Arlene
  Feminism and International Relations
    and, 184–185
  International Scholarship Around the
    World and, 117–118, 124, 162
  International Studies Quarterly article
    (1997) of, 92, 175, 180
Tobias, Sheila, 29
Todorov, Tzvan, 167
Toulmin, Stephen, 86–87, 103, 163, 171
transversal politics (Yurval-Davis), 144
Treaty of Westphalia, 120, 153–154,
  162–163
Tribe, Laurence, 134
True, Jacqui, 123–124, 179

United Front. *See* Northern Alliance
United Nations
  Beijing Platform for Action and, 69
  Conference on Population and
    Development (1994), 142
  data collection by, 67–68, 114–115
  Decade for Women and, 27, 39,
    67–68, 114
  gender empowerment measure
    (GEM), 114
  gender mainstreaming and, 68–69
  gender-related development index
    (GDI) and, 68, 114
  Human Development Program and, 68
  Human Development Reports and,
    62–63, 114
  religious fundamentalist hostility
    toward, 149–150
  Women's Conference (1995), 142
United States
  Christian identity in, 153, 154n12
  concerns about the feminization of,
    132–134, 136–137, 140, 150
  concerns about the multiculturalism
    of, 132–133, 150
  Convention on the Elimination of All
    Forms of Discrimination Against
    Women (CEDAW) and, 146

gendered economic inequality in, 44
Gulf War (1991) and, 131
international hostility toward,
  150–151
international relations academic discipline and, 72–73, 77–78, 81–82,
  90, 116, 118–120, 124, 154, 162,
  184–185
military tribunals in, 134
notions of gender in, 8–9
Patriot Act in, 136
September 11, 2001 terrorist attacks'
  impact in, 127, 133, 135–136
South Korea and, 23, 105–107, 111
women in the military in, 5–6, 21,
  131–133, 141–142
University of Southern California, 184
Uppsala University, 20n4
USA Patriot Act, 136

Van Evera, Steve, 110n28
Verba, Sydney, 93n3, 95n7, 102n20
Vietnam War, 31
Visscher, Janszoon, 167
Vitalis, Robert, 121

Waever, Ole, 117–119, 124, 162
Wallensteen, Peter, 29
war
  children and, 30
  gendered conception of, 19–22,
    25–27, 29–30, 79, 98, 127, 131,
    134, 142, 146
  impersonal nature of, 23
  intimacy of, 23
  as learned behavior, 34
  masculinity and, 20–22
  rape and, 23, 101
  the state and, 20–21, 23
  women and, 23, 30, 145
War and Gender (Goldstein), 20
Waring, Marilyn, 101, 111–112
Warriner, Ina, 25–26, 113n33
Waylen, Georgina, 176–177, 183
Weber, Max, 104n22
Weldes, Jutta, 178–179
Welsh School, 20n3
"Westoxification," 135
Westphalian Synthesis (Philpott),
  153–154

"Why Is There No International Theory?" (Wight), 78

Wight, Martin, 78–79, 81, 84

Wildman, Sarah, 137

Willinsky, John, 121–122

witchcraft, 165, 170

WomanStats project, 99n17, 181–182

women. *See also* feminism; gender; gender inequality

in Afghanistan, 128, 131–132, 134, 136–139, 142, 146

in corporate leadership positions, 62–63

in early modern era, 165

fertility rates and, 66

as foreign policy leaders, 5–6, 22, 30

historians' neglect of, 164–165

increased workforce participation of, 66–67

in Islam, 143–144, 151, 157–158

in militaries, 5–6, 21, 25–26, 29–30, 131–133, 141–142

part-time and home-based work of, 65–66, 68

as political leaders, 21, 75, 85, 113, 114

poverty and, 62–63

religious worldviews and, 142–143, 157, 165

role in reproduction and, 47, 66, 100–101, 112, 166

in the Third World, 39–40, 44–45, 48

war and, 23, 30, 145

Western political philosophy on, 80

Women Living Under Muslim Laws (WLUML), 143–144, 157

Women's International League for Peace and Freedom (WILPF), 185

Women's International Peace Conference, 27

Woolf, Virginia, 106n26

World Bank, 69, 150

World Trade Center attack (1993), 156n15

World War I, 27, 145

World War II, 11, 81, 145, 154

You Just Don't Understand (Tannen), 73–74

Youngs, Gillian, 64

"You Still Don't Understand" (Waylen), 176

Yugoslavia wars (1990s), 23, 127n1

Yuval-Davis, Nira, 144

Zalewski, Marysia, 74n5, 177, 179

Zimbabwe, 101